Workout

ADVANCED

STUDENTS' BOOK

Paul Radley

Kathy Burke

Longman

Pearson Education Limited
Edinburgh Gate, Harlow,
Essex CM20 2JE, England
and Associated Companies throughout the world.

www.longman.com

First published by Addison Wesley Longman Ltd. 1996
Seventh impression 2001

ISBN 0-17-556519-8

Printed in China
GCC/07

*The publishers and authors would like to thank the following for
their participation in the reading and piloting of course material:*

Suzie Rudling (CEL, Amiens); Richard Kiely and Seamus O'Riordan
(Thames Valley University, London); Penny Busetto, Penny Grieve
and G Heyworth (The British School, Pistoia); Lyn Harris, Siân
Preece and Jacqui Eacott (King's School, London); Nick Shaw and
John Walker (Cambridge English Studies, La Coruña); Audrey
Morris (Hampstead Garden Suburb Institute, London); Guy Heath
(LinguaSec., Madrid); Deborah Spencer (Alphamega, Montpellier);
Andrew Kinselle; Kirk McElhearn; Margaret Fowler.

*The publishers would also like to thank all those who took part in
recordings and supplied photographs, and are grateful to the
following for their permission to reproduce copyright material on
the pages stated:*

The Independent: Judy Jones, pages 8, 9; Julia Thorogood, page 99;
Tim Wapshott, pages 98, 117, 118; Steve Crawhaw, page 111
Private Eye: pages 6, 11, 12, 19, 47, 59, 60, 61, 66, 67, 77, 86, 92, 108
Elle (UK): William Langley, page 12
The Irish Independent: page 12
Hamish Hamilton/Penguin: reprinted by permission of the Peters,
Fraser and Dunlop Group Ltd, page 25
Mel Calman: pages 29, 41, 73, 78, 79, 82
The Guardian: © Malcolm Smith, page 33
British Airways Holidays: pages 35, 36
Virago Press: © Deborah Tannen, published by Virago Press 1992,
page 43
Black Swan: *Tales of the City* by Armistead Maupin, page 45;
A Sensible Life by Mary Wesley, published by Black Swan, a
division of Transworld Publishers Ltd, at £5.99, page 91
Methuen London: *Families and How to Survive Them* (1983)
© John Cleese and Robin Skynner, page 49; *Love and Friendship*
(1962) © Alison Lurie, page 51; *The Secret Diary of Adrian Mole
Aged 13¾* © Sue Townsend, page 95; *Educating Rita*, © Willy
Russell, page 96

Critical Quarterly: Barbara Conrad, page 52
House of Colour: page 55
Amnesty International: page 58
The Big Issue: page 62
The Spectator: page 62
The Observer Magazine: © Nonie Niesewand, page 65; © Dr John
Collee, page 75, reprinted by permission of the Peters, Fraser
and Dunlop Group Ltd; © Lucy Ellmann, page 89
Penguin Books Ltd: © James Thurber 1939, 1951, page 67; *Driving
in the Dark* by Deborah Moggach © Penguin Books 1989, page
91; *The Accidental Tourist* by Anne Tyler © Penguin Books 1986,
page 91
Carol Publishing Group: From *Color Psychology and Color Therapy*
by Faber Birren. © 1951, 1960 Faber Birren. Published by
arrangement with Carol Publishing Group. A Citadel Press
Book, pages 81, 83, 122
Time Out: pages 84, 117
Punch Library: page 86
Tony Husband: page 87
Hodder & Stoughton Ltd: *The Woman Next Door* by Joy Cowley,
first published in *Heart Attack and Other Stories*, Hodder &
Stoughton, 1984, page 98
Macmillan London Ltd; *Some Tame Gazelle* by Barbara Pym,
page 98
Serpent's Tail: *Seeing in the Dark,* ed. Ian Breakwell and Paul
Hammond, pages 105, 107
The Hampstead and Highgate Express: page 107
Sheil Land Associates Ltd: *The Fake's Progress* by Tom Keating,
Geraldine and Frank Norman (Part I © Tom Keating and Frank
Norman), published by Hutchinson, page 113
Faber and Faber Ltd: *Paris by Night* by David Hare, page 115; *We
are still Married* by Garrison Keillor, page 128
The European: 'The Weekly Newspaper for Europe', pages 120, 121
The Telegraph: © *The Telegraph* plc 1992, pages 120, 121
Casarotto Ramsay Ltd: For permission to record on cassette
Educating Rita © Willy Russell, published by Methuen London.

*Every effort has been made to trace owners of copyright, but if any
omissions can be rectified, the publishers will be pleased to make
the necessary arrangements.*

Photographs

Steve Benbow Photography: 8.2, 8.3; The Bridgeman Art Library:
14.1a, 14.1d, 14.3b; The British Broadcasting Corporation: 13.1d;
The British Film Institute/The Walt Disney Company: 13.1b;
Bubbles Photo Library: 14.1a; The Ronald Grant Archive/Cinema
Museum: 13.3b, 13.3d; The Robert Harding Picture Library: 4.8;
Robert Holden: 1.2, 1.3; The Hulton Picture Company: 9.1a; The
Image Bank: 4.9, 7.1, 7.3; *The Independent* Newspaper: 2.4, 2.6,
2.7; *The Irish Times:* 11.2; The Kobal Collection: 3.3, 3.4, 3.5,
13.3a, 13.3e, 13.4; The National Gallery: 14.3a; Network
Photographers: Paul Lowe 2.5, Martin Mayer 12.2; Paul Radley:
1.1, 3.6, 3.7, 3.9, 5.1, 13.2; Retna Pictures: 9.1c; Rex Features: 2.1,
2.1b, 2.2b, 2.3c, 4.2, 4.3, 4.7, 5.2, 5.3, 7.5a, 7.5b, 7.6a, 7.6b, 7.7a,
7.7b, 8.1, 9.5, 10.1, 11.1a, 12.1a, 13.1c, 13.3c, 14.2a, 14.2b, 14.3c,
p120; John Ridley Photography: 2.9; Frank Spooner Pictures: 2.8,
6.2, 9.1b; Tony Stone Worldwide: cover photographs, 4.1b, 4.4, 4.5,
4.6, 4.10, 7.4, 9.2, 9.3, 9.4, 10.5, 12.1b, 12.1c, 12.1d, 13.1a; Michael
Sturley/SDA: 10.6, 11.1a–f, 11.3a–c; *The Telegraph* Colour
Library: 10.2, 12.1e; Topham Picture Source: 6.4, 6.5, 6.6; Zefa
Picture Library: 7.2, 10.3, 10.4

Illustrations

Illustrations by Paul Catherall, Harvey Collins, Ann Farall, Sophie
Grillet, Tony Hall, Gecko Limited, Pantelas Palios, Sarah Perkins,
Martin Saunders, Nick Ward

Contents

Map of Workout Advanced

'Humour is emotional chaos, remembered in tranquility.'
JAMES THURBER

Vocabulary: humour

What is humour?

1 Write your own dictionary definition of **humour**.
Compare in groups and try to agree on a *definitive* definition.
Now look up **humour** in your dictionary.
How does your definition compare?

Types of humour

2 Match the different types of humour and jokes with their definitions.

1 Amusing without appearing to be so; quietly ironic.
2 Humorous acting that depends on fast, sometimes violent actions.
3 Humour dealing with the unpleasant or dark side of life (e.g. death, people's problems).
4 Showing the foolishness or evil of a person, organisation or practice, in an amusing way.
5 Unnaturally, unhealthily cruel or morbid, this kind of humour is unsophisticated, often quite juvenile and offensive.
6 Showing dislike or intolerance of people of different races.
7 Concerned with sex, sometimes in an unpleasant way.
8 A joke played on someone to embarrass them and amuse others.
9 Unfairly dismissive of the opposite sex; showing them as stupid or inferior.

a black (*adj*)
b practical (*adj*)
c dry (*adj*)
d satire (*n*)
e racist (*adj*)
f sexist (*adj*)
g sick (*adj*)
h slapstick (*n*)
i dirty (*adj*)

How funny?

3 Put the following ways of describing humour in order of funniness. Discuss in pairs.

> amusing   hilarious   a giggle
> a good laugh   funny

Some of these can be used with modifiers like *very, really* and *quite*. Combine the modifiers with the words and expressions and try to decide which combinations sound 'right'.
One of the words is rarely used without a modifier. Which one – and why?

Common mistakes

4 Choose the correct word in each sentence.

1 We told/played a practical joke on Tom. We put all the clocks back so he thought he was an hour late.
2 Sarah was annoyed when we laughed at/with her after her fall.
3 I like to tease/joke him about his bad pronunciation, but sometimes he gets annoyed.
4 Phil can really say/tell a joke well. He always makes me laugh.

Discussion

What makes you laugh?

Look at the types of humour in Exercise 2. What type of humour do you enjoy most?
Discuss your answers in groups, using the words you have studied on this page.

Listening

Before you listen

1 Look at the photograph and predict what happened in the anecdote that you are about to hear.

First listening

2 In which order do you hear these words and phrases for the first time? Listen and write a number in the box.

☐ black cab   ☐ down the hill

☐ tiny little man   ☐ Edinburgh

☐ let's just get in   ☐ such a shock

☐ running along backwards

Second listening

3 Listen again and complete these sentences with the correct word.

1 I was living in Edinburgh with this _____ of mine.

2 We phoned a _____ and it took quite a long time to arrive.

3 The cab driver got out and came to the _____ .

4 We went to the cab, got in and we sat in the _____ .

5 And then suddenly the cab started _____ backwards.

6 He ran round to the _____ of this huge, heavy, black cab.

7 My friend had the presence of mind to slide back the _____ and pull on the handbrake.

8 It could have been a really, you know, really _____ situation.

Pronunciation: vowel sounds

4 In continuous speech the weak vowel /ə/ is often used. Look at this sentence from the text. Underline the vowels which you think are weak, as in the example.

> 'We w<u>e</u>re sitting in the back of the cab looking out the back window, by this time finding the whole thing really funny, which was stupid because, you know, we were hurtling towards our deaths.'

T3 Now listen and check your answers. Why do you think the weak vowel is used in some cases and not in others?

Listen again and repeat.

Speech features: giving yourself time to think

We often use certain words and phrases which have the function of allowing us time to think about what we are going to say next, and order our thoughts. Listen to T4 and find two such words or phrases.

Reading

Before you read

1 Look at these suggested ways of overcoming stress.
How effective would they be for you?
List them in order of efficiency.

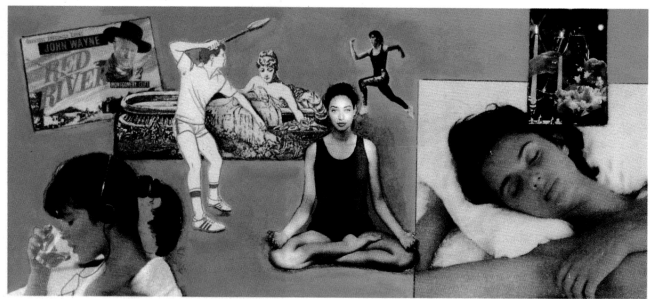

Now compare your order with another student and discuss:

What other ways are there of dealing with stress?

How do you deal with stress?

While you read

2 You are now going to split up into two groups, each reading a different text about an unusual way of dealing with stress.
Student A look at the text on this page. **Student B** look at the text on page 9.

Student A

The first time you read the text answer these questions.

1 What sort of problems do the people mentioned in the text have?

2 How are they learning to deal with them?

3 What do you say that makes you think the therapy is effective?

Compare answers with another student from the same group.

Then look at Exercise 3 on page 9.

Facing life's terrors armed with a smile

'AUDITIONS cause me a lot of anxiety,' said Tony Polidori, a nightclub and restaurant singer, who works all around the country and abroad. 'Family problems, stress, and pressure – you name it. I've always lived for tomorrow, saved up my money. It's hard for me to enjoy the moment.'

After his fourth therapy session, Mr Polidori appears relaxed and swaps banter with other group members. He fears that his son, 11, will also grow up to be as anxious as he is, unless he tackles his stress problem. 'I found myself smiling more the week after the first session, and feeling happier. I know I have to be more positive, and I've picked up some good ideas.'

Ashok Patel's first encounter with laughter therapy came when he entered a health shop in search of texturised vegetable protein and herbs. He came out with a leaflet about a stress counselling service.

Ashok Patel: 'Most people I see are lonely'

'Some people deal with their stress by smoking or drinking, which doesn't do you much good,' Mr Patel, who runs a hostel for the homeless in Handsworth, said. 'Most people I see these days are lonely. It's a product of living in big cities. People become insulated, cut off from one another. They forget how to enjoy themselves. Laughter is one way of getting people to relate better to one another, particularly in a small group like this. It helps you to look introspectively, and to sort out problems.' Jenny Broadhurst, who is divorced with two children, has had 'quite a few' problems as a result of a close relative who was alcoholic. 'I like the comradeship I get coming to these sessions. Some of the tips do stick in the mind. Today, for instance, we were told about a businessman who dealt with the stress of meetings by imagining everyone present in pink pyjamas, and that made him stop worrying. Things like that I find useful.'

© *The Independent*

Stress sufferers learn to laugh at misfortune

1 A NEW remedy for countering stress and despair is being pioneered in inner-city Birmingham. The treatment costs nothing, has no harmful side effects and its applications are virtually limitless. It is called laughing.

2 Robert Holden, a psychotherapist and counsellor, chose one of the most downtrodden parts of the country to open the first NHS laughter clinic. He reckoned that if it worked in Handsworth it could work anywhere.

3 His group laughter therapy is based on scientific research, common sense and observation. Doctors have known for years that laughing reduces muscular tension, improves breathing and regulates the heartbeat. It pumps adrenaline into the bloodstream, along with endorphins, the body's chemical painkillers. The contribution of laughter to mental health, although self-evident, has resisted psychologists' attempts to unravel its mechanisms.

4 The idea of devoting whole therapy sessions to laughter and smiling occurred to Mr Holden when he was doing one-to-one counselling. His clients were trying to cope with traumas including bereavement, divorce and sexual abuse. 'The turning point in these sessions tended to come when they could laugh about it,' he said. 'That was the moment when their perception of the problem changed, and they could begin to take control of their lives again.'

5 Mr Holden persuaded the West Birmingham health authority to back a pilot project at its advice and counselling centre off the Lozells Road, where he was running stress management sessions.

The old adage about laughter being the best medicine has become reality at a unique clinic.
Judy Jones *reports*

6 Five months on, the fortnightly midday laughter sessions bring about a dozen people together, and there is a waiting list of 50 for planned evening courses. The only charge is for tea or coffee.

7 A typical session starts with closed eyes, breathing exercises and exhortations to 'breathe in molecules of happiness'. Clients are invited to smile, on the grounds that even simulated smiles can improve mood. Mr Holden runs through some of the theories on why people lost the knack of laughing. One centres on the conflict between the 'parent, adult and child' in all of us; and the tendency, as people grow up, to suppress the playful instincts.

8 People then split into groups and are asked to tell each other what made them laugh recently, a question which leaves some stumped for an answer. Sometimes the session ends with tape recorded, and infectious, laughter.

9 Clients are also given exercises to do between sessions. One is to start the day by standing in front of a mirror and giving out a rip-roaring laugh. Another is to smile whenever you speak on the phone.

10 Mr Holden, who is preparing to give GPs training in laughter therapy, is aware of its limitations. 'If you've got a lousy relationship, or you've lost your job, of course laughter is not going to cure it. But it will make you better able to deal with it.'

© *The Independent*

Student B

The first time you read, match this information to the paragraphs in the text. Write the paragraph number(s) in the boxes.

☐ Activities which members of therapy groups are given to do at home.

☐ A description of how the therapy works in practice.

☐ Limitations of this type of therapy.

☐ How Robert Holden discovered the idea for this type of therapy.

☐ Robert Holden's reason for opening his clinic in Handsworth.

☐ Scientific reasons which explain why the therapy is effective.

☐ Information about the number of people attending therapy sessions.

Compare answers with another student from the same group. Then look at Exercise 3 below.

Vocabulary comprehension

3 Choose six unfamiliar words from the text that you have read, which you think are important for a complete understanding of the text.
By looking carefully at the context try to work out what the words mean.
Then discuss your list with other students who have read the same text.

Grammar: the present

1 Do you remember the different uses of the present tenses?
In groups, prepare a questionnaire using only the present tenses in your questions.
Write six questions and use as many of the various functions of the present tenses as you can.

Example: *What do you do when you get angry?*
    a keep it to yourself
    b shout and make a fuss
    c get violent
    d other (please specify)

Choose a topic from the following or invent your own if you prefer:

personality   emotions   humour   free time
        holidays   bad/good habits

Now work with a student from another group and try out your questionnaire.

Grammar reflection

2 Look at the verb tenses in these sentences, then find and compare them to the original ones in the texts on pages 8 and 9. What is the difference in meaning between the sentences in each pair? Which of the sentences in the box are unlikely or incorrect? Why?

---

1 Auditions are causing me a lot of anxiety … (*text A*)

2 After his fourth therapy session Mr Polidori is appearing relaxed … (*text A*)

3 People are becoming insulated … (*text A*)

4 Mr Holden, who prepares to give GPs training in laughter therapy, is aware of its limitations. (*text B*)

---

3 Look at the sentence pairs from Exercise 2, and match each sentence with one of the uses.

A general truths
B talking about the moment of speaking
C general time (e.g. habits and states)
D dramatic narrative
E synopses of books, films, plays etc.
F temporary situations
G commentaries
H demonstrations/instructions/describing sequences
I describing progressive change

---

4 Find pairs of sentences in lists A and B which have the same form and use of the present tenses.

A

1 Pollution is getting worse every year.
2 Although we may not always be able to see it, hot air rises.
3 It's raining.
4 They drink too much.
5 I'm waiting for the light to change when this guy jumps in my car …
6 I'm staying with friends at the moment.
7 Agassi serves – it's out!
8 You put the cheese in the hot pasta and stir it well.
9 It's about this American who travels to India and …

B

a Al Pacino looks at Michelle Pfeiffer and says …
b He's a doctor.
c She's not going out much these days.
d Gascoigne passes the ball to Smith … It's a goal!
e You just press the button and wait.
f People are looking after their health more nowadays.
g He's making dinner at the moment. Can he ring you later?
h This bear goes to the cinema and …
i Deciduous trees lose their leaves in the autumn.

5 In pairs, match the sentences above to the uses listed in Exercise 3. Then write another sentence illustrating each of the uses. For further information see the Grammar Reference on page 137.

Practice

The car

6 Look at the two pictures which are the first and last in an original sequence of eight pictures.

Discuss in pairs what you think happens in the rest of the cartoon.

Ask your teacher questions to find out about the rest of the sequence. You can only use the present tenses.

Example: *What are the people in the car saying to the man on the right?*

The Martian joke

T5 7 The present tenses are often used to tell jokes. In groups of three, look at the following information: **Student A** page 119, **Student B** page 121 and **Student C** page 122.

Without showing each other, discuss and decide the correct order to make the complete joke. When you have finished, listen to someone telling the joke and check your answers.

"Sorry, we don't serve food."

Say the right thing!

"Good Lord, Fenton, I had no idea you had died!"

Reacting

1 Match these reactions to the situations 1 – 12 below.

a	pleasure	g	surprise
b	anger	h	joy
c	sympathy	i	relief
d	sorrow	j	boredom
e	irritation	k	excitement
f	praise	l	interest

1 A colleague comes in and tells you that someone has reversed into your car.

2 Your best friend tells you she is going to have a baby.

3 A neighbour tells you his cat has been run over.

4 Your boss says she has got a cold.

5 A member of your family phones you at work and tells you that you have won a free holiday to the States in a competition.

6 Someone tells you that they went parascending at the weekend.

7 Someone you don't like very much explains at great length how he bought a new stamp for his collection.

8 A friend tells you that there is a new film by your favourite director starting at the cinema in your town.

9 Someone tells you that you haven't got to work at the weekend after all.

10 A colleague comes in and announces that he/she has just found out that your 60-year-old boss got married at the weekend to a 20-year-old rock singer.

11 Someone buys you a cake on your birthday and you comment after tasting it.

12 A friend phones up at half past seven and says that he or she can't come to dinner that evening.

2 In pairs, work out what you would say in each situation.

T6 3 Listen to Part 1 and identify the reaction for each of the situations.

Now listen to Part 2, and react to what you hear.

Listen to Part 3 and note down the exchanges where you think the person replying is being sarcastic. How can you tell that they are being sarcastic?

4 Invent statements for each of these situations. You can use real or invented information if you prefer.

1 You have just heard some very good news about . . .

2 You have just returned from a very enjoyable and exciting holiday.

3 A family pet has not been well recently.

4 Talk about your favourite hobby – give plenty of details about it.

5 Give some surprising news about your teacher or another student in your class.

Now move round the class and give your information to other students. React to each other's statements.
You can decide how you want to react to others' statements, either sincerely or sarcastically.

*'People everywhere confuse
what they read in newspapers with news.'*

A J LIEBLING

Vocabulary: the press

Find the categories

1 Look at this list of words connected to the press. Divide them into four categories. (The categories do not contain equal numbers of words.)

> tabloid good/bad taste features designer
> periodical financial comment reporter
> home editorial quality columnist
> freedom photographer travel popular
> critic review journalist picture editor
> censorship daily contributor leader
> magazine sub-editor weekly politics
> editor sport foreign newspaper monthly
> sensationalism ads correspondent
> journal article arts invasion of privacy

Pairwork

2 In pairs, compare your lists. Take it in turns to choose pairs of words from your lists and ask each other to explain the difference between the words. For each satisfactory explanation, give one point. (If in doubt, check your answers in a dictionary.)

Newspaper headlines

3 Here is a brief guide to the 'rules' by which English newspaper headlines are written:

The article and the verb *to be* are omitted.

The present tenses are used to describe something which has happened, is happening, or happens repeatedly.

When the present continuous is used, the auxiliary verb *be* is omitted.

To refer to the future, the infinitive with *to* is used.

Passive sentences are written without their auxiliary verbs.

There are a number of words which are specifically used in headlines, e.g. *quit* is often used instead of *resign*.

Look at the headlines below and write them out in full.

Discussion

Scandal!

Some of the headlines on this page are sensationalist. Discuss in groups:

Why do you think newspapers use headlines like these?

What sort of newspapers use them?

What is your opinion of censorship in the press?

Which of the headlines would also be published in your country?

What do you think about the right of well-known people, like celebrities, politicians or the monarchy, to keep their personal life private?

Can you think of any occasions in your country when famous people use the media to get free publicity?

Princess denies rift in the Family

CD PRICES ATTACKED BY DIRE STRAITS

Kisses cost the boss $30,000

Man fined for $3m tip to belly dancer

BISHOP QUITS OVER WOMEN

BEER CANS TO CARRY HEALTH WARNING

BABY'S TOES AND EAR BITTEN OFF BY SISTER

Listening

Before you listen

1 Madonna, the pop and film star, published a book which caused a lot of controversy over the photographs and the text.

All the major British newspapers were offered the chance to publish some of the photographs before the book went on sale, and *The Observer*, a Sunday newspaper, published some of them in its colour supplement.

In groups, discuss and list the reasons why you think a quality newspaper like *The Observer* decided to publish these pictures.

First listening

2 You are going to hear an interview about the Madonna pictures with Tony McGrath, picture editor of *The Observer*. The first time you listen, make a note of his reasons for publishing the photographs. Are any of his reasons the same as the ones you listed?

Second listening

3 Read these questions, then listen again and make notes to answer them.

1 What conditions did the publishers impose on people who wanted to see the pictures?

2 Why, in Tony's opinion, did they impose these conditions?

3 Why did he find the discussion in New York 'incredibly difficult'?

4 What does Tony say about the price of the book and CD?

5 What was the asking price for the pictures and how much did *The Observer* have to pay?

6 What extra condition did *The Observer* include in its offer for the pictures?

Discussion

4 What do you think of Tony's reasons for going ahead and publishing the pictures? Do you think *The Observer* was justified in doing so? What would you have done in their position?

Pronunciation: *th*

 5 Listen to a section of the conversation with Tony again and make a note of all the words you hear containing the sound '*th*'.

Now divide the words into two categories – voiced '*th*' as in *this* and unvoiced '*th*' as in *thing*.

Listen again and check your answers.

Students sometimes also have difficulty hearing and pronouncing the difference between '*d*' and voiced '*th*', and '*t*' and unvoiced '*th*'.

Listen and tick the word you hear.

	A	B			A	B
1	doze	those	5		taught	thought
2	dare	there	6		tread	thread
3	den	then	7		tree	three
4	day	they	8		team	theme

Now listen and repeat, concentrating on the accurate pronunciation of '*th*'.

Speech features: *well*

The word *well* can have many meanings in spoken English, including these:

- to indicate that you are changing the topic
- to indicate that you intend/want to carry on speaking
- to indicate that you are about to say something
- to indicate that you have reached the end of the conversation
- to make a suggestion, criticism or correction less definite
- just before or after you pause, to give yourself time to think about what you are going to say
- to modify or correct something you've just said
- to explain or justify something.

Listen to [T10] and pay particular attention to Tony's use of the word *well*.
Discuss which of the meanings above correspond to the examples you hear.

Grammar: past tenses (1)

Lateral thinking

The Two Barbers

1 Listen to the story your teacher is going to read. Make notes of the main facts. Then ask your teacher questions to which the answer is either 'Yes' or 'No', to find the solution to the riddle.

Grammar reflection

2 The diagram represents the period of time around the publication of the Madonna pictures. Look at the events on the line to decide which tenses to use in order to complete the sentences below. Choose the correct tense for the verbs in brackets.

> 1 When *The Observer* people (see) the pictures in New York, the other newspapers (already/see) them.
> 2 From September, when the publisher (accept) their offer, until October, Tony (wait) for the photos.
> 3 Tony (be) very surprised when the page proofs (arrive) as he (expect) original photographs.
> 4 The book (come) out on 12 October.

3 Now complete these rules with the name of the correct tense.

a When you want to describe the situation in which a particular event occurred, or to describe more temporary situations, you use the _____ .

b When you want to talk about a particular event which happened at a specific time in the past, something which took place regularly in the past, or something which happened over a period of time in the past, you use the _____ .

c When you are looking back from a specific moment in the past and you are describing the effects of something which happened at an earlier time in the past, you use the _____ .

d What's the difference in meaning between the following sentence pairs?
   a I'd been living/I'd lived in France for years.
   b I'd been seeing him for a long time./I'd seen him before.

Now check your answers in the Grammar Reference on page 138.

The diagram (timeline)

JULY
- The Observer views pictures in New York 21st July
- Other newspapers view pictures in London 15th July

AUGUST
- The Observer makes offer 3rd August

SEPTEMBER
- Harper Collins accepts offer 7th September
- Publishing deadline 16th September
- Page proofs in London 28th September

OCTOBER
- Original photos in London 3rd October
- The Observer publishes Madonna pictures 11th October
- The book comes out 12th October

Practice

The Haircut

4 Look at these notes based on an anecdote by the American novelist, Garrison Keillor, from his book *We Are Still Married*.

Work in groups. Write a version of the complete story, using each of the verb tenses you have studied in Exercise 2, at least twice. When you have finished, read the complete story on page 128.

> St Paul - toothache - woman dentist - painless - decide to have haircut - Hair One Day and Gone the Next - Personal Hair Stylists - young woman - pink hair - chew gum - Candy - Just a trim round the edges and not too short - finish - glasses back on - old clown - How's that? - That's fine - $16 - $4 tip - bought a cap at the drugstore - Care for some haircream? - home - angry - wife - You have the most beautiful green eyes, do you know that?

Reading

Before you read

1 If you were the picture editor of a newspaper, which of these photographs would you be prepared to publish?

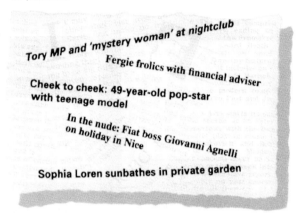

Tory MP and 'mystery woman' at nightclub

Fergie frolics with financial adviser

Cheek to cheek: 49-year-old pop-star with teenage model

In the nude: Fiat boss Giovanni Agnelli on holiday in Nice

Sophia Loren sunbathes in private garden

Grief-stricken Princess Caroline at husband Casiraghi's funeral

While you read

2 Look at the captions above, and the title of the article on page 17. Write three facts and one opinion which you expect to find in the article. Now skim-read the article to find out if your expectations were accurate.

Vocabulary comprehension

3 Find the words on the left in the text and match them to the synonyms and definitions on the right.

1 *Para. 1* smudgers	a	annoyed
2 *Para. 2* gnat	b	attraction
3 *Para. 3* stop-at-nothing	c	photographers
4 *Para. 5* do-gooders	d	prevented from doing something
5 *Para. 7* glimpsed	e	well-meaning but interfering people
6 *Para. 9* miffed	f	kept at a safe distance
7 *Para. 11* take in their stride	g	small flying insect
8 *Para. 12* thwarted	h	risk-taking
9 *Para. 13* kept at bay	i	caught sight of
10 *Para. 14* lure	j	accept calmly without considering to be a problem

Phrasal verbs

4 Choose the correct meaning for these phrasal verbs, for the context in which they appear in the text.

1 go about *(3)* – *a* continue to do *b* approach *c* dress or behave in a certain way

2 burn out *(3)* – *a* stop burning *b* stop working *c* become exhausted or ill by working too hard

3 pull off *(4)* – *a* succeed in *b* drive off the road and stop *c* start moving forward

4 run into *(6)* – *a* begin to experience unexpectedly *b* hit *c* meet unexpectedly

5 take up *(8)* – *a* get to and stay in (a place) *b* start *c* draw attention to

6 give up *(9)* – *a* stop *b* allow someone to have *c* allow oneself to be arrested

7 blow up *(15)* – *a* be destroyed by an explosion *b* approach suddenly *c* fill with air

4 ▶

Writing: formal letter of complaint

Imagine that you are a well-known person. How would you feel if you were being constantly followed by a paparazzo? Write a letter to the editor of the *Daily Sun*, complaining about harassment by photographers.

When you write a formal letter you need to know:

- where to write your address and the date
- where to write the name and address of the person you are writing to
- how to address the person you are writing to
- where, in relation to the opening, to start the first line of the letter
- how to finish the letter, bearing in mind whether you know the person's name or not
- how to write your name at the end.

If you are still in doubt about any of the above, look at the example letter at the back of the Workbook.

Well-organised letters are written in paragraphs. In a letter of complaint you could write a paragraph for each of the following:

– an introduction giving information about yourself,

– details of the incident(s) you are complaining about,

– any other relevant information,

– the action that you would like the person to take.

The power of the paparazzi

In the celebrity fish pond the paparazzi are the killer sharks – quite distinct from the amiable, bottom-feeding 'smudgers' who lurk outside popular nightclubs at unpopular hours. Distrustful by nature, solitary by inclination, and impervious to conventional discipline, they approach their work like surgeons preparing for an operation.

Like opera singers and waiters, many of the best paparazzi come from Italy. The term was invented by Federico Fellini for his film *La Dolce Vita*, and is a mixture of *papatacci* (a uniquely irritating Italian gnat) and *razzi* (the popping of flash-bulbs).

Anyone who doubts the seriousness with which the paparazzi go about their work should take a look at Sestini's Florence-based operation. He employs four stop-at-nothing photographers, each equipped with a high-speed inflatable dinghy, diving equipment, underwater cameras, portable telephones, binoculars and a motorbike. All of them must be able to swim, scuba-dive, drive like Ayrton Senna, resist lie-detector tests and climb trees. None earns less than £50,000 a year: Most burn out after a year.

It is Sestini himself who pulls off the most memorable coups. Two years ago he smuggled himself inside Monte Carlo's cathedral for the funeral of Princess Caroline's husband, Stefano Casiraghi. Using a tiny buttonhole camera and an infra-red remote control he photographed weeping relatives kneeling at Stefano's coffin.

Well, no one ever said it was a profession for do-gooders. Sestini made £20,000 for his day's work. The smudgers standing outside made maybe £100 each.

It was one of Sestini's Italians who I ran into outside Bill Wyman's house near Vence in the South of France a few years back. At the time the middle-aged Rolling Stone's relationship with 16-year-old Mandy Smith was being studied by Scotland Yard, and referred to in highly incriminating terms by most of the popular press.

Stone-faced Wyman was looking even stonier than usual on the rare occasions he was glimpsed through the barred and guarded gates of his villa. After two days of fruitless waiting, Sestini's man decided to try something different.

Overlooking the estate was a huge pine tree, up which the Italian shinned with cat-like dexterity. He took up position on a high branch, offering a view not just over Wyman's place but over most of Provence, and waited confidently for his chickens to come home to roost.

But home to roost instead came a gigantic Mediterranean eagle, already deeply miffed at failing to catch anything for its supper, and about to be made more so by the discovery of an uninvited Italian paparazzo squatting next to its nest. Those of us on the ground were wearily getting ready to give up for another night when the terrible commotion began.

Clouds of feathers, pine needles, shreds of Armani trousers, squawks, oaths and screams for mercy were followed by the fastest tree descent in history. The next day Sestini's man, wrapped in more bandages than anyone since Tutankhamen, was dutifully back in position. Instead of a camera he was carrying a shotgun.

Serious paparazzi take such hazards in their stride. Ron Galella (yet another of those names that ends in a vowel), the much-feared New York celebrity photographer, started wearing an American football helmet after his jaw was broken by Marlon Brando. When Jackie Onassis obtained an injunction prohibiting Galella from coming within 100 feet of her, Galella successfully counter-sued for restraint of trade.

How can the paparazzi be thwarted?

Sir James Goldsmith has tried citizen's arrest, and Madonna, mob violence. But the paparazzi are not kept at bay for long.

With magazines happy to pay £50,000 for candid pictures of celebrities, the lure is nearly always stronger than the deterrent. In any case, many paparazzi say that, like romance, the real thrill is the pursuit. 'When I get someone in the viewfinder it is the most exhilarating experience you can imagine,' says Jean-Claude Ratteuil, a wily Frenchman who works the French Riviera, specialising in the Monacan royal family.

He once spent 53 hours on a floating Lilo waiting for Princess Stephanie and actor Rob Lowe to appear together on an isolated beach. Paddling with his hands back towards the shore a storm blew up, swamped the Lilo, ruined his best rolls of film and nearly drowned Ratteuil, who spent several days in hospital suffering from sunburn and exposure. 'I still count it as a great coup,' he says, cheerfully.

Faced with this sort of determination, many celebrities have accepted that, short of taking up residence in bank vaults, complete privacy isn't possible and, sooner or later, the paparazzi will get them.

The paparazzi – fed by a public whose curiosity is matched only by its sense of disapproval – have changed the nature of fame. Instead of vainly trying to hide, most sensible targets now take their cue from Dudley Moore's nonchalant billionaire in the movie *Arthur*:

Dudley Moore: 'I think I'll take a bath.'
John Gielgud: 'I shall alert the media, sir.'

Speaking

Problem-solving: Front page

Work in groups of three or four. You are the editorial team of *The Independent* newspaper. You have to design and produce the front page of the Sunday edition of the newspaper. Here is a list of your tasks:

> 1 Read the list of news items and decide which to include.
> 2 Decide the relative importance of the items and write them on the layout grid provided on page 117.
> 3 Re-arrange the words provided to make the headlines.
> 4 Decide which photographs to use in the spaces allocated to them.

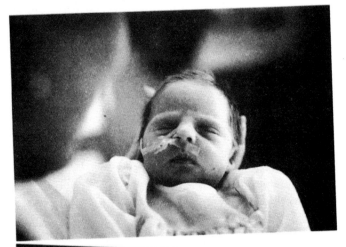

1 Here is a brief summary of news items which were used in this particular edition of *The Independent*.

a warning about the sale of pornography on computer disc to children

b progress report on plans to privatise British Rail

c revolutionary operation conducted on an unborn baby which saved her life

d plan to place adult prisoners with younger ones in the hope of reducing the number of riots

e news of student loans and grants for part-time students

f prediction of the government's financial plans and the date of the general election

g report of a bomb attack on a bus in Northern Ireland

Now look at the front page layout grid on page 117 again. There is space for five articles based on the items listed above. Discuss in your groups which five to include.

2 Now that you have decided what to include, work out where to fit them into the layout grid according to their relative importance.

3 Rearrange the words to make the headlines for the articles you have chosen:

a exposed porn children computer to

b impasse BR cabinet hits sell-off

c tall she saved was two when inches

d young mix jails to and old plan

e students part-time in for sight loans

f tax cuts poll April odds on and shorten

g Ulster on troops after bombing backlash alert bus for

4 Look at the photographs on this page and decide which one you would use in the large space provided.

When you have finished, look at page 126 and compare your answers with the actual front page of *The Independent*.

Grammar: the noun phrase

Before you read

1 How do you feel about travelling by air?
Have you ever had a bad experience on a plane?
In the United States a prize called the Frankenstein Award
is awarded every year for the worst plane journey of the year.
What sort of journey do you think wins the prize?

While you read

2 Now read the article and find out about a Frankenstein
Award prize-winner's experience.

Accepting the Frankenstein award for the worst journey of the year, Mr James Williams of Toronto said: "I was the only passenger on a commuter flight from Boston to Master Plain.' Ten minutes after take-off there was the sound of an explosion from the flight deck and a blue flame flashed through the passenger cabin.

Then the pilot, whose name turned out to be Captain Lowenburg Chank, appeared and said: 'Pray to whichever God you hold most dear.' Then he went back to his job and landed us safely fifteen minutes later.

There was no explanation of any kind, and when I got into the terminal I found my luggage had been lost on the flight."

The noun phrase: giving more information

3 To give more information about the person or thing
you are talking about – and to make written
language more descriptive – you can use modifiers
(in front of the noun) or qualifiers (after the noun).

Complete this chart with the information that goes
before and after these nouns in the text above.

	journey	
	passenger	
	flight	
	flame	
	cabin	
	pilot	
	job	
	minutes	
	explanation	

4 Match the modifiers and qualifiers used in the
chart, to these categories.

Compound noun
Adjective
Prepositional phrase
Determiner (a, the, my etc.)
Relative clause

Check your answers in the Grammar Reference on
page 138.

Practice

Sentence expansion

5 Work in pairs. Take turns to add modifiers and qualifiers to the
noun nouns in this sentence:

The man bought the book.
Example:
Student A: The **old** man bought the book.
Student B: The old **postman** bought the **leather-bound** book.

You have a time limit of ten minutes. When you have finished,
compare final sentences with other students.

Writing: newspaper articles

You are going to write a newspaper article based on this photograph.

1 Here is a check-list of characteristics specific to newspaper articles. Make sure that when you write your article you include all of them, if appropriate:

- headline
- sub-heading (where appropriate)
- introduction
- organised in paragraphs
- factual information (what? when? where? why?)
- eye-witness reports (written in direct speech)
- conclusion
- writer's opinion (if appropriate to the subject)

2 Before you write your article, invent some factual information about the two men and the situation. Answer these questions as a basis for this information.

What are the names, ages, professions of the two men?

What is the family or social background of the man on the right?

What had happened just before the scene in the photograph?

What happened after the scene?

What happened when the case went to court?

Invent any other information that you think is relevant to the subject.

3 Now write your article. It should be between 250 and 400 words long. When you have finished, check it thoroughly for spelling, vocabulary and grammar mistakes and also for appropriacy of style.

Exchange articles with other students. Compare your different interpretation of the facts and check each other's work for mistakes. Then discuss them with the writer.

(See Workbook pages 56–57 for guidelines to appropriacy in writing.)

Vocabulary

Humour

Complete these sentences with *one* appropriate word:

1 His students often played silly _____ jokes on him, like tying his shoelaces together when he wasn't looking.
2 The Woody Allen film I saw last night was _____ funny. I had tears in my eyes from laughing so much.
3 We often _____ Alice about her crooked teeth, until we realised how much it upset her.
4 I'm no good at _____ jokes and besides, I've got a lousy memory.
5 A lot of the jokes that you hear men telling about mothers-in-law and secretaries are very _____.
6 Most countries have _____ jokes about their own minorities; in Britain, for example, there are many jokes involving the Irish and the Scots.
7 Charlie Chaplin was perhaps the greatest exponent of _____ humour who has ever lived.

The press

Make a list of at least three words for each of these categories of words associated with the press.

types of publication	occupations	sections of a newspaper
8 _____	11 _____	14 _____
9 _____	12 _____	15 _____
10 _____	13 _____	16 _____

Grammar

Present tenses

Complete this joke by writing the correct form of the verbs in brackets in the space on the right.

This man (send) his dog to the bar every day to buy his cigarettes. One day a friend (come) to his house, so the man (decide) to show his friend what his dog can do. He (put) a five pound note under the dog's collar because he hasn't got any change and (send) him off to the bar and they (wait) for him to come back. They wait and wait and the owner (get) more and more anxious. So they go to the bar and when they go in the dog (sit) there with a glass of whisky in front of him. The owner (say), 'What (you/do) with the whisky? You've never done this before!' And the dog answers, 'I never had the money before.'

17 _____
18 _____
19 _____
20 _____
21 _____
22 _____
23 _____
24 _____
25 _____
26 _____

Past tenses (1)

Read this newspaper article. In each line followed by a numbered space, there is a verb in the wrong tense. Write the verb in the correct form in the space.

Addressing Judge Houghton in the Dublin District Court, Mrs Marie Bothwell had said: 'My clients, Molloy and Joyce, are both fishermen. They admit that they were deciding to drive the minibus they find outside the Zenith nightclub across Ireland to their home in Cork. But they were having great difficulty in getting it going and they entirely failed to notice that the bus had been completely full with the sixteen people who hired it to drive them home, and who had a sing-song while Joyce and Molloy were trying to open the bonnet.

27 _____
28 _____
29 _____
30 _____

31 _____
32 _____
33 _____

'After some time, three of the passengers get out, asked Molloy and Joyce what they did, and getting only silence as their answer, raised the alarm. Both men were at sea for three months.'

34 _____
35 _____
36 _____

The noun phrase

Make four logical sentences using the nouns and a combination of the words in the box below.

37 A car:
38 A journey:
39 A man:
40 A girl:

> forty-three year old
> whose name was Rita
> gleaming   red   long
> to London   pretty   train
> with a beard
> parked outside the house
> young   from Twickenham
> £4000

Check your answers in the Answer Key on page 124.

21

'Life is a maze in which we take a wrong turning before we have learned to walk.'

CYRIL CONNOLLY

Vocabulary: life choices

1 How many of the words in the box do you associate with the images in these photographs? List the words under the appropriate photograph. Give your list a title and compare in groups.

> boredom
> self-confidence
> freedom   safety
> adventure   thrill
> rhythm   routine
> continuity
> flexibility
> excitement
> career   security
> risk   enthusiasm
> stability
> independence
> responsibility
> danger

Now write down the adjective forms for the words in the box.

Idiomatic phrases

2 What do these expressions mean?

I really *get a kick out of* climbing. I spend all my free time in the mountains.

He was forty years old, had a massive overdraft and a boring job. He really wanted to *escape the rat race*.

I can't stand *the nine to five* lifestyle. I need variety.

With a partner, discuss what you get a kick out of, and whether you agree with the other sentences.

3 Do you have similar phrases to these in your language? Do they have a positive or negative connotation, or could some have both? Discuss with a partner.

a I need *a solid base*.
b She likes to see *new horizons*.
c He needs someone *to cling to*.
d 'Who was there?' 'Oh, *the same old faces*.'
e I like not knowing *what's round the next corner*.
f I need to have *a sense of purpose*.

Discussion

Taking risks

Some people are happier when their lives involve risk-taking, while others need a more secure lifestyle. In groups, discuss and write a questionnaire of five or six items to find out whether the people in your class are risk-takers. Use the vocabulary from Exercise 1.

Example: *When you chose your present occupation, was the most important consideration:*

a job security?
b 'adventure?
c independence?
d other (please specify)

Invent a points system and a key explaining the significance of the score.

Now try your questionnaire out on students from other groups.

Speaking

Which of these hitch-hikers would you give a lift to?
Discuss your choice in pairs.

Listening

Before you listen

1 How old do you think the man in the photo is?
What sort of job does he do? What kind of shop is
this? What sort of holiday do you think he usually has?

First listening

T11 2 Listen and number this information from 1–6 in the
order in which you hear it.

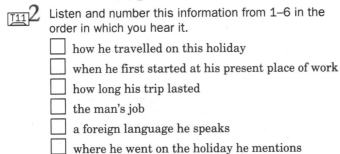

- [ ] how he travelled on this holiday
- [ ] when he first started at his present place of work
- [ ] how long his trip lasted
- [ ] the man's job
- [ ] a foreign language he speaks
- [ ] where he went on the holiday he mentions

Second listening

3 Now listen again and note down as much
information as you can about the points listed.
Compare notes with a partner.

 5 ▶

Pronunciation: weak forms – prepositions

T13 4 In English certain words are pronounced in their
weak forms. Listen to Part 1 and make a note
of the five prepositions which are pronounced in
this way.

Now listen to Part 2. What do you notice about the
pronunciation of these prepositions? What rule can
you deduce about their position in the sentences
and the way they are pronounced?

Listen again and repeat.

Speech features: emphasis

There are various ways in which Vic gives greater
emphasis to what he says. Listen to T14 and
complete these sentences with one or two words.

It _____ is – it's a _____ time for me too.
... with a _____ well-known name in England.
It worked _____ well _____.
I _____ manage to make a trip there.
... very countrified, but _____ enjoyed it.

In pairs, discuss the advantages and disadvantages
of hitchhiking, referring to your own experiences or
those of people you know. Try to use one or two of
the above devices to emphasise what you say.

23

Reading

Before you read

1 Ted Simon was a *Sunday Times* journalist when he decided to ride round the world on a 500cc Triumph motorcycle. Imagine that you are Ted Simon, and answer these questions.

What route will you take, if you want to see as many countries as possible?

What sort of information will you collect before you set off?

What are your strongest feelings about making the journey?

How do you think making the journey will affect your life afterwards?

Now discuss your answers in groups.

While you read

2 Read the text and make notes about:

Ted Simon's route

the information he collected before he set off

his feelings about the journey

what he imagined the effect would be on his later life.

Are there any similarities between the notes you made in Exercises 1 and 2?

Vocabulary comprehension

3 Explain the meaning of these phrases from the text.

Para. 1 to do justice to

Para. 2 you have to crawl ... stay on the ground and swallow the bugs

Para. 3 in great awe of

Para. 4 being loose in the world

Para. 5 at heart

Para. 6 heading for   within my grasp

Para. 8 flaunted   folly   the man outside in the gutter looking in

Para. 9 the great void   a rush of exultation

6 ▶

Improve your language learning: dealing with difficult vocabulary

One of the difficulties of reading in a foreign language is dealing with unfamiliar words.

Here are four important ways in which you can improve your technique:

1 **Context**
Can you guess the meaning of the word *light-weight*?

Now look at the word in its context in the text and try to work out the meaning. This should make your guess more accurate.

2 **Part of speech**
What part of speech is *light-weight* – an adverb, a noun, a verb, or an adjective?

In this context it is used as an adjective. Substituting other adjectives for the word may help you to understand its meaning.

3 **Base Words**
The 'root' of the new word may be familiar to you, and may help you to work out its meaning. In the same way, the two parts of the word *light-weight* will lead you to its meaning.

4 Another way of working out the meaning of a word is to compare it with similar-looking words in your own language. This can often give you an *idea* of the area of meaning.

Remember:
It is quite possible to read and understand most texts without knowing all the words. If you *do* want to check the meaning of words in a text, use a monolingual dictionary. If you are still in doubt, check your answers in a bilingual dictionary.

Reading

It was going to be the journey of a lifetime, a journey that millions dream of and never make, and I wanted to do justice to all those dreams. **1**

In spite of wars and tourism and pictures by satellite, the world is just the same size it ever was. It is awesome to think how much of it I will never see. It is no trick to go round the world these days, you can pay a lot of money and fly round it non-stop in less than forty-eight hours, but to know it, to smell it and feel it between your toes you have to crawl. There is no other way. Not flying, not floating. You have to stay on the ground and swallow the bugs as you go. Then the world is immense. The best you can do is trace your long, infinitesimally thin line through the dust and extrapolate. I drew the longest line I possibly could, that could still be seen as following a course. **2**

Generally the great overland journeys follow the Asian land mass East until the traveller is at last forced to take to the water at Singapore. I chose a different way because I was powerfully attracted by the challenge of Africa, and in great awe of it too. If I could conquer Africa, I thought I would be able to face the rest of the world with confidence. **3**

So I chose Africa, and logic prescribed the rest. Cape Town led naturally to Rio de Janeiro. A cruise ship sailed that route three times a year at very reasonable rates, and as an act of faith I booked my passage for 24 February 1974. From Rio a long loop of fifteen thousand miles round South America would bring me up the Pacific coast to California. Across the Pacific the picture was more confused. China was only interested in receiving coach parties, and South-East Asia was seething with the war in Vietnam, but there was Japan, Australia, Indonesia, Malaysia and Thailand. Coming home through India seemed absolutely right. That was a challenge I would be better prepared to meet after being loose in the world for a while. **4**

Dutifully I collected information about Pacific fares and sailings, about road conditions in the Andes, ferry services in Indonesia, the weather in Northern Australia, but it was all foolishness and at heart I think I knew it. When I spread the Michelin maps of Africa on the living room floor (and they must be the most beautiful road maps ever made), when I gazed down at the enormity of that continent, the physical variety and political complexity of it, and when I considered my complete ignorance of it, Cape Town seemed as distant as the moon. **5**

What point, then, in worrying about the stars. It was enough to know they were there and that I was heading for them. I thought myself to be the most fortunate man alive to have the whole world almost literally within my grasp. There was no one on earth I would have changed places with. **6**

Or so I thought – until that black night on the pavement of Gray's Inn Road, when I stood dripping rain water, sweat and despair, crushed by the unwieldiness of the monster I had created, and the enormity of the prospect I had invented for myself. **7**

Only three yards away, behind the thick glass doors of the *Sunday Times* lobby, was the bright and comfortable world that suited most people well enough. I could see the commissionaire, smoothly uniformed behind his desk, looking forward to a pint of beer and an evening with the telly. People in sensible light-weight suits, with interesting jobs and homes to go to, flaunted their security at me and I felt my gut scream at me to strip off this ridiculous outfit and rush back into that light and the familiar interdependence. It struck me very forcefully that if I went on with this folly I would forever after be the man outside in the gutter looking in. For a moment I was lost beyond hope, utterly defeated. **8**

Then I turned away from all that, somehow fumbled my packages away, got on the bike and set off in the general direction of the English Channel. Within minutes the great void inside me was filled by a rush of exultation, and in my solitary madness I started to sing. **9**

Speaking

Discuss in groups:

Why do you think Ted Simon went on his journey?

Do you think he was irresponsible to attempt it?

Are you one of the 'millions who dream' of making a journey like his?
What stops you from making it?

How do you think a journey of this sort changes a person's life?

What sort of problems do you think Ted Simon faced when he finished his journey?

Grammar: past tenses (2)

Sentence generation

1 Write a new sentence to replace each one below. Don't change or move the word in bold. Change all the other parts of the sentence, making sure that the original functions of the words remain the same.

Example:

1 I've **been** working in London for ten years.
 ↕   ↕   ↕   ↕   ↕   ↕
 She's **been** living at home since 1966.

2 I first started here **in** 1957.

3 Have you **ever** been to France?

4 I got interested in French fifteen or sixteen years **ago**.

Now compare your sentences in groups. Are all the sentences grammatically correct?

Grammar reflection

2 Look at these extracts from the interview with Vic and answer the questions.

> A How long have you been working here?
>   I think I first started here in 1957.
>
> B I got interested in French fifteen or sixteen years ago.
>
> C Have you ever been to France?
>   Yes, I did manage to make a trip there.
>
> D How did you travel?
>   I hitchhiked all the time.

Extract A

1 Why did the interviewer use the present perfect continuous rather than the present perfect simple?

2 Why did Vic use the past simple in his answer?

Extract B

3 Why did Vic use the past simple rather than the present perfect?

Extract C

4 Which words in this extract are often used with the past simple? Can you think of any other words often used with this tense?

5 Why did the interviewer use the present perfect?

6 Which word in the question is often used with the present perfect? Can you think of any other words often used with this tense?

Extract D

7 Why did Vic use the past simple in his answer?

8 Why did both speakers use the past simple?

Check your answers in the Grammar Reference on page 139.

Practice

Sentence correction

3 Rewrite these sentences correcting the verb tense mistake in each of them.

1 In August last year I've been to Brazil for my holidays.

2 She worked on her car for the last three hours and she still hasn't finished.

3 He was here since six o'clock and he's still waiting.

4 Did you see the latest Rohmer film yet?

5 They lived in Canada for nearly four years now.

6 Vic has been getting up at six o'clock yesterday morning.

7 In his long career Charlie Chaplin has starred in hundreds of films.

8 They've lived in New York for five years and before that they've spent 15 years in Europe.

Lies!

4 Write a profile of yourself, using each of these tenses at least twice – the past simple, the present perfect simple and continuous. Include four 'lies', i.e. invented or incorrect information.

In pairs, read your profiles to each other and try to spot the four lies in your partner's profile.

Say the right thing!

Agreeing and disagreeing

1 Work in groups of six students. Copy these topics onto separate strips of paper. Fold them and mix them up. Each student takes a topic, and makes a statement supporting it. The others in the groups have to agree or disagree with the statement.

- The police should be armed.
- Trains are better than buses.
- Smoking should be banned in restaurants.
- Cats are better pets than dogs.
- You should never give money to people begging in the street.
- Buying and wearing fur coats is immoral.

2 In the same groups, make a note of the language you used for agreeing and disagreeing during your discussions.
Are any of the expressions used for disagreeing, considered offensive or impolite? How do people express strong disagreement during a discussion?

T15 3 Listen to these people discussing three of the topics above. The first time you listen, decide how well the people know each other in each conversation. Is there any difference in the way they express agreement and disagreement in the three conversations?

Listen again and tick the phrases that they use to agree and disagree with each other.

You must be joking!	Come off it!
Yes, I suppose you might be right.	Absolutely! Absolutely!
I'm sorry, but I really don't agree.	Never! Never!
Mmmm. But …	I agree …
Sure.	Yes, I'm sure that's true, but …
Really?	Well, yes, I suppose so.
Yea …	I take your point, but …
Oh no! Come on!	Like you said …
But …	You do?
Do you think so?	Actually …
In fact …	

Now mark the phrases A (agree) or D (disagree) according to how they were used in the conversations.

Look at the remaining expressions, and decide whether they are formal or informal. What is the effect of intonation on the degree of formality of the expressions?

Speaking

Vic Spenser and Ted Simon are both very independent travellers and have never relied on the help of travel agencies or other tourist organisations to prepare their journeys. On the other hand, many people prefer tour operators to organise their holidays.

Package tours

1 Work in pairs or groups of three, and prepare arguments for or against package tours. Make notes (not whole sentences) which you may want to use in your discussion.

Group A: look at page 117.
Group B: look at page 121.

2 Now form groups of four or six students, with half in favour of and half against package tours. Discuss the issue, using the arguments you have prepared. (The language you studied on page 27 will be useful.)

Writing: composition

What is a 'good' composition?

1 Write a check-list of advice for students writing compositions, including specific information about overall structure; sentence and paragraph length; examples or illustrations.

Language points

2 The ability to write clearly also depends on your familiarity with the language necessary for linking, referencing, sequencing, giving examples and illustrations, generalisations and summaries, quotations.

Which of these categories do the words and phrases in the box correspond to?

linking; sequencing; giving examples; summarising; making generalisations; quotations.

all in all ...	by and large ...
all things considered ...	on the other hand ...
ultimately ...	as reported in ...
furthermore ...	as in the case of ...
as X wrote/suggested ...	The first point ...
for instance ...	such as ...

Can you think of any other language to fit the categories?

(*Note:* 'Referencing' is the ability to ensure that it is clear what words such as *this, it* or *they* refer to.)

3 Before you start writing, look at the composition and questions on page 123.

4 Now write the composition based on your discussion about package tours. You have the choice of either writing your real feelings and opinions or adopting the opposite point of view to your own.

Write the composition, bearing in mind all the relevant issues you have discussed up to now. When you have finished, exchange work with another student and try to work out whether the opinions you read are his/her own or not.

'The whole object of travel is not to set foot on foreign land. It is at last to set foot on one's own country as a foreign land.'

G K CHESTERTON

Vocabulary: another country

Attitudes

I say – you're NOT foreign, are you?

ONLY WHEN I'm ABROAD...

1 Cartoonists often use humour to say something serious. What do you think the cartoonist's intention is in this case?

Well, I really enjoyed my year abroad. It was a bit hard to get used to a different culture at first, but I learnt a lot. It's made me look at my own country from a different perspective ...

It was awful. They haven't even heard of fast food there ... I hated the food! And you wouldn't believe the disorganisation of everything. I couldn't wait to get back home ...

2 How would you describe these attitudes? Write down four or five adjectives for each one.

How fascinating!

3 Choose the correct word in each sentence.

1 We were fascinated/interested by the traditional harvest ceremony. We just couldn't leave!

2 I'm very interested/curious in Islamic art so I spent hours in the museum.

3 People from other cultures are often intrigued/interested by the custom of arranged marriages. They wonder how they are arranged and if they are generally successful.

4 They were quite curious/interested about us, because of the way we were dressed.

What is the difference in meaning between the four adjectives above?

Which other adjectives and verbs have the same 'roots' as *fascinated, interested, intrigued*? Write a sentence to illustrate the way they are used.

4 If you complain about a problem, you want something to be done about it. The following informal words also mean 'complain' – often just for the sake of it and often in a way that annoys others.

He moaned/grumbled/went on about the food.

Which words mean:

a complain in a low voice, nor forcefully?

b criticise the same thing repeatedly?

In what circumstances do you do any of these things, if at all?

Discussion

Adapting

Work in groups. Look at this list of problems which face people who go to live in another country. Put the problems in order of difficulty.

☐ unusual food   ☐ bureaucracy

☐ doing without good coffee   ☐ racism

☐ different social customs   ☐ finding accommodation

☐ language difficulties   ☐ different climate

☐ feeling lonely

Are there any other problems which you have experienced, which are not listed?

Now compare answers with other groups.

Listening

Before you listen

1 What is the difference between a traveller and a tourist?

What are the advantages and disadvantages of being one or the other?

What do you consider yourself to be when you travel?

First listening

2 [T16] Listen to Kathy asking Sheila about her travel experiences. The first time you listen tick (✓) the places that Sheila has lived in and cross (✗) those she hasn't been to yet, but would like to go to in the future.

Spain	France	Mozambique	Australia
Italy	Greece	Norway	United Kingdom
China	USA	India	South Africa
Belgium	Brazil	Namibia	Turkey
Ireland	Portugal	Chile	Eastern Europe

Second listening

3 Read these questions, then listen again and answer them.

1 What personal information do you find out about Sheila during the conversation?

2 What's Kathy's reaction to the length of time that Sheila spent in the first country she mentions?

3 Which country was Sheila particularly enthusiastic about and why?

4 What distinction does Sheila make between travellers and tourists?

5 Do you think that Kathy is the same sort of traveller as Sheila? Give reasons for your answer.

6 What are Sheila's long term plans?

▶ **7** ▶

Pronunciation: weak forms – conjunctions

4 [T18] Listen to the four sentences in the conversation between Kathy and Sheila. Write the number of the sentence in which you hear these conjunctions:

and   but   than   as   that

Now listen again. The word *and* has two pronunciations. How does the pronunciation differ in each case?

Listen to the pronunciation of *but* in the sentences. Can you explain why it is different in each case?

Why is *that* pronounced differently in the sentences?

Now listen again and repeat, concentrating on producing the weak or strong forms of the conjunctions according to what you hear.

Speech features: *yes* and *no*

In English, other words are often used instead of *yes* and *no*, especially when speakers are either very sure, or not sure at all about their answers.

Listen to [T19] and make a note of the ways Sheila says yes to Kathy's questions.

Here are some other ways of saying:

yes   *of course – agreed – Mmm – certainly*

no   *no way – definitely not – of course not – certainly not – uhuh*

When do you think you would use the expressions above?

Invent some questions which would make you want to use them in your reply. (*Note:* If you are uncertain, use *Yes and no ...*, *Mmm ...* or *Well, ...*)

Grammar: the future

Interview

1 Think of eight questions you would like to be asked about your future. Write two questions for each of these categories: hopes/desires; predictions; plans/intentions; arrangements. Work in pairs and interview another student, using your questions.

Grammar reflection

2 Look at these sentences about the future. Write the numbers of the sentences under the appropriate heading below.

hopes/desires	predictions
plans/intentions	arrangements

> 1 I think that eventually I'll stop moving around . . .
> 2 I'd like to go to Brazil.

3 I'm intending to return to France at the end of the year.

4 Don't worry. I expect you'll soon make friends there.

5 I might be working for the same company in ten years' time.

6 Perhaps she'll change her mind and agree to the proposal.

7 I doubt if they'll turn up now: it's nearly nine o'clock.

8 I'm meeting Tony at three o'clock.

9 They're thinking of selling their car.

10 They certainly won't come before the end of the year.

11 I'm exhausted. I don't think I'll go out tonight after all.

12 I'm sure he'll ask her this time.

13 I'm really busy right now, but I'll give you a ring this evening.

14 I'm definitely going to the States some time in the new year.

15 I should think he'll go back to India eventually.

3 Look at the different forms used for predictions. Order them according to how certain the speaker is. How can predictions be made more, or less, certain?

Look at the forms for plans/intention and order them according to the degree of certainty they suggest. Which of the expressions are the most formal?

4 Match each sentence a–d with its corresponding background information:

1 I've just spoken to the doctor.

2 He's very strong and has a positive attitude.

3 I work with him.

4 I've arranged to meet him.

   a He'll recover.
   b He's going to recover.
   c I'm seeing him tomorrow.
   d I'll be seeing him tomorrow.

Check your answers in the Grammar Reference on page 139.

Practice

Right or wrong?

5 Are these sentences grammatically correct? Put a tick or a cross next to each one. Now discuss them with a partner and explain what is wrong.

1 I'm planning to go to the States some time in the new year.

2 I'll let you know when I will have organised everything.

3 They will have a party next week.

4 I don't think he'll find another job that easily.

5 She hopes to earn enough money to buy a new car.

6 When you will come to my house I'll show you my stamp collection.

7 I'm tired. I think I'm going to bed.

8 I'm sure you will be enjoying your visit to the cathedral.

9 They definitely won't come before the end of the year.

10 I'll have finished the book by next Wednesday.

Speech!

6 Imagine you are a politician in your country just before an election. Prepare a speech lasting about three minutes stating your plans and intentions for making improvements in one or more of these areas:

social services   transport
education   economy   taxes

Try to use as many of the future forms that you have studied as possible.

In groups of four or five, take turns to give your speech. Make a note of the number of future expressions each speaker uses, and award a point to each one. The winner is the person with the most points.

Speaking

Look at these photographs of people on holiday. In each case an environmental problem is being exaggerated by their presence. Can you work out what the problems are?

Reading

Before you read

1 You are going to read a text about the environmental damage caused to the Alps by the skiing industry. Which of the following information do you expect to find in the article?

a An account of disasters caused by skiing developments.

b The amount of money that skiing earns for countries.

c Information about attempts to solve the problem.

d The history of skiing.

e The first-hand account of an avalanche survivor.

f Statistics about the number of skiers visiting the Alps.

g An explanation of how skiing damages the environment.

h The amount of money that the EEC has spent on solving the problem.

While you read

2 Now read the text and check to see if it contains the information in Exercise 1.

Vocabulary comprehension

3 Find words in the text which have a similar meaning to the words or phrases below.

Para. 1 assistant

Para. 2 summits

Para. 4 useful, beneficial
            cut down

Para. 6 small movement of soil and rocks
            absorb   thickly and uncontrollably

Para. 8 completely destroyed

Para. 9 trying to solve
            young

Para. 14 dangerous
            allow to fall off

Para. 15 freed from control

8 ▶

Reading

Is the skiing industry losing its grip? **Malcolm Smith** on moves to minimise the avalanche threat

Paring the piste resistance

1 WHEN Doctor Paulcke, a German physician, and a young apprentice named Branger bought Finnish skis at the Great Exhibition in Paris in 1889, no one could have guessed where the purchase would lead.

2 The Branger family pioneered Alpine skiing at the Swiss resort of Davos, where the world's first funicular took skiers to the now famous Parsenn runs. Within a few decades, the high peaks – once the reward of a half-day's climb – could be skied five times before lunch. Other resorts soon followed; even more were purpose-built.

3 This year's ski season is now nearing its peak, fuelled by a multi billion-pound Alpine skiing industry, with 40,000 ski runs and 14,000 ski-lifts for 12 million skiers. Austria's ski runs would circle the globe if joined end to end.

4 But the industry that proved a boon for poor Alpine farmers is damaging the environment. Forests have been felled to make way for more runs, car parks and hotels; pistes have been bulldozed and reshaped, destroying their fragile vegetation; and Alpine meadows have been abandoned by farmers keen to exploit tourism.

5 According to Javed Ahmad, executive director of Alp Action, international co-operation is needed to save the Alps.

6 Forests are the lifeguards of these snowy peaks. They provide a natural barrier against avalanches and landslips, but they also prevent them. Trees soak up rain while their leaves cushion the fragile soil below from heavy raindrops, making destructive landslips and flash floods rare. Alpine hay meadows also play a vital role. Their rough-cut surfaces hold snow; uncut meadow grows rank, allowing snow to slide off the smooth vegetation.

7 The avalanche is now a common and damaging phenomenon. Forestry experts estimate that two thirds of the several thousand avalanches that descend into inhabited parts of the Austrian Alps each year are the result of forest depletion.

8 In just three weeks in 1987, landslips in the Italian and Swiss Alps killed 60 people, made 7,000 homeless and damaged 50 villages and holiday centres. Italian villages such as Morignone and San Antonio Morignone were wiped out by 10 million tons of treeless mountainside.

9 SWITZERLAND and Austria are now grappling with the problem. Several schemes are under way to plant new forests and to keep skiers out of existing forests, where their skis can slice off sapling trees.

10 In Switzerland, an environmental-impact study is needed for new ski-lifts and cable cars in virgin areas.

11 Some Swiss centres, such as Grindelwald, have put a stop to any further ski-lift and hotel construction.

12 The Austrian provinces of Vorarlberg and Tyrol have passed a law to prevent new development. 'It's the result of local Alpine communities saying enough is enough,' says Werner Fritz, director of the National Tourist Office.

13 The French and Italians are doing little forest replanting, symptomatic of what Dominique Rambaud, at the International Centre for Alpine Environment, refers to politely as their lack of interest in managing the Alpine environment.

14 Experts say the concentration of purpose-built French ski resorts is also hazardous. The last big landslide in Les Arcs in 1981, caused £5 million of damage when 300,000 tons of mountainside washed away. Too much piste bulldozing and forest felling, coupled with vast areas of roofs and concrete car parks which shed the heavy rain, were blamed.

15 The French, in particular, are storing up an environmental disaster that could be unleashed any time.

© *The Guardian*

Role-play: Ski resort

The problem: The old village of Altberg in the Alps has a largely agricultural economy, but in recent years agriculture has been in decline, as farmers have been finding it harder and harder to make a living from the land. There is a small ski resort on the outskirts of the village with two pistes, largely used by local people. A large development company has been trying to buy up farm land above the resort with the aim of expanding skiing activities in the area. There would be advantages and disadvantages for the village if this were to happen. A public meeting is to be held in the town hall to discuss the issue.

Look at these roles and decide which one you relate to most. (The planning officer is the person who chairs the meeting and has to make the final decision according to how well people have made their case.)

villager   Alpine farmer   environmentalist
planning officer   skiing developer

Now work with a partner who has chosen the same role and prepare arguments to make your case at the public meeting. Prepare them in note form so that you can refer to them while you speak.

Grammar: adjectives

In Unit 2 you studied ways of giving more information for description by using modifiers or qualifiers. In this unit you are going to take a closer look at the use of adjectives as modifiers.

Structure

1 Adjectives can be in an attributive position with nouns, or in a predicative position with verbs like *be* or *become*.

Example: hot coffee   (attributive)

          This coffee is hot.   (predicative)

(*Note*: Some adjectives e.g. *afraid, asleep, sorry* are only used predicatively.)

Example: He's asleep now.

(NOT: ~~There's an asleep man on the floor.~~)

Look at the extract from a tourist brochure and find an example of a predicative and an attributive adjective.

THAILAND, once Siam, is today deservedly known as the land of smiles. The Thai people are naturally charming and polite and the standard of service you receive in hotels and restaurants is universally high.

The capital, Bangkok, has something for everyone. Tiny sampans and long-tailed taxi boats swarming all over the river and klongs ... saffron clad monks making their way to their devotions ... and *Wats* (temples) everywhere. At night, the city really comes to life – pitch-black bars and discothèques in Patpong, sumptuous restaurants and nightclubs in the big hotels, and typical Thai restaurants featuring local cuisine with accompanying classical dance performances or Thai boxing.

There is, without question though, a lot more to Thailand than busy and bustling Bangkok. On the following pages will be found beach, hill and idyllic island resorts, all perfect to combine with this magical city.

MALAYSIA'S lovely coast line is beginning to give way gently to resort development and one of the more recent 'finds' is the island of Pangkor with its little neighbour Pangkor Laut.

Although access may be a trifle difficult – an interesting 4 hour drive from Kuala Lumpur followed by a 45 minute ferry ride – the effort of reaching these tranquil havens is truly worthwhile.

Also off the west coast are the 99 legendary islands of Langkawi, the largest of which is also named Langkawi – an island which is all one might wish of a tropical paradise ... exotic flowers, long stretches of stunning white beaches and hideaway coves shaded by lofty palms.

Across on the beautiful east coast, washed by the south China Sea, Kuantan and Cherating also have excellent beaches and surroundings which offer great scope for exploration.

Off the west coast of Peninsular Malaysia, Penang is a mere 15 miles long and 9 miles wide, washed by the waters of the Straits of Malacca.

An island of superb uncrowded beaches, the best of these is Batu Ferringhi, a 2 mile stretch along which are located most of the major resort hotels. The island's colonial past is utterly fascinating and reminders are everywhere in the interesting little capital of Georgetown.

In the lush, hilly interior, there are many points of interest like Kek Lok Si Temple and a must is the funicular railway that will take you to the top of Penang Hill.

Types of adjectives

2 Qualitative adjectives identify qualities which someone or something has, e.g. a *happy, intelligent* person.

Classifying adjectives identify someone or something as a member of a 'class', e.g. *financial* help (as opposed to *emotional* or *physical* help). Some adjectives can be used as both classifying and qualitative adjectives.

Compare: *an emotional person* (qualitative) and *the emotional development of a person*.

(*Note*: Classifying adjectives do not take comparative and superlative forms, and cannot be used with modifiers, like *very, quite, rather*, etc.)

Now look at the extract from the travel brochure again and find examples of qualitative and classifying adjectives.

Order of adjectives

3 When two or more adjectives are used before a noun, the adjectives follow a certain order:

Opinion adjectives	Descriptive adjectives
general/specific	size/age/shape/colour/nationality/material

Example: *They bought a lovely, stylish, large, old, rectangular, brown English oak table.*

Find examples in the texts of nouns preceded by more than one adjective, and notice the order of the adjectives.

Practice

Types of adjectives

4 Divide the words below into classifying and qualitative adjectives.

> nice pretty east popular south hot
> funny international comfortable historical
> basic expensive free modern quiet
> daily alternative small attractive golden

Order of adjectives

5 Use the adjectives in the correct order before each noun to make noun phrases.

Example: beach – white, sandy, soft
a soft, white, sandy beach

hotel – modern, large, expensive
climate – sunny, warm, Mediterranean
water – blue, clear, clean
restaurant – international, open-air, clean
rooms – spacious, comfortable, twin-bedded

Writing: describing places

Holiday brochures

1 Look at the photograph, and read the description of the holiday resort in the extract from a travel brochure. Complete the description of the place and its facilities using the adjectives given.

> vivid translucent tourist rainbow-coloured
> tranquil gleaming independent simple
> coral unique white tiny Indian
> inhabited unspoilt blue simple small

Some 400 miles south west of Sri Lanka lie the Maldives, an _____ republic of 4000 _____ coral islands scattered across the _____ _____ waters of the _____ Ocean.

In this _____ environment, where visiting another hotel means taking a boat, only about 200 of the islands are _____ – some by _____ fishing communities, others with just one _____ _____ hotel.

Here the visitor will find a _____, _____ setting of _____ _____ beaches ringed by _____ _____ reefs teeming with _____ fish – a haven for the watersports enthusiast and for those seeking to do nothing more than totally unwind with the emphasis on sunshine, the beach, the ocean and _____ living ...

See page 126 for the correct version of the extract, and check your answers.

A favourite place

2 What is your favourite place on earth? Make notes about it, including suitable adjectives, and write a description of it in the style of a travel brochure, making it sound as attractive as possible.

Work in groups. Take it in turns to read your 'brochures'. Decide which one was the most attractive, and what made you want to visit the place described.

Vocabulary

Life choices

Use one of these words to complete each sentence.

kick thrill career security boredom
freedom rat-race responsibility

1 The film was three hours long and was subtitled. Many people left out of sheer _____.

2 He goes rock-climbing every weekend on his own. He shows no sense of _____ towards his family.

3 She has just left her present job and gone on a yachting trip – she doesn't care about her _____ at all.

4 I really get a _____ out of motorcycling even though I know it's dangerous.

5 I think most people need a mixture of excitement and _____ in their lives.

6 They sold their house, gave up their jobs and went to live abroad. They were fed up with the _____ .

7 Few people can resist the _____ of downhill skiing once they have tried it.

8 If you work for yourself you have more _____, but less security.

Another country

Write the words which correspond to these definitions.

9 To complain about something in a bad-tempered way, usually in a low voice, and not forcefully.

10 Interested and delighted, so much so that your thoughts are concentrated entirely on one thing.

11 All the rules and procedures followed by government departments.

12 Interested and eager to learn about.

13 To deal successfully with a difficulty.

14 The ideas, customs and art that are shared by a particular society.

15 The practice of treating one person or group of people less fairly than others.

16 To complain about something in a way which might irritate others.

Grammar

Past tenses (2)

Complete this biography of a writer by writing the verbs in brackets in the correct form.

Mary Wesley (be) born near Windsor in 1912. Her education (take) her to the London School of Economics and during the war she (work) in the War Office.

17 ____
18 ____
19 ____

She (also/work) part-time in the antique trade. Mary Wesley (live) in London, France, Italy, Germany and several places in the West Country. She (live) in Totnes for a number of years now where she says that she lives 'rather a hermit's existence'. She (previously/write) for children and claims that her 'chief claim to fame is arrested development, getting my first novel published at the age of seventy.' Black Swan (publish) this first novel, *Jumping the Queue* in 1983 and it (be) an immediate success. Black Swan (also/publish) her late novels, *Harnessing Peacocks*, *The Vacillations of Poppy Carew* and *Not That Sort of Girl*.

20 ____
21 ____
22 ____

23 ____

24 ____
25 ____
26 ____

The future

Write a sentence about:

27 Something relevant to you which will be in progress next summer.

28 A future fact described on a timetable which is relevant to your working day tomorrow.

29 An arrangement which you have made with someone for the coming week.

30 Your intentions for this evening.

31 A decision, which you have just made, to take the bus home.

32 A prediction about the economy next year.

33 A prediction about the weather later today, based on conditions now.

34 A hope or desire that you have for the future.

35 Something which has not yet happened in your life, and which will happen by the end of this year.

Adjectives

For each of the following, choose two different descriptive adjectives from the box and use them in the correct order to write a description.

36 a _____ _____ armchair

37 an _____ _____ village

38 _____ _____ food

39 a _____ _____ man

40 an _____ _____ film

sun-tanned interesting leather
hot historical Indian luxurious
tall important little

Check your answers in the Answer Key on page 124.

'No man would listen to you talk if he didn't know it was his turn next.'

EDGAR WATSON HOWE

Vocabulary: communication

1 Look at the cartoon.
Have you ever found yourself in a similar situation with someone?

What causes this type of problem? How can it be solved? Discuss in groups.

Adjectives

2 Divide the list of adjectives in the box into two groups – characteristics of *a* good communicators, and *b* bad communicators.

| tactful   abrupt   blunt   forthright   direct   open   standoffish   reserved   approachable |
| over the top   expressive   arrogant   off-handed   dismissive   articulate   argumentative   pompous |
| understanding   tolerant   opinionated   frank   straightforward   outspoken   sensitive   supercilious |

Idiomatic expressions

3 Match the idiomatic expression relating to communication, with sentences 1 – 7. Then replace the relevant words in each sentence with the expressions.

a rub someone up the wrong way	1 It's so frustrating talking to her! She talks and talks, but it takes her ages to say what she's really *trying* to say.
b get to the point	2 I'm really glad we've discussed this and been honest about our feelings. I feel much better about it now.
c clear the air	3 I just couldn't make him understand what I wanted.
d get the wrong end of the stick	4 I thought it best to tell them what the disadvantages would be.
e bring something up	5 When he started talking about style I thought he meant those things you climb over between fields in the country …
f point something out	6 In the meeting I decided to start talking about the sensitive issue of staff cuts.
g get through to someone	7 I don't know why, but he always manages to irritate or offend me whatever he does; maybe it's his manner.

Discussion

Successful and unsuccessful communicators

Work in two groups. **Group A** complete the 'successful' part of the mind map, and **Group B**, the 'unsuccessful' part. Include all the words and expressions you have studied so far.

Work with a partner from a different group. Compare and discuss your mind map.

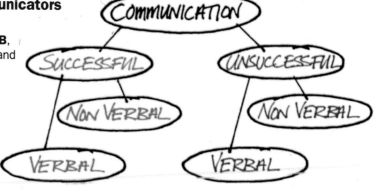

Listening

Before you listen

1 Have you ever been persuaded to buy something you didn't need?
What techniques did the person use to convince you?
How did you feel afterwards?
Do you think you could make a living out of selling things? Why, or why not?

First listening

T20 2 You are going to listen to Graham Maynard, now a senior Sales Manager for Nestlé, talking about two incidents he remembers from the beginning of his career, when he was a sales representative. Listen and decide the order of these pictures which describe his **second** anecdote.

Second listening

3 Read these questions and make notes while you listen so that you can give complete answers.

1 What was Graham's first job?
2 What did he sell?
3 What idea did he have for beating his competitors? What went wrong?
4 What weather conditions does Graham really hate?
5 Where did the 'snow' incident take place?
6 Why did Graham's car stop?
7 What did the policeman ask Graham?
8 How did the story end?

9 ▶

Pronunciation: weak forms – adjectival words

T22 4 There are seven adjectival words which are usually used in their weak forms in conversational English:
a, an, the, some, his, her, saint.

Listen to each sentence and write down the weak form of one (or more) of the words listed above.

Now listen and repeat, concentrating on using the weak forms accurately.

Speech features: *in fact*

Listen to T23 and listen to Graham say **in fact**. Decide which of these meanings his use of the phrase corresponds to in each case:

• in reality, in truth – often used as emphasis or to check something which has just been said
• to emphasise or introduce a contradictory opinion to something which has just been said
• to introduce more detailed information related to what has already been said
• to introduce new – often surprising – information related to something already discussed.

Now work in pairs and write sentences for the meanings of **in fact** which are not illustrated by Graham's sentences.

Grammar: verbs with *to* + infinitive, or *-ing* clause

Same or different?

1 Work with a partner. In which of the sentence pairs is there no change in meaning? In sentence pairs where there *is* a change in meaning, explain the difference between the two versions.

1 a I used to go back every two years.
  b I'm used to going back every two years.

2 a It started raining.
  b It started to rain.

3 a I remembered discussing it before the meeting.
  b I remembered to discuss it before the meeting.

4 a I didn't like to ask him.
  b I didn't like asking him.

5 a I love reading the Sunday papers.
  b I love to read the Sunday papers.

6 a He began to tell me about his childhood.
  b He began telling me abut his childhood.

7 a I forgot seeing him about the flat.
  b I forgot to see him about the flat.

8 a He regretted saying that he thought you were stupid.
  b He regretted to say that he thought you were stupid.

9 a I tried to phone him.
  b I tried phoning him.

10 a Sally went on to study at university.
   b Sally went on studying at university.

11 a They need to cut their hedge.
   b Their hedge needs cutting.

Grammar reflection

2 Look at the way the verbs are used in these sentences.

1 I used to have one or two farm shops that I was responsible for.
  I'm used to driving in bad weather but I hate snow.

2 I was driving off along the road and it started to cough and splutter ...
  I was driving off along the road and it started coughing and spluttering ...

3 'Young man, are you trying to start that vehicle?
  'Young man, have you tried pushing the car to get it started?'

4 I needed to turn the car round to leave, to go back to the next store.
  The exhaust of the car needed cleaning.

List the following verbs in two groups:
verbs with *-ing* or *to* where there is

a no change in meaning, and
b a different meaning.

like begin attempt forget regret fear
remember continue try prefer love
go on start need bother hate

Now answer these questions.

1 Do you use *-ing* or *to* after verbs in the first group, when they are used in the continuous tense?
Example: *I am trying _____ French in the evenings. (learn)*

2 Which of these two sentences refers to a habit, and which refers to a memory?
  a I'm used to getting up early every morning.
  b I used to get up early every morning.

Check your answers in the Grammar Reference on page 141.

Practice

Childhood

3 Complete these sentences about your childhood.

1 Your earliest memory. *I remember ...*
2 Something you did often, but no longer do. *I used to ...*
3 Something you disliked doing. *I hated ...*
4 A hobby you had, and still have. *I started ...*
5 A place or person you enjoyed visiting. *I loved ...*
6 Something you enjoyed eating. *I liked ...*

Now compare and discuss your sentences with a partner, using the verbs you have studied in Exercise 2.

Someone like me ...

4 Write down your habits under the following categories, using the verbs *like/used to/ try/hate/start*:

sleeping habits (get up/go to bed)
weekly sporting activities
meals and mealtimes
reading habits
study

Now ask other students questions about their habits until you find someone who has at least two habits in common with you.

Speaking

Role-play

Read about this problem which has arisen between two old friends.

> Peter and Jeremy have known each other for nearly twenty years, and until two years ago, were very good friends. Five years ago Jeremy met Lucy and they started going out together. Peter didn't like Lucy but because he didn't want to hurt Jeremy's feelings he kept this to himself.
>
> Jeremy's company sent him to live in Argentina for a year, and when he came back, he and Lucy decided to get married. He confessed to Peter that one of his reasons for getting married was that he was afraid of being 'left on the shelf'. Since then Peter's relationship with his friend – and above all, with Lucy – has gone from bad to worse.

Choose one of these roles and turn to the relevant page.

Student A: Peter (page 118), **Student B:** Jeremy (page 119), **Student C:** Lucy (page 119), **Student D:** Sally – a friend of all three (page 119).

Writing: informal letter

Read the first draft of a letter Peter wanted to write to Jeremy, to make peace with him. Can you identify where Peter has been too abrupt? Rewrite the letter, changing the content to make it more conciliatory and diplomatic. Include any solution you found to the problem during your discussion.

Now write Jeremy's reply to Peter's letter. Again, try to be diplomatic, and take into account the points that arose during your discussion. Don't forget to lay out your letter correctly.

> 23 Railway Road
> Surbiton
> Surrey
>
> Tuesday 15th Feb.
>
> Dear Jeremy,
>
> Seeing as how you are such an obstinate person and would never have got in touch I thought I'd better write to you if I ever wanted to see you again. If it hadn't been for Lucy none of this would have happened. I really don't know why you married her and let's face it, time is not improving matters, if you know what I mean.
>
> Anyway, Sally suggested that I write to you, so I thought I'd give it a try, even though I know it's unlikely you'll say yes as you're afraid Lucy will disapprove. How about meeting for a drink sometime? We could maybe go out and have a good time when Lucy is away at her mother's. At least that way she won't interfere with you having fun and she need never know.
>
> Anyway, whatever you decide, write to me or give me a ring (jailer permitting) and let me know how things are going. Better not mention this letter to the old lady or she might have a tantrum.
>
> See you
> Peter

41

Reading

Before you read

1 Here are the beginnings of some of the paragraphs of the text you are about to read. What kind of information do you expect to find in the text? List as many ideas as you can alongside each sentence beginning.

The danger of misinterpretation is greatest …

An American woman visiting England …

To the American, politeness requires …

The fate of the earth depends …

Despite the fact that talking to each other …

While you read

2 Read the text and compare the content with your predictions in Exercise 1.

Vocabulary comprehension

3 Choose the best definition for each of these words from the text.

1 *Para. 1* tongue
  a soft, moveable part inside the mouth, used for tasting and talking
  b language
  c pieces of leather underneath the laces of a boot or shoe

2 *Para. 2* imposing
  a unreasonably expecting someone to do something or spend time with you when they don't really want to
  b using your authority to make sure a rule is kept
  c grand, impressive

3 *Para. 3* setting
  a surrounding in which an event takes place
  b particular set of circumstances or conditions
  c piece of metal in jewellery, which holds a precious stone

4 *Para. 3* booth
  a stall for the sale or display of goods
  b small, enclosed, or partially enclosed room, e.g. a telephone booth
  c in a bar or restaurant, two high-backed benches with a table between them

5 *Para. 4* inclined
  a with a disposition/tending towards
  b sloping; slanting
  c bent; lowered

6 *Para. 8* yield
  a supply; produce
  b surrender; give up
  c energy released by the explosion of a nuclear weapon

4 Now look at these words in the context of the text and try to work out the meaning.

Para. 3 enraged *Para. 4* ruse *Para. 5* fleeting
Para. 6 snubbed *Para. 7* pitfalls *Para. 10* crave

10 ▶

Speaking

There are many cultural differences regarding when to speak to strangers. In your country, would you say anything to a stranger in these situations?

Have you noticed any other situations where there are cultural differences in attitudes to communication?

Reading

Mixed Metamessages across Cultures

[1] The danger of misinterpretation is greatest, of course, among speakers who actually speak different native tongues, or come from different cultural backgrounds, because cultural difference necessarily implies different assumptions about natural and obvious ways to be polite.

[2] Anthropologist Thomas Kochman gives the example of a white office worker who appeared with a bandaged arm and felt rejected because her black fellow worker didn't mention it. The (doubly) wounded worker assumed that her silent colleague didn't notice or didn't care. But the co-worker was purposely not calling attention to something her colleague might not want to talk about. She let her decide whether or not to mention it: being considerate by not imposing. Kochman says, based on his research, that these differences reflect recognisable black and white styles.

[3] An American woman visiting England was repeatedly offended – even, on bad days, enraged – when the British ignored her in settings in which she thought they should pay attention. For example, she was sitting at a booth in a railway-station cafeteria. A couple began to settle into the opposite seat in the same booth. They unloaded their luggage; they laid their coats on the seat; he asked what she would like to eat and went off to get it; she slid into the booth facing the American. And throughout all this, they showed no sign of having noticed that someone was already sitting in the booth.

[4] When the British woman lit up a cigarette, the American had a concrete object for her anger. She began ostentatiously looking around for another table to move to. Of course there was none; that's why the British couple had sat in her booth in the first place. The smoker immediately crushed out her cigarette and apologised. This showed that she had noticed that someone else was sitting in the booth, and that she was not inclined to disturb her. But then she went back to pretending the American wasn't there, a ruse in which her husband collaborated when he returned with their food and they ate it.

[5] To the American, politeness requires talk between strangers forced to share a booth in a cafeteria, if only a fleeting 'Do you mind if I sit down?' or a conventional, 'Is anyone sitting here?' even if it's obvious no one is. The omission of such talk seemed to her like dreadful rudeness. The American couldn't see that another system of politeness was at work. By not acknowledging her presence, the British couple freed her from the obligation to acknowledge theirs. The American expected a show of involvement; they were being polite by not imposing.

[6] An American man who had lived for years in Japan explained a similar politeness ethic. He lived, as many Japanese do, in extremely close quarters – a tiny room separated from neighbouring rooms by paper-thin walls. In this case the walls were literally made of paper. In order to preserve privacy in this most unprivate situation, his Japanese neighbours simply acted as if no one else lived there. They never showed signs of having overheard conversations, and if, while walking down the hall, they caught a neighbour with the door open, they steadfastly glued their gaze ahead as if they were alone in a desert. The American confessed to feeling what I believe most Americans would feel if a next-door neighbour passed within a few feet without acknowledging their presence – snubbed. But he realised that the intention was not rudeness by omitting to show involvement, but politeness by not imposing.

[7] The fate of the earth depends on cross-cultural communication. Nations must reach agreements, and agreements are made by individual representatives of nations sitting down and talking to each other – public analogues of private conversations. The processes are the same, and so are the pitfalls. Only the possible consequences are more extreme.

We Need the Eggs

[8] Despite the fact that talking to each other frequently fails to yield the understanding we seek, we keep at it, just as nations keep trying to negotiate and reach agreement. Woody Allen knows why, and says, in his film *Annie Hall*, which ends with a joke that is heard voice-over:

[9] "This guy goes to a psychiatrist and says, 'Doc, my brother's crazy. He thinks he's a chicken.' And the doctor says, 'Well, why don't you turn him in?' And the guy says, 'I would, but I need the eggs.' Well, I guess that's pretty much how I feel about relationships."

[10] Even though intimate as well as fleeting conversations don't yield the perfect communication we crave – and we can see from past experience and from the analysis presented here that they can't – we still keep hoping and trying because we need the eggs of involvement and independence.

Say the right thing!

Persuading

1 Work in groups of three. **Student A:** Try to persuade **Student B** to do one of the things listed below. **Student C:** Make a note of the language used for persuasion. Now change roles, until you have all had a turn as **A**, **B** or **C**.

- You want to go out for a drink but your friend wants to stay at home and watch TV.
- You think your boss should take the rest of the day off as he or she has flu.
- You want a friend to change previously made holiday plans and go to the USA with you this summer.

Language

2 This is the pattern of communication often followed when someone is persuading/being persuaded.

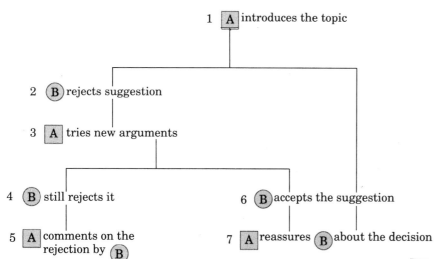

1 [A] introduces the topic

2 (B) rejects suggestion

3 [A] tries new arguments

4 (B) still rejects it

5 [A] comments on the rejection by (B)

6 (B) accepts the suggestion

7 [A] reassures (B) about the decision

Situation

3 Work in pairs. Use the language you learnt in Exercise 2 in your conversation.

Student A: Your friend – whose car has just broken down again – is intending to buy a bicycle for the journey to the city centre every day. Try to persuade your partner *not* to get a bicycle, but another car instead. Include these points:

- dangers of city traffic
- the weather
- not being able to give friends lifts
- cycle thieves

Student B: You have decided to buy a bicycle to go to the city centre every day as your car has just broken down again and you are fed up with it. Your friend will try to persuade you to buy another car instead. Find arguments to persuade your partner that your decision is the right one. Include these points:

- ecology
- cost
- health
- time-saving

What was the pattern of the conversations you had in Exercise 1?

What language did you use at the various stages?

T24 Listen to two conversations and map out the communication, using the numbers in the diagram.

Which of the conversations is more formal?

What are the differences in vocabulary and verb tenses that tell us this?

In which phases of the conversations are the following phrases used? What is their function?

It's just that ...	Sorry, ...
Oh, go on ...	As a matter of fact ...
Oh, all right then ...	Quite ...
It's about ...	I was wondering ...
the problem is that ...	I really think ...

Listen again and complete the phrases.

> 'A family is a unit composed not only of children, but of men, women, an occasional animal, and the common cold.'
>
> *OGDEN NASH*

Vocabulary: the family

Explain the difference

1 Work in pairs. Explain the difference between the words in each group, either by defining them, or inventing a sentence which demonstrates their meaning in context.

1 relations/relatives/kin
2 wife/spouse/bride
3 husband/groom/partner
4 brother/child/sibling
5 divorce/separate/split up
6 adopted child/foster child/orphan
7 marry/get engaged/get married
8 wedding/marriage/matrimony
9 nuclear family/extended family/single-parent family
10 ancestors/descendants/heirs/offspring
11 love/ be in love/fall in love
12 upbringing/background/environment
13 bring up/raise/grow

Common problems

2 Choose the correct word or expression for each sentence.

1 It's important for parents to encourage _____ their children.
   a dependence on *b* independent of *c* independence in *d* dependence of

2 He prefers to be _____.
   a with himself *b* on his own *c* by his own *d* on himself

3 She's never been unhappy living alone, as she's very self-_____.
   a adjusted *b* completed *c* reliant *d* satisfied

4 You _____ your parents far too much. You'll have to start doing things for yourself – they can't do everything for you …
   a account on *b* trust *c* rely on *d* depend

5 She decided to rent a flat, because she thought she needed _____ from her family.
   a freedom *b* liberty *c* independence *d* liberation

6 Children need to learn to _____ themselves.
   a look for *b* look up *c* fend for *d* offend

3 Read the extract below quickly, and decide on an appropriate title.

'Mom, that's sort of why I called.'
'Yes, darling?'
'I want you to call Mr Lassiter and tell him I won't be in on Monday morning.'
'Oh … Mary Ann, I'm not sure you should ask for an extension on your vacation.'
'It's not an extension, Mom.'
'Well, then why …'
'I'm not coming home, Mom.'
Silence. Then, dimly in the distance, a television voice began to tell Mary Ann's father about the temporary relief of haemorrhoids. Finally, her mother spoke: 'Don't be silly, darling.'
'Mom … I'm not being silly. I *like* it here. It feels like home already.'
'Mary Ann, if there's a boy …'
'There's no boy … I've thought about this for a long time.'
'Don't be ridiculous. You've been there five days!'
'Mom, I know how you feel, but … well, it's got nothing to do with you and Daddy. I just want to start making my own life … have my own apartment and all.'
'Oh, *that*. Well, darling … of *course* you can. As a matter of fact, your daddy and I thought those new apartments out at Ridgemont might be just perfect for you. They take lots of young people, and they've got a swimming pool and a sauna, and I could make some of those darling curtains like I made for Sonny and Vicki when they got married. You could have all the privacy you …'
'You aren't listening, Mom. I'm trying to tell you I'm a grown woman.'

Now answer the questions.

1 Where do you think Mary Ann is calling from?
2 What has she decided to do?
3 What's her mother's attitude to Mary Ann's decision?

Discussion

Family life

Family life isn't always easy. Parents and children often have disagreements. Which of these problems can be the main cause of conflict between parents and children?

Do – or did – you have any of these problems with your parents or children? What other issues can cause conflict in families?

fashion   going out at night   household chores   the opposite sex   leaving home

Listening

Before you listen

1 Which of these statements could apply to your family?
Which of them do you believe are valid? Discuss in groups.

a 'Children have to help with the housework.'

b 'Children are only allowed out alone during the daytime.'

c 'If teenagers go out alone they have to let their parents know where they are going.'

d 'Children are expected to work at weekends and during holidays and give part of their earnings to the family.'

e 'Boys have more freedom than girls.'

f 'Teenage girls are never allowed out alone at night.'

g 'When a son marries, he lives with his wife in the same house as his parents.'

h 'Children have a responsibility to look after their ageing parents.'

First listening

 2 Neevita was born in England, although she was brought up in an Indian culture. The first time you listen, tick the statements above which apply to Neevita's family.

Second listening

3 Read these questions, then listen again and write down the answers.

1 What, if anything, doesn't Neevita like about her family life?

2 In what ways does Neevita's brother have more freedom than she has?

3 Which differences between Pakistani and Indian families does Neevita mention?

4 In which ways are Neevita's parents different from typical Indian parents?

5 In Indian families, what happens when the children get married?

11 ▶

Pronunciation: weak forms – pronouns

 4 When English is spoken at normal conversational speed, there are six pronouns which are usually pronounced in their weak forms.

Listen to these sentences from the conversation between Jonathan and Neevita. Make a note of the pronoun which is pronounced in its weak form in each sentence.

The pronouns *there, us* and *he* are sometimes used in their strong forms. When do you think this could happen?

Now listen and repeat, paying attention to your pronunciation of the pronouns.

> ### Speech features: *right*
>
> The word **right** can have several different functions in conversation:
>
> - to attract the speaker's attention, especially when a different speaker wants to say something
> - to express agreement or approval
> - to show that something has been understood
> - to check that someone else has understood or agreed
> - to reassure the speaker that she or he is being listened to.
>
> How do you think the intonation of **right** differs for each of the functions listed?
>
> Listen to T28 . Whenever the speakers use the word **right**, tick the corresponding function from the points above.

Grammar: wishes

> ### Families
>
> **1** If you had three wishes about your family or your childhood, what would they be?
>
> **Example**: *I wish I had a brother.*
>
> *I wish my sister would come and visit me more often.*
>
> Work in groups. Read out your sentences. Does anyone in your group have similar wishes?

Grammar reflection

2 Look at these sentences from 〔T25〕, and the other types of wishes below.

> 1 I wish I wasn't the eldest.
> 2 I wish I had more freedom.
> 3 I wish my brother wasn't spoilt.

4 I wish my parents would give me more freedom.
5 I wish my sister could come and live with me in Paris.
6 I wish my sister would come and live in Paris.
7 I wish I'd been the youngest child in my family.

Now decide which kind of wish is expressed in each of the sentences.

> A a regret that a present situation is not as we would like it to be
>
> B a regret that something happened, or didn't happen, in the past
>
> C a desire for someone to change, or to do something
>
> D a wish that someone was able to do something

3 Answer the following questions.

1 Which verb tenses are used in each of the sentences?
2 Which sentences refer to the future/present/past?
3 Which other two words can be used instead of *I wish …* in some of the sentences?

Check your answers in the Grammar Reference on page 141.

"I wish you'd use the nutcrackers, dear."

Practice

Sentence puzzle

4 Use a word from each column in the chart below, and make as many complete, logical sentences as you can. Compare your sentences with a partner.

I wish	she	would	come out	tonight
		had	here	
	I	was		
		could		

Perfect world?

5 Write three regrets about things that have happened in the world, and three wishes for the present or the future.

Example: *I wish the internal combustion engine had never been invented.*

I wish there was a fairer distribution of wealth between nations.

I wish people would stop judging others by their appearances.

Now discuss your regrets and wishes in groups. Which ones are the most common? How realistic are they?

Reading

John Cleese, one of the writers of the book *Families and how to survive them*, from which the extract is taken, is better known as an actor. He directed and starred in the film *A Fish Called Wanda* and became famous as a writer and actor in the *Monty Python's Flying Circus* and *Fawlty Towers* TV series. Some years ago he participated in a therapy group run by psychotherapist Robin Skynner. They published this book as a result of their experiences in the group.

Before you read

1 The text you are going to read is about something called the 'Family Systems Exercise', which the psychotherapist Robin Skynner sometimes uses at the beginning of a series of group therapy sessions.

If you were a therapist, what sort of information would you be interested in finding out at the beginning of a series of sessions? Discuss in pairs.

While you read

2 Read the text quickly and find out what happens in the 'Family Systems Exercise'. What does the exercise try to prove?

a that families are all basically the same
b that people don't need to talk to each other to be able to get on
c that a person chooses a partner because this person is similar to himself or herself
d that people need to be part of a family in order to be happy.

Vocabulary comprehension

3 List six unfamiliar words from the text which you think are important for a complete understanding of the text. Look at the words again and try to write a definition for each one. Compare your lists in groups, and help to explain the meaning of any words you know. Now look up the words on your list in a dictionary.

Phrasal verbs

4 Find phrasal verbs in the text which have the same meaning as the following words and phrases.

choose	discover
happen	try to find
subject to	raise
postpone	get on one's feet

Reading

1 **Robin** Let me explain. I should say this whole idea was perhaps the most startling discovery I encountered in years and years of working with families, and I only gradually came to accept it as true. But the most dramatic piece of evidence for it is called the Family Systems Exercise. The first time I saw this was in 1973, when some visiting American family therapists demonstrated it to us. We've now incorporated it into our training methods at the Institute of Family Therapy.

2 **John** What's the exercise for?

3 **Robin** Its purpose is to show what lies behind the way that couples pick each other out across a crowded room! And it demonstrated to me more clearly than I'd ever realised how unconscious attractions work, and what they're about.

4 **John** You mean it shows how we pick each other without knowing anything about each other?

5 **Robin** Yes. The trainees do this exercise very early on – in fact ideally when they're still complete strangers. They're put together in a group and asked to choose another person from the group who either makes them think of someone in their family or, alternatively, gives them the feeling that they would have filled a 'gap' in their family. And – here's the interesting bit – they're not allowed to speak at all while they're choosing.

They just stand up and wander around looking at all the others. When they've all chosen someone, that is when they're in pairs, they are told to talk together for a time, to see if they can find out what made them pick each other. They're encouraged to compare their family backgrounds. Next, each couple is asked to choose another couple, in order to make foursomes. And then, each foursome is asked to form itself into a family of some kind, agreeing with each other what role in the family each person will take. Then they talk together about what it was in their family backgrounds that led to their decisions. And finally, they report to the whole group what they've discovered.

6 **John** Which is what?

7 **Robin** That they've somehow, each one of them, picked out three people whose families functioned in very similar ways to their own.

8 **John** How do you mean 'functioned in very similar ways'?

9 **Robin** Well, they'll find that all four of them are from families where there was difficulty in sharing affection; or perhaps in expressing anger, or envy; or where there had been a lot of near-incestuous relationships; or where people had always been expected to be optimistic and cheerful. Or they might discover that all four of them had fathers who were away from home during the years when that mattered a lot to them; or that all their families had suffered some big loss or change of a similar kind when they were all at similar ages.

10 **John** Couldn't this just be because they are looking for things they have in common?

11 **Robin** That's not really a good enough explanation for the *number of connected* similarities they always find. I know it may sound unconvincing to anyone who hasn't actually tried it, but it's quite uncanny when you experience it for yourself.

12 **John** But what about all the 'wall-flowers'? How do you explain the ones who don't get chosen?

13 **Robin** Well, funnily enough, it was the 'wall-flowers' that clinched the argument for me – finally convinced me that there was something extraordinary going on. The very first time that I was in charge of putting about twenty trainee family therapists through this exercise, I suddenly got worried that the ones who came together last would feel they were all rejects. So, when we asked the groups to report on their experiences – the family similarities they'd discovered – I put off asking the 'wall-flower' group till last, as I was rather dreading what their reaction would be. But they were just as fascinated as the rest of the trainees. They had discovered that they had all been fostered, adopted, or brought up in children's homes. They had *all* felt rejected early in their lives, and had somehow, in this exercise unerringly picked each other out!

Speaking

This cartoon from the book by Cleese and Skynner seems to suggest that the person we choose as a partner often has the same defects as we have. Discuss in groups:

Do you agree with this point of view? What other factors are important in influencing people to choose a partner?

What are the qualities *you* look for in another person?

Make a list of the five most important ingredients of a happy relationship.

♡ *What a divinely damaged person.* ♡

Grammar: the passive

Quotation quiz

1 Each box in the grid below represents a word which will help to complete a famous quotation by Oscar Wilde.

Work in two teams. Take turns to invent sentences using the verb tenses specified by each box. For each correct and logical sentence you invent, your teacher will reveal the word for that box. The winner is the first team to find out the quotation.

' __A__ course, __B__ had __C__ been __D__ before __E__ but __F__ had __G__ been __H__ up.'

Oscar Wilde

present simple passive A	present continuous passive B	past simple passive C	past continuous passive D
past perfect passive E	future simple passive F	present perfect passive G	future perfect passive H

Grammar reflection

2 Look at these examples of the passive from previous texts in this unit.

> 1 I was dropped and picked up.
> 2 It is called the 'Family Systems Exercise.'
> 3 Indian girls are not allowed to go out.
> 4 I wasn't pressurised to leave home.
> 5 I can always remember being very strongly encouraged to leave home.

Which kinds of passive tenses – from the grid in Exercise 1 – can be found in these sentences? Write the corresponding letter A – H alongside each sentence.

Now invent your own sentences for the rest of the passive tenses in the grid.

Answer these questions about the passive.

1 How does a passive construction change the 'focus' or emphasis in a sentence?

2 Why is the agent (person or thing responsible for the action) often omitted in a passive sentence?

Example: *They are told to talk together for a long time …*

3 To introduce the agent, we use the preposition *by*. What does the preposition *with* introduce?

Example: *It was celebrated with a party, by my parents and friends.*

In which of these contexts would you expect to find a large number of passives?

> novels   instructions   newspapers   scientific texts
> speeches   advertisements   official forms

Check your answers in the Grammar Reference on page 142.

Practice

Rapid reading

4 Work in pairs. **Pair A** turn to page 120, and **Pair B**, to page 121. Read the texts, and write a question for each one, using the passive.

Now exchange questions with another pair of students. Read your partners' texts and answer the questions as quickly as possible. The first pair to answer the questions correctly is the winner.

Writing: describing people

Link verbs

1 A link verb links a subject and 'a complement'. The complement tells you more about the subject.

Example: *Fred **was** an opera singer*.

Here is a list of link verbs which are used for describing subjects.

appear	feel	grow	prove	smell	taste
be	get	keep	remain	sound	turn
become	go	look	seem	stay	

Adjectives and noun groups can be used as complements after link verbs.

Example: *She felt very **contented**.*
*He seemed **an ideal person for the job**.*

After the following link verbs, *to* + infinitive clauses can be used as complements:

appear get grow prove seem

Example: *They seemed **to like** us.*

Link verbs with adjectives

2 Make a list of adjectives which can be used to describe a person's character and appearance. Choose five link verbs and use them with the adjectives you have listed to describe the appearance and character of a student in the class.

Example: *She is tall, slim and very good-looking. She seems quite optimistic – she always looks cheerful when she comes to lessons.*

In pairs, read your sentences and try to guess the identity of the person being described.

Link verbs with noun groups

3 Complete these sentences with the appropriate link verb.

1 Even though he always _____ a very relaxed sort of person, I found out later that he uses tranquillizers.
2 After studying languages at university he _____ an interpreter at the United Nations.
3 She _____ not the right person for this job.
4 Despite the efforts of the media, her private life still _____ something of a mystery.
5 To most people they always _____ a happy sort of couple.
6 I hope he gets elected; he'll _____ a very good Prime Minister.

Structuring descriptions

4 These are three main areas which are often focused on during descriptions of people.

1 physical attributes (hair, eyes, complexion, shape of face, other facial features, build, height, way of walking, gesture, clothes and accessories)
2 emotional, intellectual, and moral attributes (e.g. *cold, intelligent, dishonest*)
3 habits (behavioural and emotional habits, opinions, gesture and expression)

Read these two extracts from the novel *Love and Friendship*, by the American writer, Alison Lurie. Underline the descriptive words and phrases, and match them to one of the numbers above, as in the example.

As she spoke, Emmy looked at her husband again, and suddenly he looked *unattractive* to her, a heavy young man with a red face and blurred features, standing in the frame of the door, blocking her way out. Actually, most people found Holman good-looking, in an agreeably unobtrusive way. Even Emmy's family had to admit that there was nothing in his appearance to suggest the weakness and over-refinement of the academic stereotype. Neither fair nor dark, he had broad shoulders and a compact, athletic build. His face was boyish in design but serious in expression; he could have been a junior executive in a big company which manufactured something of industrial importance, such as mining machinery.

'Come into the parlour,' Julian said to his guests in an unconcerned manner. 'Would you like a sherry? I think there still is some.' He ran his hand through his hair, which was as long and as dark as Richard's. He was tall and very thin, with an exaggerated, almost theatrical Black-Irish face. He had thick charcoal eyebrows and high, hollow cheeks; he looked overexcited, as if he were about to die of consumption or lead a small raid for the Sinn Fein. On his jaw was an X-shaped duelling scar (the result of a bicycle accident at the age of eleven). Emmy noticed with disfavour that both his neck and his nails were dirty.

Developing descriptions

5 Work in groups. What other attributes could Holman or Julian have, which are not included in their descriptions in Exercise 4? Choose one of the characters and complete a description, by using link verbs, adjectives and noun phrases. Compare descriptions with students from other groups.

Extension

6 Read this poem.

My father's house

My father's house is a junk shop of juxtaposition
Strangely ordered sensitivity and stubbornness.
Closed windows holding dogmatic ideas and dust
Opera, holidays abroad and the panic of lost glasses.
It is shrunken with age and antiques
Overgrown with obsessive collecting.
Pink china tea cups, piles of letters and papers
Kind hands saving money laced with worms.

The stairs have arthritis, winding with difficulty
To drawers stuffed with my grandparents and other relations
Gathering cobwebs, harbouring guilt.
He is everywhere in the wardrobes and furniture
Narrow, oddly clothed, ranged on the picture rail –
It is easy to fall down. But out in the street
When you go to collect a lost ball
The houses are young and empty and blank.

BARBARA CONRAD

Which of the photos on this page shows the man described in the poem?

In pairs, make a list of adjectives, noun phrases etc. which you would use to describe his character, his appearance and the clothes he wears.

Write a description of about 250 words based on the notes you have made. Write the description as if it was part of a novel, using the passages in Exercise 4 as a model.

Vocabulary

Communication

1–8 Find eight pairs of words in the box which have similar meanings.

supercilious	eloquent
tactful	brusque
pompous	tolerant
opinionated	reserved
diplomatic	abrupt
open-minded	reticent
articulate	self-important
dogmatic	condescending

The family

In this paragraph the underlined words have been put in the wrong places. Write the correct word in the spaces.

Things were very different when my <u>relatives</u> met. They both came from very large families which was nice for me when I was a child because lots of <u>parents</u> came to visit us all the time, in fact my <u>adopted</u> family runs into hundreds of people.

My parents met and <u>got married</u> during the second World War and they <u>got engaged</u> after only three months. They didn't even bother to <u>fall in love</u>!

My sister and I had quite an easy-going <u>partner</u> and we were both quite happy, but when she left home my sister had several unhappy relationships, although she now seems quite happy with her latest <u>upbringing</u>. In fact they now have an <u>extended</u> child.

9 _____
10 _____
11 _____
12 _____
13 _____
14 _____
15 _____
16 _____
17 _____

Grammar

Verbs with -ing and to + infinitive

Some of these sentences contain mistakes in the clause which follows the verb. Tick the sentences which are correct, or rewrite the sentences where necessary.

18 Wendy loves to spend her summer holidays in Jersey.
19 Harold went on to study English at university after he left school.
20 I tried seeing him last night but he was out.
21 I'm used to playing football every Saturday morning when I was a child.
22 We need buying a new plug for the television.
23 They began arguing about euthanasia again, so I got bored and left.
24 I'm trying learning French at night school.
25 We're used to having to work hard at this time of year.

Wishes

Rewrite these sentences with the correct form of the verb in brackets.

26 I wish my sister (not ask) my parents for money all the time.
27 She wishes she (not go) to Malta for her holidays, as it was too hot for her there.
28 I wish you (can) come and spend a weekend with me, but if you've got too much work, there's nothing to be done about it, I suppose.
29 This island is really beautiful and we wish you (be) here to enjoy it with us.
30 I wish he (phone) me to say that he wasn't coming to work today.
31 I'm really tired today; I wish I (go) to bed earlier last night.
32 He wishes his boss (not give) him so much work to do on Friday afternoons.
33 They wish they (can) afford a new car, but they just haven't got enough money.

Passives

Write complete sentences using the correct halves from the two columns below.

34 Hotel bills have to ...   ... had been stolen.
35 The National Gallery ...   ... were damaged during the Gulf War.
36 Fifty people ...   ... be paid the day before departure.
37 I phoned the police when I
     found out the painting ...   ... have been invited to the reception.
38 Next year our salaries ...   ... is not allowed in this part of the building.
39 Many oil wells in Kuwait ...   ... will be paid in sterling.
40 Smoking ...   ... is being restored at the moment.

Check your answers in the Answer Key on page 124.

'Style is knowing who you are, what you want to say, and not giving a damn.'

GORE VIDAL

Vocabulary: style

Adjectives

1 Divide the following adjectives related to style into those which are generally positive (P) and negative (N).

> frumpy stylish dowdy drab chic elegant
> classy scruffy cosmopolitan sloppy
> sophisticated over the top tacky tasteful
> gaudy tasteless unkempt dishevelled

Which of these adjectives can only be used to describe clothes, or people, or both? Which can only be used predicatively? Are there any adjectives which cannot be used in the following sentences?

1 She's wearing a(n) _____ pair of jeans.
2 Her clothes are very _____.
3 He's a really _____ person.
4 He's really _____.

Verbs

2 Choose the best alternative to complete these sentences.

1 There's something reassuring about Lisa. She has such a lovely _____.

   a style *b* manner *c* position

2 She's got a lot of style. It's not only her clothes or anything like that, it's just that she _____ well.

   a walks *b* moves *c* goes

3 He's always careful about what colours he wears and he's very well-groomed. I think that's why he comes _____ as such a stylish person.

   a up *b* through *c* across

4 I like that sweater. That colour _____ very well with your hair.

   a fits *b* suits *c* goes

5 That colour _____ you perfectly – you ought to wear blue more often.

   a suits *b* matches *c* fits

6 I don't know why I bought this jacket. It's not really _____.

   a me *b* myself *c* I

7 There's a trend amongst Hollywood stars at the moment to dress _____, perhaps because they feel guilty about having so much money.

   a up *b* down *c* off

8 They don't enjoy rock concerts and parties much – they're more _____ yoga and Zen Buddhism.

   a out of *b* into *c* up

Idioms

3 Five of these words and phrases mean *fashionable*, in informal English. Which one means *unfashionable*?

the latest thing	trendy
all the rage	in
the latest craze	out

Use the words and phrases to discuss what is fashionable – in clothes, restaurants, music, free-time activities – at the moment in your country.

Discussion

Style

What constitutes 'style'? In groups, discuss and put the following in order of importance. Add anything else you think is important.

☐ clothes and accessories
☐ hair style and cut
☐ accent
☐ posture, movement
☐ facial expression
☐ vocabulary
☐ actions

Listening

Before you listen

1 In your opinion, which of the people in the photographs on these pages have got style? Discuss your answers in pairs.

First listening

T29 2 You are going to hear a conversation with Alice Prier, a founder of a company called House of Colour, which advises people on the colour and style of their clothes. Read this page from the company brochure. The first time you listen, underline the items on the brochure that she mentions in the recording.

Second listening

3 Listen again and complete these sentences from the conversation.

1 Well, I have a colour … a company called _____ London and we have two consultations that _____ mainly women.

2 We also do made-to-measure _____ so we know a lot about them, so we know _____ in the clothes.

3 I think somebody has style … is somebody _____ makes them feel good.

4 We spend about an hour and a half _____ during that time _____ likes and dislikes …

5 If you have _____ you were the other way around.

6 All the lines _____ reflect that.

7 Well, if you feel good _____ comfortable with yourself.

8 And very often people really do _____ tell them, to give _____ in trousers than a skirt.

13 ▶

Pronunciation: assimilation

4 It is possible to pronounce some words in two ways, depending on the style you want to adopt. The first pronunciation of these words is more common in conversational English, while the second is more formal and studied.

/tʃ/	/tj/
ma<u>t</u>ure	ma<u>t</u>ure

/dʒ/	/dj/
e<u>d</u>ucation	e<u>d</u>ucation

/ʃ/	/si/
asso<u>c</u>iation	asso<u>c</u>iation

T31 Listen to these extracts from Alice Prier's talk and tick the pronunciation of these words that you hear.

		A	B			A	B
1	indivi<u>d</u>ual	/dʒ/	/dj/	3	<u>d</u>uring	/dʒ/	/dj/
2	tex<u>t</u>ure	/tʃ/	/tj/	4	furni<u>t</u>ure	/tʃ/	/tj/

Now listen again and practise using the opposite pronunciation of the words.

STYLE

The structure of your body determines the shape of the clothes that can make you look your best. A House of Colour STYLE consultation aims to help you make a confident imaginative choice of clothes by analysing your body's frame and its outline.

Our fully trained consultants take detailed measurements to determine your body proportions. They demonstrate the fabrics, patterns and textures that most compliment your face and figure. They show you the styles of clothes and accessories that will conceal any problem areas and enhance your best features.

A natural compliment to colour analysis, your STYLE consultation includes:

- full analysis of the body frame
- practical demonstration of necklines, fabric textures and patterns
- the lengths, outlines and details that best suit you
- examples of shapes and details for jackets, coats, tops, skirts, dresses and trousers
- advice on hairstyles
- advice on jewellery, glasses frames and accessories

You will receive a compact file containing all the information about your own personal style that will prove invaluable when choosing clothes. You may also like to take advantage of our exclusive DESIGN service.

BOOK AN APPOINTMENT NOW

Speech features: *so*

How many sentences can you think of which demonstrate the many uses of the word *so*? Apart from the more conventional uses of *so*, it is also used in conversational English to

- ask a question about something that has just been discussed
- check that you have understood something that has just been said
- summarise something
- give an account of something
- draw attention to what you are about to say.

Listen to T32 . Discuss the meaning of the word *so* in each case.

Reading

Before you read

1 What do you think are the three most important problems that the 'rich and famous' face? Discuss your answers in groups.

Now look at the headline of the article on page 57 and the photographs of the stars. What does 'to dress down' mean? Why do you think the stars need to 'dress down'? Skim the text to find out why.

While you read

2 Read the article and see if your predictions in Exercise 1 were correct.

Vocabulary comprehension

3 Find words and expressions from the article which have a similar meaning to these:

to walk casually (*column 1*)
clothes (*column 1*)
natural/unpretentious (*column 1*)
to show fear or shock (*column 2*)
the activity of collecting money for a charity (*column 2*)
short-lived (*column 2*)
a dress (*column 2*)

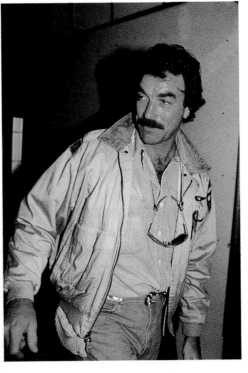

4 Can you work out the meanings of these words and expressions in the article?

tramp-like figures (*column 1*)
conspicuous wealth (*column 1*)
burden (*column 1*)
ilk (*column 1*)
trainers (*column 1*)
check out the latest line (*column 1*)
hottest (*column 1*)
snooty (*column 2*)
going bust (*column 2*)

14 ▶

Reading

Why the stars think it's chic to dress down

His face a mixture of horror and outrage, the maitre'd summons waiters to throw out the two tramp-like figures who have sauntered into his oh-so-trendy domain.

But just as the scruffy pair are being propelled through the door, there's a gasp of recognition and an immediate flood of apologies.

These are not bag people, as America calls its down-and-outs. Beneath the floppy felt hats and grotty army greatcoats are Hollywood megastar Julia Roberts and bearded beau Jason Patric.

Not that Julia and Jason are too indignant at their less than cordial greeting. They want the world to know that they've abandoned fabulous designer clothes for the sort of gear that costs 50p at an Oxfam shop.

It's called Extreme Celebrity Guilt – the latest trend among film stars for whom conspicuous wealth has become a burden.

America is in the grip of the worst recession since the Thirties. Empty order books, massive redundancies, 23 million people on food stamps and galloping home repossessions tell the sad story.

Solidarity

Even in the golden state of California, television supermarket ads are a constant round of discount offers and money-off coupons.

Up in Beverly Hills, the problems are different.

ECG demands movie stars show solidarity with the common man, but how do you do it when you are still earning £3 million a picture?

In Julia's case, she demonstrates her concern by wearing scruffy clothes and turning up at places like Morton's Restaurant in Hollywood in a battered pick-up truck, then refusing to choose from the £70 a head menu.

For Julia and her ilk, sequinned evening dresses are out and dressing down is *de rigeur*. TV interviews, premieres and evenings out are an excuse for them to appear in old trainers, torn T-shirts and cycling shorts.

They check out the latest line in clothing created by Jim Trenton, better known to listeners of LA's KROQ radio station as the DJ who calls himself The Poorman. His Poorwear – 'Recession Clothing for the Nineties' – is the hottest fashion ticket around. The range of loose-fitting sweatshirts, shorts, hats and trousers sells for between £3.50 and £8 – and the stars love it.

Trenton says: 'People here are sick of the pretence. Clothes are expensive here but nobody has any money. I don't think the stars want to impress any more. Dressing up and having an attitude is out.

'My best pal is Emilio Estevez and he drives an ordinary jeep or Bronco. He lives in Malibu but is totally earthy. Wearing this line, you can be cool *and* have money.

'I know dozens of stars and they feel guilty about having so much money. The common man doesn't relate to people who think they are better than him.

'It's all related directly to the economy. Celebs like to go to ordinary dance clubs and mingle with the ordinary people instead of ritzing in Beverly Hills.'

But ironically the charity shop look sometimes carries a Rodeo Drive price tag. Fashionably worn out jeans can cost up to £1,000 and an old denim

from GERARD EVANS and KEVIN SMITH in Los Angeles

jacket £2,000 in the antique denim shops which have sprung up on LA's trendy Melrose Avenue. A pair of cowboy boots which have been clumping around on someone else's feet for forty years is priced at £600.

Mark Fox, whose namesake stores are favoured by Julia Roberts, Guns 'N Roses, Arnold Schwarzenegger, George Michael, Sylvester Stallone, Jon Bon Jovi and Mickey Rourke, says the big names don't flinch at the price tags on his shredded denims.

History

'They are buying a piece of American history. Jeans are as American as apple pie and old jeans show a touch of class.

'It is supply and demand. Everyone wants these jeans now but you can't step up production – you only have the rare few left from decades ago.'

Beverly Hills mansion parties are out now too. When the stars get together it is invariably at a fund-raising bash for Aids causes, the homeless or under-privileged.

Los Angeles Times society writer Jeannine Stein says: 'The point here is not just to hear about people suffering, but to represent it yourself.' She recalls a recent Hunger Benefit organised by Oxfam where stars like Cybill Shepherd, Lou Diamond Phillips and Jackson Brown sat on the floor eating rice and beans with their hands to dramatise the inequality of world food distribution.

At weekends in Santa Monica, Tom Selleck and his pals drive over from their £3 million Malibu beachfront properties to drop off leftover food at a celebrity soup kitchen which even offers a vegetarian selection.

When stars themselves eat out, Spago on Sunset is still popular. But many prefer to slum it on Melrose Avenue – the equivalent of London's King's Road – at Trumps or Angel City Grill.

On Rodeo Drive snooty couturiers are going bust fast and others have put up Sale signs. Charles Jourdan will knock 40 per cent off a party frock.

But in the world of showbiz, a trend is as fleeting as fame.

Lance and John are known as The Hollywood Kids and have forged TV and magazine careers out of spotting the latest crazes.

They are in no doubt that the merest upswing in economic fortunes could see ECG rapidly revert to the more traditional Extreme Celebrity Greed.

'After the 'me' decade, the Nineties are non-glamour. These guys and girls are getting millions per picture but what they are saying is "Hey, I'm just like you. I work out in my Reeboks and drive my jeep with the Evian bottle in the back and no make-up."

'But it could all change once things start picking up again.'

'Most of them feel guilty because they're so rich'

Today

Improve your language learning

Appropriacy: speaking

It is sometimes difficult to know what language to use to say something, especially if you want to avoid appearing rude or offending someone. There are no hard and fast rules dictating when to say what you say. You must become sensitive to appropriacy, particularly in these areas.

Intonation
Potentially blunt, informal and impolite replies can be modified by the correct intonation.

Choice of words
Students are always keen to learn and use informal language but they can get into difficulties if they use this language in inappropriate situations. Find out in what circumstances words and expressions are appropriate at the time you learn them.

Length and choice of structure
Length is a useful indicator of how polite a structure is. Longer structures are usually more polite than shorter ones, but don't forget that a long structure can become quite blunt or impolite if it is said with the wrong intonation.

Learn to identify when a more (or less) formal style is appropriate. This is partly a cultural problem. Some societies are more formal than others. You will get better at choosing the appropriate register, the more contact you have with native speakers. Here are some factors to consider:

- your status, relative to the person you are speaking to
- the age difference
- how well you know the other person
- the delicacy of the request, complaint etc.
- the emotional state of the other person

Speaking

Role-play

Work in groups of three or four: **Students A, B, C/D**. Study your roles on page 118 and act out the interview between a journalist, the owner of a shop which sells expensive secondhand clothes, and two film stars.

Writing: formal requests

1 Read this short description from publicity material produced by the human rights organisation, Amnesty International.

Amnesty works!

Since 1961, Amnesty International has adopted or investigated more than 42,000 cases – some of which involved many individuals. Of these, over 38,000 are now closed. We have looked into the human rights record of every country and, unfortunately, have had cause to criticise most.
Amnesty International does not just work for the release of Prisoners of Conscience;
• Amnesty also seeks fair and prompt trials for all political prisoners.
• Amnesty opposes torture and executions.
• Amnesty also makes certain that victims of unjust imprisonment, torture and execution are not forgotten – so that no one can say: 'We didn't know.'
• Amnesty provides help and advice to Governments genuinely seeking to improve conditions in their own countries, and is now working particularly hard in Eastern Europe.
• Amnesty seeks to help provide younger generations with an understanding of human rights for a better future.
• Amnesty advises on the drafting of international legal instruments in the field of human rights protection.

2 Plan a letter to one of the stars mentioned in the article on page 57, asking for their support for the Amnesty International campaign against the repression of the native Indian population of the USA. This support could take the form of a donation, a public appearance at a function or the inclusion of a statement and photograph on campaign material.

Here is a list of possible items to include in the letter. In pairs, discuss which items to include, and whether you would like to include anything else.

- Introduce yourself and the work of the organisation.
- Mention the newspaper article in which you read about the stars 'dressing down'.
- Comment on the star's films and any past work for charity he or she has done.
- Explain why you are writing and make your request.
- Close your letter, thanking the star in advance for his or her co-operation.

3 Now write your letter, paying attention to the correct layout and register for a formal letter, and the most suitable opening and closing lines.

Grammar: the article

Check your articles

1 Without looking at page 57, fill in the gaps in this section of the text with *a/an/the* or leave the space blank.

His face _____ mixture of _____ horror and _____ outrage, _____ maitre'd summons _____ waiters to throw out _____ two tramp-like figures who have sauntered into his oh-so-trendy domain. But just as _____ scruffy pair are being propelled through _____ door, there's _____ gasp of _____ recognition and _____ immediate flood of _____ apologies. These are not _____ bag people, as _____ America calls its down-and-outs. Beneath _____ floppy felt hats and _____ grotty army greatcoats are _____ Hollywood megastar Julia Roberts and her bearded beau Jason Patric.

Not that Julia and Jason are too indignant at their less than cordial greeting. They want _____ world to know that they've abandoned _____ fabulous designer clothes for _____ sort of gear that costs 50p at _____ Oxfam shop.

Compare answers with a partner. Justify your choice where you have different answers.

Grammar reflection

2 These rules for the use of *the* and *a/an* or no article have been mixed up. Write *a/an*, *the* or *no article* in the space before each rule. Then write an example from the text on page 57 to illustrate the rule, or invent one.

1 _____ when both the speaker and listener know what is being referred to
2 _____ with professions
3 _____ when making a general statement, before uncountable nouns or plural countable nouns
4 _____ when talking about something which is unique in the world, or of which there is only one in a particular place
5 _____ with adjectives when referring to certain groups or categories of people
6 _____ when talking about the ability to play musical instruments
7 _____ between the preposition and the noun in certain common phrases
8 _____ when talking about some public places, systems or services
9 _____ when a singular countable noun is mentioned for the first time
10 _____ in exclamations in which there is a singular countable noun
11 _____ in exclamations in which there is an uncountable noun or plural noun
12 _____ when making a general statement about all things of that type
13 _____ with certain categories of nouns (school subjects, games, names of meals and abstract nouns).

Check your answers in the Grammar Reference on page 142.

Practice

Spot the mistake

3 Find the mistakes in these sentences and correct them. Give an explanation for your correction.

1 I don't like using a train to go to work – I prefer a bus.
2 'What beautiful day!' exclaimed one of the tourists at the Lake Geneva.
3 A Queen of England is going to have to start paying the taxes soon.
4 When she left a school she went to the university but I don't know which one.
5 We went to the reception by the car. It was the really luxurious car.
6 I always do the exercises in morning when I get out of the bed.
7 Did you hear about accident this morning? Hundreds of the people were taken to a hospital.
8 He plays guitar and piano very well. I wish I could play the musical instrument.

The article game

4 Play this game in two teams. The aim of the game is to win a row of three noughts or crosses for your team. The row can be horizontal, vertical or diagonal in any direction. Team A starts. Select a square, and make a correct, grammatical and logical sentence containing the articles in the order listed, on the topic given. If the sentence is correct, draw **X** (or **0**) in that square. Team B continues.

the the a	animals	a a the	school	a a a	novels
the a the	music	the zero the	transport	the the zero	love
a the zero	holiday	a the a	jobs	a the the	weather

Say the right thing!

Clarification

Have you ever found yourself 'lost' in a conversation with someone? You have these alternatives:

* pretend that you have understood and carry on
* stop the person immediately and ask for clarification
* wait till they have finished and then ask them to repeat.

Whatever you decide, it is important that you use appropriate language, taking into consideration the speaker, the situation, and the importance of what the other person is trying to explain.

It may also happen that another person doesn't understand what *you* are saying, or has not been listening.

This section will help you to deal with these situations.

"All right, I'll go over the strategy just once more: Get in There and Smash His Face to a Pulp."

 1 Listen to the phrases and write them under the correct heading.

a checking that you have understood
b asking for clarification or repetition
c checking that others have understood
d saying that you don't understand
e correcting other people when they misunderstand you

2 Can you notice anything wrong with this exchange?

Politician: So that's a brief summary of the government's plans for reshaping the economy over the next five years.
Journalist: Come again?

What should the journalist have said if he hadn't understood?

3 Work in pairs. Choose something from this list to explain to your partner.

* Explain exactly what your job involves.
* Give directions to your house.
* Explain your favourite recipe.
* Explain how to operate your computer/video-recorder/fax/camera etc.
* Summarise your philosophy of life.

Spend a few minutes on the preparation before giving your talk. Your partner will be interrupting you frequently. Be prepared to clarify anything your partner queries. Try to use as much of the language studied in this unit as possible.

'Money is better than poverty, if only for financial reasons.'

WOODY ALLEN

Vocabulary: money

Questionnaire

1 Ask a partner these questions and note down the answers. Then turn to page 126 for the score and decide which interpretation best fits your partner.

Money! Can you handle it?

1 I'm the kind of person who
- a spends money like water.
- b likes to splash out every once in a while.
- c budgets and saves up for things.

2 I would like to
- a be loaded.
- b be well off.
- c have enough to live on.

3 My bank balance is usually
- a in the red.
- b quite healthy.
- c in the black.

4 I rarely pay for things
- a in cash.
- b by cheque.
- c by credit card.

5 I think my friends would describe me as
- a foolhardy with money.
- b usually generous.
- c mean and stingy.

6 When I'm feeling low I treat myself to
- a a bottle of champagne and a night out on the town.
- b a nice meal in a reasonable restaurant.
- c a new English language dictionary.

7 If I am short-changed in a shop I
- a say nothing.
- b point out politely but firmly what has happened.
- c immediately start shouting at the assistant.

8 I would like to live in a country with
- a a high cost of living and a good standard of living.
- b a high cost of living and a poor standard of living.
- c a low cost of living and a high standard of living.

What's the difference?

2 Explain the difference between the words in these pairs.

1 poverty/destitution
2 spend-thrift/thrifty
3 hard up/penny-pinching
4 generous/charitable
5 grasping/tight-fisted
6 well off/wealthy
7 stingy/careful

Check your answers in your dictionary.

"Take a card, any card."

Discussion

Getting rich quick

What's the best way of making a lot of money in a hurry?

Discuss in groups. Add two other items to the list, and then put the list in order.

go gambling in Las Vegas	invest in stocks and shares
marry someone rich	buy and sell property
work hard	write a best-selling novel
rob a bank	write a number one pop song

Now work in pairs with someone from another group and compare results. Justify the order of items on your list.

Before you listen

1 In many big cities people are living and sleeping in the open.

In groups, discuss these questions:

Who are they? Why do they live like this? Are there any homeless in your city? What solutions can you think of to alter this situation?

Look at the front page of a weekly London newspaper. Who do you think produces the paper? Why do you think they chose the title *The Big Issue*?

First listening

2 Listen to the interview with A. John Bird. Are any of your views on the question in Exercise 1 shared by him?

Second listening

3 Listen again and make notes about what A. John Bird says about homelessness and *The Big Issue*. Use the following headings as a guide:

1 *The Big Issue*
   a Where it is sold
   b Who it is sold to, and by whom
   c Where the money goes
   d The number of people living on the streets in London
   e The content of the newspaper
   f The contributors to the newspaper
   g The number of copies sold
   h Gordon Roddick and the idea for *The Big Issue*

2 A. John Bird's background and experience
3 The problems and causes of homelessness, with regard to industry; education; family.

Now compare notes in pairs. What do you think about *The Big Issue*? Is it an answer to the problem of homelessness?

15 ▶

Pronunciation: word boundary (1)

4 In which cases do you think there is elision or 'blending' of -*t* and -*d* with vowels of other words? Look at these sentences from A. John Bird's talk.

1 'It's sol<u>d</u> to the general public by homeless people who use i<u>t</u> as a means of employment.'

2 '… so therefore I ha<u>d</u> a kin<u>d</u> of social understanding of some of the problems tha<u>t</u> people were going through …'

3 '… if the governmen<u>t</u> needs to be doing anything …'

T36 Listen and check your answers.

Now do the same thing for -*h* in these sentences.

4 'The charities obviously have a higher, er … estimate and the governmen<u>t</u> <u>h</u>as a lower estimate …'

5 'Well, <u>h</u>e could <u>h</u>ave returned to selling drugs which <u>h</u>e was doing before, but <u>h</u>e chose not to and <u>h</u>e made his way to the Street News office and started to sell the paper and started to get <u>h</u>imself together …'

Finally, decide what happens to -*r* when followed by -*h* in this sentence.

6 '… all the traditional industries that kept people in work fo<u>r</u> <u>h</u>undreds of years …'

Now listen and repeat.

Speech features: *sort*

Listen to T37 where the word ***sort*** is used several times in one particular phrase. What is the function of this phrase?

Can you think of any other uses of ***sort*** in informal English?

Grammar: conditional sentences

The conditional generator

1 'If this is the way Queen Victoria treats her convicts, she doesn't deserve to have any.' (Oscar Wilde, standing handcuffed in the pouring rain on his way to prison.)

In pairs, produce as many variations on this sentence as you can in ten minutes. Use as many types of conditional sentences as possible.

Now compare with other pairs, to see who has the highest number of logical, correct sentences.

Grammar reflection

2 Look at these examples of conditional sentences from the interview with A. John Bird, and classify them according to the tenses used in the *if*-clause and the main clause.

> 1 It depends if you're looking at government estimates or on the estimates of some of the charities.
>
> 2 If we were to aim the paper simply at the big social issues then no one would read it.
>
> 3 We also have writers who just send in material and if we like it, we publish it.
>
> 4 If you put them all together there are very rare occasions when people have such a general range.
>
> 5 If you were in the government, what would you do to help the homeless in Britain?
>
> 6 If the government needs to be doing anything, it needs to be trying to rejuvenate some of ... replacing some of the large industries.

3 Match the sentences to the uses A – E listed below. (Some of the uses listed are not covered by the sentences in the box. Change the tenses in sentence 2, and write a conditional sentence for those uses.)

Make a note of the tenses used in each case.

> A Talking about a situation which sometimes exists or existed.
>
> B Talking about a situation which you know does not exist.
>
> C Talking about a situation when you do not know whether it exists or not, or when it is unlikely to exist.
>
> D Talking about a situation which may exist in the future.
>
> E Talking about something which might have happened in the past, but did *not* happen.

(*Note*: In spoken English it is now possible to find combinations of tenses which were traditionally considered 'wrong' in conditional clauses.

Example: *If I **had known** you were coming, the tea **would be** on the table now.*

*If I **didn't have** a licence, I wouldn't **have bought** a car.*)

What effect does the use of *if only* and *unless* have on the meaning of conditional sentences?

Which verb do you use in the *if*-clause in type D, to talk more formally about a possible future situation?

Check your answers in the Grammar Reference on page 143.

Practice

A tricky moment

4 Listen to what happened to Martin when he was out for a day's motorcycling in the mountains.

Work in groups. Check that you understand what happened, then discuss what you would have done in his position.

Begin: *If I ...*

Now listen to what Martin actually did.

On page 118 there are some more difficult, real-life situations. Using conditional clauses, discuss what you would do in these situations.

Reading

Before you read

1 The British are very sentimental about animals (and often treat them better than they treat humans!). How are animals treated in your culture? Tick or cross the following questions.

Do you think domestic animals should ...?

have free access to all rooms in the house ☐
eat food from people's plates ☐
go on holiday with their owners ☐
be given special food ☐
sleep on or in the bed with their owners ☐
sleep inside the house ☐
be allowed to go out unaccompanied ☐

Now discuss the points you have ticked. Are these views all commonly accepted in your country?

While you read

2 Read the text quickly and decide which of these titles was the original title of the article.

a Desirable Residences
b Creature Comforts
c Hamsters' Houses
d Crazy or Caring?

Vocabulary comprehension

3 Look at these words and phrases in their context and work out what they mean.

Para. 1 on the brink of
last ditch
tail-docking
ear-cropping
Para. 2 shuffle off their mortal coils
tossed
Para. 3 hutch
Para. 4 fluff
Para. 5 several rungs further up the property ladder
plunged
slumming it
rub off on
Para. 6 suck up to
Para. 8 shelled out

Now look at the list of synonyms and definitions on page 119 and match them with these words.

16▶

Speaking

As you have read in the article, many British people spend a lot of money on pets and pets' accessories. Look at the illustration. Which of these do *you* consider 'luxuries' and which would you not be prepared to do without? Discuss in groups.

Reading

With the pound in your pocket worth next to nothing and your house on the brink of repossession, you might be forgiven for being tempted to seek out a dog's life. Humans may be having a rough time but some pets are having a good recession. Pet food sales are up, with particularly promising growth among expensive brands like Cesar and Sheba. At the last election, as a last ditch vote-getter, the Liberal Democrats proclaimed itself the Party for Pets with its 'A Pet is for Life' policy document which promises, among other things, to outlaw 'tail-docking and ear-cropping'.

Nor need pets worry about financial problems. The Sanwa Bank of Japan has recently opened its books for pet bank accounts which will prove useful to pay for the water beds, stress therapy and flush toilets that are now on sale for the more fortunate beasts in Japanese society. Each account comes complete with a cheque book and cash card. And when they shuffle off their mortal coils, pet cemeteries like Evelyn Waugh's Happier Hunting Ground from *The Loved One* are springing up all over the world, although not always with happy results. Recently, a couple from New York sued the Long Island Pet Cemetery for $1.2 million after it tossed Ruffian, a deceased 10-year-old sheepdog, into a mass grave instead of burying him under a $1.083 headstone with his pink blanket and toys.

More fortunate than Ruffian is Rosemary, an angora rabbit from Stoke Newington in London currently enjoying a luxurious lifestyle. To call Rosemary's garden dwelling a 'hutch' would be to undersell the property. Its complex construction by a sculptor took three days. Built from timber, it is over eight feet in length, with a corrugated plastic roof. The front door is decorated with an eye, a heart and a rabbit to signify 'I love bunnies', according to owner Miss Robins. The interior boasts walls decorated with plastic lettuce leaves and pictures of different types of rabbits. If the temperature falls too low in winter, Miss Robins places a hot water bottle in a cake tin to keep the house warm.

Rabbits will have to learn, however, that money cannot buy you everything. Life is no bowl of lettuce and carrots for Rosemary, as she may be suffering a gender crisis. 'Rosemary may be a man because he does growl when upset,' says Miss Robins. 'I had another look today. But it's so hairy back there I just can't tell. It's all fluff.'

Ferrari the hamster is several rungs further up the property ladder than Rosemary the transsexual rabbit. Not only does he come from a more up-market part of the city – just off London's Fulham Road – but he inhabits a three-storey town house decorated by his owner's mother, society interior designer Nina Campbell. 'There's a bit of an architectural problem with the stairs,' says Campbell. 'Only two floors are connected and he gets a bit restless if he's put on the top floor.' So restless is Ferrari that while having his interiors photographed he slipped and plunged to the ground – then scuttled off, unbothered. Anyway, he is said to prefer slumming it in his wire cage. The civilising effects of Fulham have yet to rub off on him. He has to live alone, as 'he is likely to eat anyone who visits him.'

While her dwelling is hardly as spacious as Ferrari's multi-roomed townhouse, Maud the King Charles Spaniel's kennel is exotic, nevertheless. Maud has a titled owner – Lord Snowdon. All wood, fret-sawed by hand and with Byzantine windows and mouldings, the Doge's Palace, as the kennel is known, has eight coats of yellow and orange paint 'scumbled' so that each layer shows through. 'Rather than pat and stroke her, I made a shelter,' says Snowdon. 'If she wants to suck up to me she goes into the kennel to get some food.'

Marion Elliot's ginger cat, George, can look forward to a similarly convivial arrangement. Marion is planning a luxurious papier mâché basket for George 'with a litter box surrounded by velvet curtains'. A tiny prototype has already been made which started out in the style of the Taj Mahal but evolved with spires and buttresses into something resembling a reliquary.

Continuing around the Monopoly board, the Mayfair of animal life is symbolised by the bird cages of Eric Lansdown, a doll's house designer from San Francisco. 'They are architectural masterpieces without being too serious,' says decorator Robin Mackay, who imports them from the US. Six feet tall with a sliding bottom tray, the cages come finished in anything from gilded matt black to gold and coral paint. 'I always think they'd be perfect for a white cockatoo,' says Mackay. Does he know any birds who have actually taken up privileged residence in one? 'Well, no. Their prime purpose is decorative,' he replies. When you have shelled out £3,000 on a bird cage the last thing you want is a guano-emitting creature to live in it.

Grammar: inversion

Grammar reflection

1 Look at these sentences from the article on page 65.

> 1 **Not only does he** come from a more up-market part of the city, but he inhabits a three-story town house.
>
> 2 **So restless is** Ferrari that while having his interiors photographed he slipped and plunged to the ground.

Underline the sections of these sentences in which inversion occurs.

3 No sooner had he left the house than he remembered he had left his keys inside.

4 Hardly had they taken off from Heathrow when the pilot said they had a technical problem and would be turning back.

5 Little did he know that the police were after him.

6 Only when she went to live in France did she realise how much she hated England.

7 Rarely have I eaten such a disgusting meal.

8 Such is the beauty of the cathedral that there are thousands of visitors every day.

9 In no way has she ever promised to work at weekends.

2 Answer the following questions on sentences 1–9 above.

a Look at sentence 1 written in a different way:

He not only comes from a more up-market part of the city but he also inhabits a three-story town house.

What is the difference in meaning between sentence 1 and this sentence? Would you say that inversion occurs more often in written/formal or in spoken/informal English?

b ***Hardly, little, no sooner***

Which verb tense is always used after *hardly* and *no sooner*?

When a sentence starts with *no sooner* or *hardly*, what does the second clause begin with in each case?

Which verb tense is used in the second clause?

Which verb tenses can be used after a sentence beginning *Little ...*?

What does the second clause begin with?

c ***So, such***

Which verb is used after *so* and *such* when they occur at the beginning of the sentence?

d **Negative adverbials**

Look at sentence 7. Can you think of any other negative adverbials which could be used instead of *rarely*?

e **Expressions with *only* and *no***

Look at sentences 1 and 9. Can you think of any other expressions with *only* and *no* which could be used in the same way?

Check your answers in the Grammar Reference on page 144.

I'm sorry, Hodger. Having worms is no excuse for these poor sales figures."

Grammar check

3 Use the words in brackets to change these sentences into 'inverted' sentences.

1 You will never see a view like that again. (*Never* ...)

2 The lake was so big that you couldn't see the opposite bank. (*So* ...)

3 He was a famous pop musician and also the manager of a football club. (*Not only* ...)

4 Alice had hardly walked down the little passage when she found herself in a beautiful garden. (*Hardly* ...)

5 They had just left their car outside the house when someone ran into it. (*No sooner* ...)

6 The interest in the lecture was so great that they had to move to a larger room. (*Such* ...)

7 Mary doesn't know that she has won the lottery. (*Little* ...)

8 I will not accept the post under any circumstances. (*On no account* ...)

Writing: narrating a story

Features

1 In terms of form and content, fables and other short stories often have many features in common. In pairs, make a list of these features under the headings: traditional ways of beginning and ending; sequencing words and phrases; verb tenses.

Story completion

2 Choose the correct word in each case to complete this story by the American writer, James Thurber.

Once upon a (1) there as a hunter (2) spent the best years of his life looking for a pink elephant. He looked in Cathay and he looked in Africa; he looked in Zanzibar and he looked in India; (3) he couldn't find (4). The longer he looked, the (5) he wanted a pink elephant. He would trample black orchids and he would walk right past purple cows, (6) intent was he on his quest. (7) one day in a far corner of the world he came upon a pink elephant and he spent ten days digging a trap for it. He hired forty natives (8) help him drive the elephant into the trap. The pink elephant was (9) captured and taken back to America.

(10) the hunter got home, he found that his farm was (11) no place for an elephant. It trampled his wife's dahlias and peonies, it broke his children's toys, it crushed the smaller animals around the place, and it smashed pianos and kitchen cabinets (12) they were berry boxes. (13), when the hunter had had the elephant for about two years, he woke up to find that his wife had left his bed and his children had left his board and all the animals on the estate were dead except the elephant. The elephant was the same as ever (14) that it had faded. It wasn't pink any more. It was white.

1	2	3
a year	*a* whom	*a* but
b time	*b* whose	*b* so
c life	*c* which	*c* then
d day	*d* who	*d* and

4	5	6
a it	*a* longer	*a* so
b one	*b* often	*b* such
c some	*c* less	*c* hardly
d none	*d* more	*d* rather

7	8	9
a And	*a* for	*a* lastly
b So	*b* to	*b* ultimately
c Then	*c* in	*c* conclusively
d Last	*d* from	*d* finally

10	11	12
a Then	*a* truly	*a* for
b When	*b* indeed	*b* as
c Hardly	*c* really	*c* as if
d As	*d* genuinely	*d* because

13	14
a Then	*a* but
b One day	*b* apart
c Later	*c* except
d Lately	*d* only

Listening

3 You are going to hear another fable by James Thurber called *The Mouse Who Went to the Country*. You are going to hear the story only once. Make notes while you listen for gist. Here are the place-names mentioned in the story:

Beddington   Sibert's Junction   Middleburg
Pell's Hollow   Grumm   Wimberby

In groups, compare notes and write your version of the story. Exchange stories with other groups and compare versions.

"Never mind the porridge. She's taken the video."

Writing

4 The pictures below tell the story of *The Mouse and the Money,* but they are in the wrong order. Put them in order, then match these sentences to the pictures.

1 I wouldn't eat that stuff. It'll give you greenback bellyache.

2 My ancestors were of the French aristocracy.

3 When I have eaten it all, I shall return to the city and live like a king.

4 Not a mouse in our house was a common house mouse.

5 I'm already a mouse of distinction and this money will make me a millionaire.

Compare your order with a partner.

Now write your version of the story. Include some examples of inversion, where appropriate, and all the features you listed in Exercise 1.

Vocabulary

Style

Complete these sentences with an appropriate word or phrase in the right form, from the box.

dress down   dishevelled   tacky   gaudy   fit
craze   dowdy   suit   manner   match

1 He always looks _____. His clothes are always dirty and he never combs his hair.

2 People often have a very good idea of what colours _____ them but they still buy the wrong colour clothes.

3 People used to think fake fur was really _____, but now it's considered fashionably 'green'.

4 She was wearing a very elegant jacket which _____ her perfectly.

5 The latest _____ in my country is the 60s fashion for bell-bottom trousers.

6 It is fashionable for stars to _____ at the moment because, it is said, they feel guilty about having too much money.

7 I'm going to buy a new pair of shoes to _____ the sweater I got for my birthday.

8 Her clothes are very _____ – I'm sure she'd look so much better in brighter, bolder colours and styles.

9 Tony has a lovely _____ – he always gives the impression he is interested in what you're saying.

10 In general, I like your clothes, but I think that luminous green and yellow jacket you were wearing yesterday was a bit _____.

Money

Write an appropriate word for each of these definitions.

11 An adjective to describe someone who uses money in a frugal or careful way.

12 A person who spends money in an extravagant manner.

13 An adjective to describe someone who is not exactly poor but hasn't got much money.

14 A specific word to describe someone who is generous in giving to the needy.

15 An adjective to describe someone who has quite a lot of money.

16 To spend money extravagantly. (two words)

17 A phrase used to say that there *is* money in your bank account. (three words)

18 An adjective used to describe someone who likes to save the money he or she has.

19 A noun used to describe the state of having no money at all for food or shelter.

20 To be given the wrong amount of money when you buy something in a shop. (two words)

Grammar

The article

Write the missing article in the space on the right. If no article is missing, put a cross in the space.

8.15 Music From The Med

Julia Arrowsmith's voyage around __21__ Mediterranean Sea continues, with four ports of call remaining in __22__ series. The first stop is Greece and __23__ music of __24__ poor, the dispossessed and the underworld – the music of 'rebetica'. From Greece it is only __25__ short journey across to Turkey and the music of 'arabesque', despised by __26__ elite but loved by the masses.

__27__ third country is Israel, with, its musical mix of 'mittel Europe' and __28__ Middle East, which has __29__ rich heritage of styles drawn from immigrants who have made it their home.

Conditional sentences

Complete these sentences by writing the correct form of the verb in brackets.

30 If the weather (be) good, we often go the coast at the weekends.

31 Nobody would come to the concert, unless we (have) some famous names.

32 If you (be) rich, how would it change your life-style?

33 If she'd seen the cat crossing the road, the accident (not happen).

34 We (read) a lot in the evenings, if there was nothing good on TV.

35 If Mary (not like) Jim, she wouldn't have married him.

Inversion

Complete these sentences with one of the words or phrases you studied in Unit 8.

36 _____ do they earn more than me but they also won the lottery last year.

37 _____ had she started to watch the film when the phone rang.

38 _____ was the generosity of our hosts that we didn't spend a penny all week.

39 '_____ have I seen such awful homework!' shouted the teacher.

40 _____ when Harold had sat down in the cinema did he remember that he had left his car lights on.

Check your answers by looking at the Answer Key on pages 124–125.

'They live in a beautiful little apartment overlooking the rent.'

ANON

Vocabulary: the home

What's the difference?

1 Explain the difference between these words.

a shack/hut/hovel/shed
b houseboat/boathouse/narrowboat/cabin cruiser
c cabin/cottage/bungalow/villa
d mansion/palace/castle/estate
e hotel/motel/inn/guesthouse/pension
f flat/apartment/bedsit/condominium/penthouse
g mobile home/caravan/trailer/camper
h detached house/semi-detached house/terraced house/maisonette/town house
i surroundings/environment/atmosphere

Odd – or unconventional?

2 Which of the following words have a negative connotation?

> weird   unusual   unconventional   novel
> strange   bizarre   bohemian   eccentric
> odd   off-beat   peculiar

Choose any of the above words to describe someone who chooses to live permanently on a boat; in a bedsit; a tent; a hotel or a mobile home.

Discussion

Accommodation

Look at these small ads for different types of accommodation. If you had the freedom to choose (and unlimited resources), which of them would interest you? Why? Which would you definitely *not* choose? Discuss your choice in groups.

- **COTTAGE STYLE HOUSEBOAT, 40 x 12ft.** BWB residential mooring, lounge, pine kitchen, double bedroom, full bathroom, well maintained, private lakeside garden, new roof, many extras.

- **WEST KENSINGTON, large** 2 bed garden flat, fully furnished, well decorated, TV, washing machine, dishwasher, f/freezer 2 mins tube.

- **DOCKLANDS/CITY TOWER BRIDGE** Wide range of luxury furnished/ unfurnished flats inc. warehouse conversions and waterside properties with secure parking, f/f kitchens, modern baths, some with leisure facilities and river views. Easy access to City.

- **MUSWELL HILL,** dine outside, summer evenings on your own 30 ft suntrap verandah overlooking landscaped garden, comes with 4/5 bed S/D house, garage, huge cellar.

- **ST. MAWGAN, CORNWALL,** idyllic 3 bed 400 year cottage, conservatory, greenhouse, workshop, 4 acres, orchard, stream.

- **ATTRACTIVE WOODLAND** for sale. 16 acres in East Sussex and 7 acres near Ashford in Kent. Freehold. Suitable for a variety of amenity uses including camping, bird watching, horses, walking, woodstove supplies and generally getting away from it all.

- **MOBILE HOME,** housed in old London double-decker bus, parked Vauxhall Bridge private carpark, all amenities, TV, video, etc., extremely comfortable and central, sleeps 3.

- **A beautiful choice and best** selection of self-contained rooms with own kitchens and showers/WCs, and bed-sits with own kitchens situated in the North London area, all with modern, luxury furniture. Cleaning, full-time maintenance and phones are all part of the service.

- **HOLLAND PARK W11,** easy-going professional person to share fun 5 bedroom house, own double room, close to tube, all mod cons, very reasonable monthly rent.

- **UNSITED 2 SECTION** side by side, 20 x 25 ft chalet style mobile home, with dining room, lounge, kitchen, bathroom, shower, pedestal, wash basin, toilet, full ch.

- **NW6,** person to share non-smoking house with 2 couples, all mod cons.

Listening

Before you listen

1 The River Thames has a network of linked canals which were once used to transport goods to other major British cities. A number of people in London live on house-boats of various kinds on these waterways.

Read these views about living on a boat, and list the advantages and disadvantages of this way of life.

First listening

T40 2 Now listen to David and Helen talking about their experiences of living on a boat. Write down the advantages and disadvantages. Do they share any of the views expressed in the article you read in Exercise 1?

Second listening

3 Listen to the conversation again and make more detailed notes about the following points.

  a differences between living on a boat and living in a house
  b things they had to get used to when they started living on a boat
  c driftwood
  d work which needs to be done
  e a disagreement between Helen and David about one aspect of boat-dwelling

Pronunciation: phrasal verbs

4 There are variations in accent on the verb and particle in phrasal verbs according to the word order and the type of phrasal verb (those that *can* take an object and those that *can't*).

T42
Listen to Part 1. What is the difference in accent on the verb and the particle in these phrasal verbs?

  a Well, you have to *trim down* your possessions to the bare essentials, don't you, living on a boat?
  b Well, you have to *trim* your possessions *down* to the bare essentials, don't you, living on a boat?
  c I *got up* immediately and *went out* to see what was *going on*.

Can you work out the rule for the accent in phrasal verbs?

Now listen to Part 2. Check to see if your rule works with each of these phrasal verbs.

wake up	go out	go down	get out
dry out	warm up	fill up	leave out

KINDRED SPIRITS

Boat dwellers

Bob Carlton
'You can get lonely if you're stuck in an office. On the water, people are always travelling past and waving,' says the director and writer of musicals, who works on a houseboat. 'You spend more time outside, sitting on deck, so you can't help meeting people.'

Caroline Dilke
'I have lived on my boat for eight years and never regretted it,' says the short story writer. 'The boat is in the middle of London, but it feels like a country cottage. It is a bit bohemian, but has become less so: my neighbours are more middle-class than before.'

Betty Marsden
'It was my late husband's idea, and at first I was terrified. Now I'd find it very difficult to live ashore,' says the actress. 'My boat is really just a house on water, like Noah's Ark. But there's a great sense of freedom out here, the bird life is wonderful and I get lovely sunsets like Turner's.'

John Osborne
As a young actor, the playwright lived on a barge: 'The mooring fee was only 25s a week, there was a cheap electricity rate and a telephone.' He recalls throwing himself into painting the boat as if it were 'a pleasant collaboration in playmaking'.

Earl Grey
'We didn't want to live in a flat and had the romantic idea of a houseboat,' says the Liberal Democrat peer. 'It lived up to everything we had wanted. I love the sound of the water, so I adored it. It isn't a normal way of life, and that means you feel a great sense of adventure.'

Dr Conor Cruise O'Brien
'I'm used to living with lots of light, air and water, so I like to combine the city with openness to the elements,' says the journalist and former politician. 'A houseboat seemed the best way of doing that in London. Before I get another one, I'd have the plumbing rigorously inspected.'

Speech features: interrupting

Listen to T43 and make a note of the ways in which the speakers interrupt each other to say something and to change the subject.
In pairs, practise using these speech features, by discussing the advantages and disadvantages of different types of accommodation.

Grammar: Question tags

'Forgive me if I'm wrong ...'

1 Sit next to a student and prepare to find out or check details of his/her life. Write a statement with a question tag about your partner for each of the categories below.

accommodation   marital status   job
hobbies   ambitions   plans for summer
travel experience   literature/   music
    films etc.

Example: *You used to live in the centre of town, didn't you?*
How does your intonation change according to how sure you are of the information in your statements?

Grammar reflection

2 Complete these sentences from T40 with the correct question tag.

> 1 When you're living in a house you take all these things for granted, _____ _____?
>
> 2 But there are some very positive things about being on the boat, _____ _____?
>
> 3 Yes, it's much cheaper than any other way of living in the city, _____ _____?
>
> 4 The wood makes a really nice little fire in that stove, _____ _____?
>
> 5 You have to trim down your possessions to the bare essentials, _____ _____, living on a boat?

Now match the tags on the right to the sentences on the left.

1 You love tea,	a	will you?
2 Oh, you've been to North America,	b	did they?
3 Let's forget it,	c	shall I?
4 I'll tell you about the party,	d	wouldn't they?
5 Come into the kitchen,	e	hadn't they?
6 I'm a bit early,	f	don't you?
7 None of the visitors came back,	g	have you?
8 I don't suppose anyone will come now,	h	will they?
9 They'd better go now,	i	hadn't they?
10 They'd like to come to the party,	j	shall we?
11 Somebody had stolen your bike,	k	aren't I?

3 Find one example from the sentences in Exercise 2 for each of these uses of tags.

A to make an order for someone to do something, less forceful
B to make a suggestion and to check that someone agrees
C to make a statement and to check that someone agrees with you or feels the same
D to show surprise, interest or anger at something that someone has just said.

Both intonations, rising and falling, can be used with tags. Which intonation is used to express A–D above?

How do you agree or disagree with someone who has used a question tag?

T44 Listen and identify the meaning of each of the sentences you hear. Now listen and repeat. Pay particular attention to the intonation.

Check your answers in the Grammar Reference on page 144.

Practice

Controversy

4 Add an appropriate tag to these controversial statements, so that they represent *your* opinions.

Example: Animals are for the service of humanity.
Animals are for the service of humanity,
aren't they?

In pairs, take turns to read your statements and agree or disagree with each other. (Be careful to use the correct intonation.)

Example: *Animals are for the service of humanity, aren't they?*
Well, I don't think they are, actually.

'Nobody should have to take an HIV test.'
'The United Nations peacekeeping force is a complete waste of time.'
'Shakespeare was the greatest playwright of his time.'
'Property is theft.'
'The quality of pop music has got gradually worse over the last ten years.'
'TV advertising interferes with enjoyment of programmes.'
'I'm the most intelligent student in this class.'
'Animals are for the service of humanity.'
'There will be a major war in Europe in the next twenty years.'
'We'd all be happier if we had more money.'

Say the right thing!

Understanding the real meaning

Tact

Misunderstandings often occur on the part of the listener, when a speaker does not say *exactly* what he or she means.

In some cases this may be because they are trying to be tactful, especially when using these language functions:

a giving orders
b making requests
c expressing dislikes
d refusing requests
e giving someone some bad news
f refusing invitations

1 Which functions do these sentences express?

1 Well, actually, I'm not terribly sure that I'm free on Saturday.
2 You know that green cup that was in the cupboard above the fridge ...
3 Maybe you'd like to come into the kitchen.
4 I was wondering if you were using the car this evening.
5 Yes, well, I expect he has some hidden talents ....
6 Well, I think I might be using it later.

T45 2 Now listen to the exchanges in Part 1 and identify the functions.

Listen a second time and make a note of the language used to make the sentences more tactful.

What are the characteristics of the pitch and intonation in these sentences? Listen a third time and repeat, paying attention to rhythm, pitch and intonation.

3 In pairs, practise the language you have heard by inventing exchanges for the following situations.

1 Ask your partner to lend you a large sum of money.
2 Tell your partner to turn the volume of the television down.
3 When asked by your partner what you think of his or her new jacket, give a negative opinion.
4 Break the news to your partner that you have just crashed his or her car.
5 Refuse an invitation from your partner to go to dinner at his or her house.
6 Refuse a request by your partner to borrow a book that you are afraid of losing.

Sarcasm

Another area where language is misinterpreted, is when a speaker is being sarcastic, i.e. saying something which is the *opposite* of what he or she really believes. Listen to the exchanges in Part 2 and decide whether or not the speakers are being sarcastic.

What are the characteristics of sarcasm in terms of language and intonation?

Make sincere and sarcastic statements about the following:

• public transport
• British food
• the weather
• a politician
• traffic in your town or city
• a famous pop musician or film star

In pairs, read your statements and try to guess whether your partner is being sincere or sarcastic.

Reading

Before you read

1 Work in groups. Which of these statements do you agree or disagree with? Discuss your reasons.

People in cities generally only have friends from their own social and professional groups.

People in cities aren't as happy as people in the country.

People in cities tend to be more materialistic than people in the country.

You are more likely to get to know a wider range of people better if you live in the country.

The quality of life in the city is better than in the country.

City life is more stressful than country life.

You can have a more complete life in the city than you can in the country.

Country people are less neurotic than people in the city.

While you read

2 Read the article 'Sensory Overload' on page 75 opposite and decide which of the above statements the writer agrees with.

Vocabulary comprehension

3 Find these words in the text and decide which meaning is appropriate to the context.

1 loosest – *a* most vague or imprecise *b* most immoral
2 starved – *a* suffering through deprivation of something *b* suffering greatly from lack of food
3 cross-section – *a* piece or slice of something which is made by cutting across it *b* typical or representative sample of something, e.g. a population, community or opinion
4 fall short – *a* fail to reach or measure up to a standard *b* prove inadequate
5 the sticks – *a* small, thin pieces of wood from a tree *b* a quiet region in the countryside
6 edifice – *a* a large and impressive building *b* a system of beliefs

4 Look at these words and expressions in the text and try to work out a definition for each.

Para. 1 herding
Para. 3 gate-crashing
Para. 4 starved   clique
Para. 8 (life is) no picnic   fraught with   glimpse
Para. 9 hankering after
Para. 10 bulky
Para. 11 striving   nirvana

Phrasal verbs

5 Find phrasal verbs with these meanings in the text.

Para. 2 tolerate or accept someone or something, even though you find this difficult or unpleasant
Para. 5 reach a better standard or achieve a better result than previously
Para. 5 try to stop yourself thinking about a particular person, thing or feeling
Para. 8 stop working
Para. 8 try to take advantage of an opportunity, even if success is unlikely

 18 ►

Reading

SENSORY OVERLOAD I'm writing this at the house of some friends. I use the word 'house' in its loosest sense. It's really a sort of see-through shack made of gum poles, mosquito net and corrugated iron, on the side of the Boro River in Botswana. We are just on the edge of the Kalahari Desert but the view is like a painting by Constable – trees along the river's edge, cattle knee-deep in water-lilies, a boy herding goats. I've been living and working here for six weeks now and, as usually happens when I'm away, I'm wondering why on earth I spend so much of my time in London.

When you tell people that you are thinking of leaving the city, it's often regarded as an admission of failure, as though there was something worthwhile and heroic about putting up with the stress of urban life. In fact, the stress most people suffer from in the West isn't really stress at all. If you want to see someone living under stress – the genuine thing – then take a look at one of the African tribeswomen here who doesn't know how many of her children will survive or whether she'll have anything to eat from day to day. The 'stress' that middle-class townfolk like me suffer from at home is a sort of neurotic cocktail of envy, restlessness and irrational desire.

I believe there's a condition, common in hyperactive children, called Attention Deficit Disorder. Some children, exposed to too many stimuli, lose the ability to concentrate on things that really matter. It strikes me that many adults suffer from a similar disorder. With the amount of TV, news and casual interaction in London, it comes as no surprise.

I don't know anything about social evolution but it strikes me that we were designed to live in small social groups, not herds of a million or more. We were also meant to communicate in person, on a one-to-one basis.

They say that young babies can communicate simultaneously with a maximum of three people, and in adult life I can't say I've managed to improve on this. I find that in very large groups of people the noise begins to obscure the signals. The way you survive in a city is to form a small social group and shut out everyone else; but those talkative people on TV keep gate-crashing this party, and ignoring them makes your real friends feel uncomfortable. The only way to avoid it is to move to a place where people don't take TV so seriously.

Most urbanites will tell you that if you leave the big city you'll find yourself starved of stimulating company. What they really mean by stimulating company is people of the same age, race, class and profession. In a city you tend to form these artificial cliques but in a small community, you get to know a true cross-section of the population.

I recently spent some time in the Orkney Islands. During my stay I got to know a crofter, a church minister, a truck mechanic, a councillor and a theoretical physicist. These people all knew each other. They often exchanged ideas and their company was more stimulating, I guarantee, than anyone you will meet at the Groucho Club.

Life here in Maun is no picnic. Things are constantly breaking down, it's difficult for most residents to make a decent living outside the safari season, and the simplest daily activities are fraught with logistical problems. But at least everything has an immediacy. In big cities we are constantly distracted from what is real and important, by people we don't know and events we can't influence. We are exposed to too many possibilities, we glimpse too many other lives and, as a result, we are constantly grasping at things we can't attain.

I'm not speaking here as a doctor but as an inveterate, incurable grasper. And after years of futile grasping I know this for certain: you will always fall short. There will always be people who seem to be doing something more interesting and seem to be better at it. You will never look as good as the people in commercials. You will never have read enough or have had enough fun. It's obvious that hankering after what you can't have is fundamentally damaging but a lot of us are seriously addicted to it.

It's taken me about 20 years to discover that the best way to avoid this is to throw the whole bulky package away. Don't do that stuff any more. Go somewhere where you can't get hold of it, where they don't have a radio or a TV or a telephone or even a bathroom mirror to contemplate. Some people call this running away, but I've come to regard it as a basic and healthy reflex. You find what's hurting you – fantasy overload – and you move away from the source of the pain.

Living in the sticks you find, magically, that you stop thinking about how things might be and you start concentrating on the important things like how to get the Land-Rover started or whether there's enough water for a shower. You get to know all the people around you. You rely on them, and they on you – instead of everyone striving individually towards some private nirvana.

This is proper social interaction. You can focus on what you do rather than constantly being distracted by coloured lights and flashes. Once you stand far enough away from it, it is quite clear that the whole media edifice – Terry Wogan, Hollywood and *The Observer* – is a lot less substantial than this half-completed shack on the banks of the Boro River.

© *The Observer*

Grammar: relative clauses

Murder!

1 Read this account of a murder and the subsequent investigation. Complete the text with the correct relative pronouns. If two pronouns are possible, fill in both, and if the pronoun can be left out, put an X in the space.

Yesterday at 3.00 a.m. police were called to the Plaza Hotel in Camden High Road, __1__ guests reported hearing loud voices and the noise of gunshots. They found the body of a man in room 113. The man, __2__ had been shot in the back, was in his mid-50s and was named as Philip Vance, a vacuum-cleaner salesman from Coventry. Police also found the gun __3__ killed him. The murder victim, __4__ wife had left him two years ago, is said to have checked into the hotel with a blonde woman the evening before his death. Police found the woman's bag, __5__ could help them to find her. At Camden Central Police Station, __6__ witnesses were being questioned, detectives said that they were trying to find the blonde woman, __7__ identity is as yet unknown. Police believe __8__ the woman may still be in the Camden area and __9__ she may be the person __10__ they have been wanting to interview in connection with other crimes __11__ they say may be linked.

Grammar reflection

2 Look at these examples of relative clauses, and answer the questions below.

Defining clauses (explain which person or thing you are talking about)

> In fact, the stress most people suffer from in the West isn't really stress at all.
>
> The stress that middle-class townsfolk like me suffer from is a sort of neurotic cocktail of envy, restlessness and irrational desire.
>
> Take a look at one of the African tribeswomen here, who doesn't know how many of her children will survive.
>
> The only way to avoid it is to move to a place where people don't take TV so seriously.
>
> There will always be people whose lives are often more interesting than yours.

1 Which relative pronouns do you use after people, things, times and places?

2 Which of the pronouns you have listed can you replace with *that*? When can you do this?

3 When can you omit the relative pronoun – when it is the subject or the object of the clause?

Non-defining clauses (give further, optional information to identify the person etc. you are talking about)

> John Collee, who writes a column in the Observer every week, is also a doctor.
> The column, which is very popular, is usually about some aspect of medicine.

4 Can you omit the relative pronoun in non-defining clauses?

5 Which pronoun do you use to refer to a person or group of people who are *a* the subject and *b* the object of the non-defining clause?

6 Which relative pronouns do you use to refer to a thing or group of things which are the subject of a clause?

Check your answers in the Grammar Reference on page 145.

Practice

Write a test

3 In groups, prepare a multiple choice exercise, where other students have to choose the correct relative pronoun. As a basis for the exercise, look at reading texts elsewhere in the book for examples of sentences containing relative clauses. Make items containing the full range of defining and non-defining clauses. Everyone in the group should have a copy of the exercise.

Example: *It was the best restaurant _____ I had ever eaten in.*
a *that* **b** *who* **c** *whom* **d** *(no pronoun)*

Now give your copy of the exercise to a member of another group. When they have finished, check their answers and explain any mistakes they have made.

Clauses with *which*

4 Non-defining clauses with *which* often give information about 'the whole situation' in the main clause.

Examples: *She's failed her driving test for the third time. She's very upset, <u>which is understandable</u>.*

This computer can fold up to the size of a note-book, <u>which makes it very portable</u>.

I didn't get my bonus, <u>which means I can't go away on holiday</u>.

Finish these sentences in the same way.

1 I've had flu five times this year, …
2 She didn't get the job, …
3 He walked out on me in the middle of our conversation, …
4 I didn't pass the entrance examination, …
5 I've never been to South America, …
6 I never told him I loved him, …
7 The man in the seat next to me on the coach played his portable radio all night, …
8 The pilot came into the passenger cabin and passed out, …

Many, most, some, one of …

5 In formal writing when you want to refer to a group of people or things you are talking about, you can use non-defining clauses like those in these examples:

a She made a lot of good friends at university. She is still in contact with most of them.
   *She made a lot of good friends at university, **most of whom** she is still in contact with.*
b In his talk, he gave detailed descriptions of several countries. He'd been to most of these countries many times.
   *In his talk he gave detailed descriptions of several countries, **most of which** he'd been to many times.*

Work in pairs and make a sentence for each of the following expressions.

| some of which | one of whom | none of which | many of whom |
| some of whom | one of which | none of whom | many of which |

Speaking

KEVIN WOODCOCK

In his article 'Sensory Overload', John Collee makes some interesting points about so-called 'civilised' life.

Here are the key arguments from his article. Consider each one and decide if you agree or disagree. Make notes to prepare for a discussion about the statements.

• People in 'civilised' society continually dream of having material goods they are never likely to be able to possess.
• People are addicted to wanting things they can't have despite the fact that this damages them.
• Television conditions us to want to become like the stereotyped 'beautiful' people we see there.
• City life tends to limit our contact with people outside our professional circle and who are different from ourselves.
• Radio, television and telephones mean that a lot of our contact with people is casual, impersonal and meaningless and this often interferes with real communication.

How many of the five statements do you agree with?

Discuss the statements in pairs or groups, and try to convince the others of your point of view.

Writing: composition

Choose one of the statements that you discussed above and write a composition about it.

You may wish to refer to Unit 3 again, in which you studied composition writing technique.

Make a plan of your composition, then write it. Try to use as many of the relative pronouns as possible from the previous page.

Don't forget to check your composition for style, grammar, and appropriacy of language, when you have finished.

'He's turned his life around. He used to be depressed and miserable. Now he's miserable and depressed.'

DAVID FROST

Vocabulary: moods

1 Match words from columns A, B and C to form phrases which could describe someone's mood. (*Note:* Certain phrases are only used with a specific modifier.)

A	B	C
to feel to be	really completely absolutely quite	down on top of the world down in the dumps miserable in a good mood great fed up full of beans over the moon in a foul mood like a million dollars lousy

What's the difference?

2 Explain the difference in meaning between the pairs of expressions.

1 in a sulk – sulky
2 bad-tempered – in a temper
3 irritated – irritable
4 moody – in a mood
5 depressed – depressive

Idioms

3 Here are some idiomatic expressions to do with getting out of moods or helping other people to get out of them. Complete the phrases using these words.

up out snap time listener jolly

to cheer someone _____
to _____ someone along
to bring people _____ of themselves
to _____ out of it
to have _____ for someone
to be a good _____

Discussion

Advice

In this list of advice for dealing with moods, only three items are genuine. Can you spot them? (These were taken from a magazine article about moods.)

For a moment I thought I was happy – but it passed...

Now discuss in groups and write six pieces of advice for dealing with moods. Use the vocabulary you have studied in this section, and write your advice as if it were to appear in a magazine.

GOOD MOOD GUIDE

1 We are most vulnerable to catching moods when we're feeling tired, so that's the time to steer clear of others' negative emotions or you'll soak these up like a sponge.

2 Promote good moods by giving them a helping hand. Exercise, for example, can boost mood-lifting chemicals called endorphins, the brain's natural opiates, as can smiling even when sad. The change in facial muscles caused by breathing through your nose as you smile, forces cooler blood to the brain, which in turn, leads to the release of endorphins.

3 One of the best ways to get out of a bad mood is to direct your emotional energy away from yourself. Remind yourself that however depressed you are there is always someone worse off than you. If you do something for someone else, like doing their shopping or cleaning their windows, you will find that your mood disappears like magic.

4 When you are in a mood, pamper yourself. Get a bottle of your favourite wine, cook your favourite food and read your favourite book or go and see a film you've been wanting to see.

5 Talk about your mood to a friend! That's what friends are for, after all. By talking through whatever is making you depressed you may come to understand the problem better yourself and find a solution.

6 If you are one of the world's mood receivers, don't choose partners or friends who are depressives or they will pull you down with them. Instead, surround yourself with jolly types.

Listening

Before you listen

1 Rearrange the words below to complete the caption for this cartoon.

what	when	is	sad	like	are	happy	you	you're

'If this _____ _____, _____ _____ _____ _____ _____ _____ _____?'

What do you think Calman is trying to say in the cartoon?

Do you think there is such a thing as 'mood compatibility'?

First listening

T46 2 Which of these things can make you depressed?

bad news	travelling by tube
traffic	relationships
politics	being ill
weather	work

The first time you listen, tick the reasons for bad moods mentioned by Nick and Felicity.

Second listening

3 Listen again and make detailed notes about
a Nick's views on living with moody people; moody friends.

b Felicity's experience of a moody person; attempts to deal with the person.

Now look back at the list of advice on page 78. Which items seem to correspond with Nick and Felicity's views?

19 ▶

Pronunciation: linking *-r*

4 The words which follow the letter *-r* in a sentence determine whether the letter is pronounced or not.

Look at these sentences from T46 and decide whether the final *-r* in a word is pronounced.

1 Yea, I feel really down when it's sort of e*r* bad weathe*r*, but I don't take that out on othe*r* people …
2 I'd prefe*r* if they sort of live with somebody else really …
3 Does it make you feel irritated if the othe*r* person's really being moody and there's no real reason, like it's bad weathe*r* o*r* you haven't any idea really why they're moody?

T48 Now listen and check your answers. What is the rule for the pronunciation of the final *-r* in a word?

Listen again and repeat.

Speech features: *or*

Listen to T49 and make a note of the way in which Nick and Felicity use the word *or* when they are asking each other their opinion of something.

Now discuss this question in groups. Try to use the speech feature *or*. In Nick and Felicity's conversation, is there anything you agree or disagree with?

Vocabulary: colour and light

List the words in the box under the headings **colour** and **light**.
(*Note*: Some of the words may be appropriate to both headings.)

Now add as many words as you can to both lists.

high-level warm natural luminous cool hue tint primary shade pale brightness reflected subdued intensity dim illumination moderate high low loud bright soft low-level tinge glow direct artificial

Discussion

Colour

'If language is an expression of man's interest in his environment, then fine differences in color are of no great concern to him, for his dictionary has very few words for color.' (Faber Birren)

Do you agree with this point of view? Discuss in groups, and try to name as many colours and 'fine differences' in colour as you can. Now write a list of the colours in order of preference, that you'd like to use in your home.

Reading

Before you read

1 The author of this text, Faber Birren, is an expert on 'functional colour' – the choice of appropriate colours for the home, work etc. Discuss these points:

How important is colour to you in your place of work or your home? To what extent does colour affect how people feel or do their work? How do you feel about the colour scheme in your classroom? Which do you consider to be the best colours for a school?

While you read

2 Read the text and choose the summary which best describes it.

a Colour is the most important consideration when creating favourable environments for human beings.
b Both light and colour are important influences, in the home and the workplace, on how people feel and how well they will do their jobs.
c It is still uncertain to what extent colour and light affect the way people live and work, although the author has a few theories.

Vocabulary comprehension

3 Find the words on the left in the text, and match them to the definitions on the right.

1	keep abreast of	a	strong desire
2	endeavoured	b	oppose
3	hues	c	calm state of mind and attitude to life
4	alertness	d	dullness
5	sedentary	e	carried out
6	defy	f	know all the most recent facts about
7	pursued	g	stationary, immobile
8	bottle up	h	shades or tones
9	equanimity	i	tried very hard
10	craving	j	keep under control with difficulty
11	drabness	k	full consciousness

Now check your answers in a dictionary.

Speaking

Work in groups of five. Each student reads about one of the colours on page 122. Summarise what the writer says, then tell the other people in the group about your colour. (Note the American English spelling of *color*.)

Now decide what the best colours would be for the new premises of a small industrial company which consists of these areas:

corridors	toilets
offices	staff relaxation area
reception area	canteen
production area	

Appoint a spokesperson for your group and compare your conclusions with other groups.

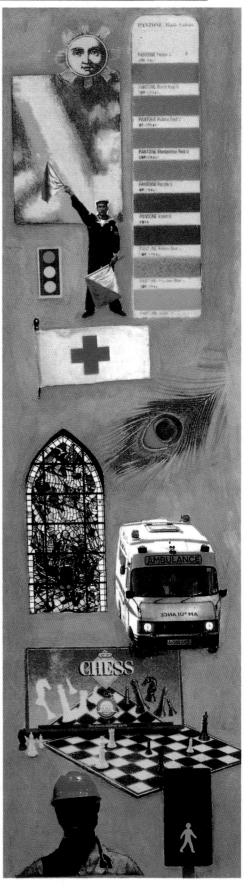

Reading

For many years it has been my profession to work with color and with people in all walks of life. I have kept abreast of color research in the fields of medical therapy, ophthalmology and psychology and I have endeavoured to put to wholly practical use some of the more theoretical findings of the scientific specialist. In all my activities I have tried to adhere to the best scientific practice and to avoid the purely speculative views which so often beset those dealing with the highly temperamental, aesthetic (and often occult) medium of color. With an eye to sound research and practical experience, my conclusions concerning the use of color in everyday life are as follows:

1 There is in color and light what might be called a centrifugal action – away from the organism to its environment. With high levels of illumination, warm and luminous colors in the surroundings (yellow, peach, pink), the body tends to direct its attention outward. There is increased activation in general, alertness, outward orientation. Such an environment is conducive to muscular effort, action and cheerful spirit. It is a good setting for factories, schools, homes where manual tasks are performed or where sports are engaged in.

2 On the other hand, color and light may have a centripetal action – away from the environment and toward the organism. With softer surroundings, cooler hues (gray, blue, green, turquoise) and lower brightness, there is less distraction and a person is better able to concentrate on difficult visual and mental tasks. Good inward orientation is furthered. Here is an appropriate setting for sedentary occupations requiring severe use of the eyes or brain – offices, study rooms, fine assembly in industry.

3 The wise color practice expressed in items 1 and 2 above, however, is not always observed. Lighting engineers, for example, are likely to deal with human environments in terms of light intensity and brightness alone. These are obviously important, but without attention to color as well the truly ideal condition is not realised. Today high levels of *general* illumination are often specified where critical seeing is necessary. While it may be granted that the eye needs a lot of light to see clearly, if this necessity leads to high brightness in the surroundings, the organism may be seriously handicapped. Brightness not only will draw attention from a task; it may defy good visual adjustment and concentration. If intense *general* illumination is required, at least the surroundings ought to be suppressed in tone. Better still, the general illumination should be moderate, and localised light sources should be added and directed immediately over the task. This will put attention where it belongs and eliminate distractions in the outer fields of view. To make a point, note how often a person will close his eyes when trying to solve a complex mental problem; the impulse here is to get rid of the environment completely.

4 In the psychological realm, experimental work in schools and hospitals has emphasised further strategies with color. Outwardly integrated persons, 'nervous' persons, small children will find relaxation in an actively colored environment. The reason is a very simple one: visual (and emotional) excitement in the environment will effectively 'match' the spirits of such persons and thereupon set them at ease. Attempts to pacify them through color or anything else may only serve to 'bottle up' such spirits to a bursting point.

5 Conversely, inwardly integrated persons will ordinarily prefer a more sedate environment – and it will provide the equanimity they innately prefer. A quiet soul told to wear a red dress or a red tie may be no means respond according to the usual pattern. On the contrary, such boldness may make him increasingly shy and embarrassed. In the case of mental disturbance, however, reverse policies may be necessary. A person with an inordinate craving for bloody red – which might lead to trouble – probably should be exposed to blue in order to counteract his temper. The melancholy person, who is tolerant only of drabness, probably should be exposed to red to animate him, physiologically as well as psychically.

And so research in color goes on and perhaps will continue to be pursued indefinitely. If that which is purely physical and biological can be combined with that which is so definitely emotional and psychical, then man's future will be a bright one indeed.

Grammar: modal verbs

Modal bingo

1 Play this game in two teams. The aim is to 'win' a complete line – horizontally, vertically or diagonally.

The first student in Team A calls out a number and the teacher gives the function which corresponds to that box.

The student has to make a grammatically correct and logical sentence to 'win' that square (✓) using an appropriate **modal verb**.

If the sentence is incorrect, team B has a chance to make the statement and win the square (✗).

1	2	3	4
5	6	7	8
9	10	11	12
13	14	15	16

Grammar reflection

2 Look at these sentences taken from listening and reading texts in this unit.

Complete each sentence with the appropriate modal verb. Where there is more than one possibility, write both alternatives. Discuss your answers with a partner.
Now match the verbs you have inserted to the functions listed below.

A	obligation/necessity	F probability
B	prohibition	G instructions, requests
C	mild obligation	H ability
D	possibility	I permission
E	suggestions/advice	

Not all the functions are covered by the sentences in the grammar box: there is a list of sentences on page 119 which contain more modal verbs. Add these verbs to the function headings above. (*Note:* Most modal verbs can be used with a variety of functions.) Check your answers in the Grammar Reference on page 146.

1 I think you _____ deal with it yourself, if you're moody, but you _____ be moody because of what other people have done to you or said to you.

2 You _____ be moody because somebody's died or something, _____ you? You know, I mean there _____ be all sorts of reasons for being moody. I mean, job-related things _____ make people feel depressed.

3 For everyone that feels good there _____ be somebody that feels bad, so that we _____ have a nice average of people feeling sort of half-way.

4 I had a boyfriend who really _____ communicate at all. There was nothing I _____ do to try to make him feel better.

5 I think he _____ _____ tried to explain the problem. Then I _____ _____ helped him or something.

6 If intense general illumination is required, at least the surroundings _____ be suppressed in tone.

7 A quiet soul, told to wear a red dress or a red tie _____ by no means respond according to the usual pattern.

8 The melancholy person probably _____ be exposed to red to animate him.

Practice

Personal happiness

3 In pairs, write a series of eight statements about the prerequisites for happiness. In each statement, include one of the modal verbs you have studied which corresponds to the functions listed in Exercise 2.

Example: *You mustn't set yourself unrealistic goals if you want to be happy.*

Include three statements which you *don't* believe in. Now work in new pairs with a different partner and read your statements. Try to guess which ones are 'false' statements.

Choose one statement (either your own or the other pair's) which you think is the most important prerequisite for happiness. Compare your statement with other students.

We'd be happier if you'd married a millionaire..

Speaking

Read this extract from Faber Birren's book and find out which colour is most suitable for restaurants.

Orange partakes of the same qualities as red. It is not generally preferred in its pure form but highly pleasing in its tints (peach, salmon) and shades (brown). For the most part tints of orange (peach) are ideal for the interiors of hospitals or homes, factories, or schools. The color is mellow, less primitive than red, and it therefore has a more 'loveable' charm. It has high appetite appeal and is quite suitable for food service. Where it may be reflected upon human skin, it casts a cheerful and flattering glow.

What other factors are important to make a restaurant an attractive place to eat in?

Look at these photographs of restaurant interiors. Which of the restaurants appeal to you, and why? Discuss your answers in groups.

Reading

Read this restaurant review. Did the reviewer like the restaurant or not?

PRIMA PASTA
Italian

Prima Pasta describes itself as 'the thinking person's pasta and pizza restaurant' and they seem to be popping up all over the place. There are now 20 in the south-east.

This latest branch is something of a show-case, behind an expanse of plate glass. Inside, it's all cream paint and objects – everything but the kitchen sink: baskets, bottles of olives, a bread bin, fire-irons and bellows round a fireplace, black and white photographs, the Elgin Marbles and lots of fake ivy. Tables are draped with pretty PVC cloths, and lit with candles. There are also smoking and no-smoking sections. They've thought of almost everything, which restaurants such as this depend on, owing as much to marketing as to a love of eating.

And what about the food? Starters include a passable, chunky mine-strone (£2.25), tonno e fagioli, Parma ham with melon, and moz-zarella, avocado and tomato salad (£3.65). Pizzas start at £3.90. Pasta shapes include penne, rigatoni, fusil-li and tagliatelle. The spaghetti with meatballs (£4.95) was all right, ditto the penne alla marinara. A special of spaghetti al cartoccio (seafood and cream cooked in foil, £5.95) was a bit bland. All the pasta was decently chewy. As a general rule, the cream-type, white pasta sauces bear little relation to real cream and are to be avoided, but the tomato-based ones are fine. There's a reasonable choice of Italian wines, several by the half bottle.

Staff are armed with pepper-grinders that should be reclassified as offensive weapons, and you get garlicky olive oil to dip dry slices of baguette in at the beginning of the meal. It cost £13 each including service.

94-98 Upper Richmond Rd, SW15 (081 785 7077) East Putney tube. Open Sun-Thur 12 noon-11pm; Fri-Sat 12 noon-11.30pm. House wine £6.95. Mineral water £1.35/460ml. Coffee 90p. No cover charge. Service optional. Fish and vegetar-ian dishes. See telephone book for other branches.

© Time Out

Was the reviewer positive, negative or neutral about these things? (Make a note of the adjectives etc. used.)

the decor	spaghetti al cartoccio
the minestrone	the white pasta sauces
the pasta in general	the tomato-based sauces
the spaghetti with meatballs	the wines

Writing

Writing a review

Look at the organisation of the review above.

How is the review structured, i.e. which four sections can you identify?

List the information that the reviewer gives the reader in the four sections.

Which is the best restaurant that *you've* ever eaten in?
Which is the best restaurant you've eaten in *recently*?
Tell the other people in your group about these restaurants.

Using the one above as a model, write a restaurant review of about 350 words.

Vocabulary

The home

Write the word which corresponds to each definition.

1 A small hut built from tin, bits of wood or other materials which are not very strong.
2 A house which has only one storey.
3 A very large house.
4 A small flat on two floors of a larger building.
5 A hotel – intended for people who are travelling by car – which has space to park the car near the rooms.
6 A small boat which people live on and which usually remains at a particular place on a river or canal.
7 A set of rooms for one family to live in, usually in a house or building which is divided into several sets of such rooms.
8 A very luxurious flat or set of rooms in a hotel, especially one near the top of a tall building.
9 One of a row of similar houses joined together by their side walls.
10 A room which is used for living and sleeping in.

Moods

One word in each of these sentences is incorrect. Underline the word, and write the correct word instead.

11 When I heard that I had passed my exam I was on top of the continent.
12 Elaine was feeling down in the ditch because she had a terrible cold.
13 It's been raining now for three days, non-stop, I'm completely eaten up.
14 You're looking full of soup today! Have you had some good news?
15 Harry is in a very good mode because Mrs James says he can leave work early today.
16 Wearing my black velvet dress makes me feel like a million lire.
17 We were over the hill when we heard that you were coming to stay with us.
18 Most mornings he's in a foul mind, so I try and avoid him.
19 Why are you in a dump? Was it something I said?
20 I was really out when my cat got run over.

Grammar

Question tags

Write the question tag for each of these sentences.

21 Let's go and see a film, _____?
22 None of the students got lost on the trip, _____?
23 Go and get me a newspaper, _____?
24 I'll make you a cup of tea, _____?
25 You'd better leave now, _____?
26 I don't suppose they will sell their house immediately, _____?

Relative clauses

Complete these sentences with the correct relative pronoun. (If the relative pronoun is *optional*, write * in the space as well, and if there is a choice of pronouns, write both).

In the test, the person being tested selects the colours in descending order of preference; the colour __27__ he likes best and places in the first position is thus the one for __28__ he has the greatest sympathy.

The airline __29__ passengers refuse to fly with any other airline, may have the best safety record or the best aircraft.

The person __30__ chooses green in the first position wants to increase his certainty in his own value, by holding fast to some idealised picture __31__ he has of himself.

The Lüscher Colour Test, despite the ease and speed with __32__ it can be administered, is a deep psychological test, developed for the use of psychiatrists, psychologists, physicians and those __33__ are professionally involved with the conscious and unconscious characteristics and motivations of others.

The physician is a busy man __34__ has little time to spare for diagnostic media, additional to those __35__ are his normal complement.

Modal verbs

In some, but not all, of these sentences the modal verb is correct. In others, the modal verb is wrong for the context. Put a (✓) in the space if it is correct, and write the correct verb if it is not.

36 You must borrow my new CD for the weekend if you like.
37 We could see a strange luminous shape at the end of the garden.
38 I may go away for the weekend as soon as I get paid.
39 I don't know where Rachel is. She can have got lost.
40 If you knew you were going to be late you may have phoned me!

Check your answers by looking at the Answer Key on page 125.

'A classic is something that everybody wants to have read and nobody wants to read.'

MARK TWAIN

Vocabulary: books

Categories of books

1 Which of these kinds of books or stories have you read in the last few months?

> saga   trilogy   fable   exposé   satire
> autobiography   atlas   manual   guidebook
> anthology   short story   textbook   biography
> fairytale   historical novel   love story
> thriller   detective novel   humorous novel
> science fiction novel   spy story   poetry

Which of the books did you enjoy reading? Can you think of any other kinds of books not listed? Compare answers in groups.

Describing books

2 Match these adjectives with two of the genres in Exercise 1.

(*Note:* Some of the adjectives are only used with specific kinds of books.)

> gripping   spine-chilling   plodding
> provocative   inane   bold   crass   witty
> hilarious   bitter-sweet   riotous   profound
> moving   trivial   predictable   intriguing
> banal   futuristic   unconvincing

Ways of reading

3 Explain the difference between these pairs of verbs.

1 browse/flip through
2 dip into/skip
3 read from cover to cover/refer to
4 scan/skim
5 leaf through/scour
6 devour/plod through

Discussion

Spot the genre!

In which kind of book would you expect to find these ten characters?

- A bitter estate owner confined to a wheelchair after a hunting accident.
- His young wife, who spends all day drinking cocktails by the swimming pool.
- Their mixed-up daughter who takes drugs.
- Their weak and neurotic son, who can never live up to his father's expectations.
- A hatchet-faced housekeeper who wears black and has a built-up shoe.
- A simple-minded stable hand who holds the key to the mystery but doesn't realise it.
- A police inspector who is marginally less simple-minded than the stable hand.
- Someone, possibly a racing driver, who is having an affair with the estate owner's wife.
- A brilliantly clever house-guest, who solves murders as a spare time pursuit.
- A dead body.

In pairs or groups, choose one of the other genres from Exercise 1 and make a list of ten characters you would expect to find in a book of that kind.

Then exchange lists with another pair or group, and try to guess which genre their list fits into.

SUMMER READING

"On your marks! Get set …"

Listening

"Tea? Coffee? Nibbles?"

Before you listen

1 Imagine that you are abandoned on a desert island. Write down three things you would most like to have with you. Compare and discuss your choices in groups of four or five.

First listening

2 You are going to hear two conversations in which people are asked which three books they would take with them if they were to spend a period of time alone on a desert island.

Write down the three books chosen by Paul in Conversation 1, and Edgar in Conversation 2.

Second listening

3 Now make more detailed notes about Paul and Edgar's books including what they are about, and why they chose them.

Which of them would you most like to read?

Pronunciation: auxiliary verbs

4 In conversational English these unaccented verbs are usually reduced to a 'contracted' weak form: *am, is, are, was, were, have, has, had, do, does, shall, will, can, must, would.*

Listen to these extracts from the conversations and make a list of the contracted auxiliary verbs you hear in each.

Check your answers, then listen and repeat.

Speech features: *I suppose ...*

T53 The phrase *I suppose* is used frequently in conversational English and can express several different meanings. The intonation used is very important. Listen to the way Paul uses it in these two sentences from the conversation and tick the corresponding uses below:

- expressing tentativeness, or reluctance to do something, even though you agree to do it
- making assumptions about something you are angry or upset about
- expressing tentatively, that you expect a negative response to something you've said
- guessing because you are unsure or can't remember
- introducing an idea which concerns a reason or explanation for something.

Think of a context and write example sentences for the uses you have not ticked.

Write down three books which *you* would take to the desert island. Discuss and explain your choice in groups. Try to use *I suppose* in your explanation.

Reading

Before you read

1 Which of these statements, if any, corresponds to the way *you* choose the books you read? Compare and discuss your answers in groups.

I usually read books that friends have recommended to me.

I just go into a bookshop and choose the first book that looks interesting either from the cover or the 'blurb' on the back.

I read the book reviews in the newspapers and choose books that the reviewers like.

I buy books which have either been nominated for or have won literary prizes.

I only read the 'classics' – that way I am sure of a good read.

While you read

2 Read the article about a person who reviews books and judges literary competitions. Then read these statements and circle the letter T (true) or F (false) according to the writer's opinion.

1 Judges of literary competitions have to work very hard for very little money.   T/F
2 The aim of writing a review is to help the author, not the reader.   T/F
3 Reviewers find it easier to criticise bad books than to praise good ones.   T/F
4 Books are usually reviewed by people who have nothing in common with the authors.   T/F
5 Sexism is not very common in the publishing world.   T/F
6 People who enter literary competitions tend to assume they will win.   T/F

Vocabulary comprehension

3 There are several idiomatic expressions in the text. Look at these expressions in their context and try to work out the meanings.

Para. 1 the down side
off the cuff
Para. 4 waiting in the wings
cop-out
the final straw
Para. 7 quid

Phrasal verbs: *bring*

4 The verb *bring up* in the sentence '... *when I brought the matter up* ...' means 'to mention or introduce a subject in a conversation'.

Which particle is used with *bring* to make phrasal verbs with these meanings?

1 produce and sell (a new product)
2 cause (a government) to lose power
3 arrange for (a meeting or an event) to be organised at an earlier date than originally planned
4 cause something to happen
5 have success in doing something difficult
6 revive someone after they have been unconscious

22 ▶

Reading

Lucy Ellmann

on the making of literary reputations

This Friday, the Irish president will present American author Norman Rush with the *Irish Times* – Aer Lingus International Fiction Prize (a cool £25,000) for his novel, *Mating*. I was one of the five judges, which involved flying First Class to Dublin several times, eating at expensive restaurants and – the down side – reading 46 books. Normally it would take me at least four years to read 46 books. Not only that, but at the discussion meetings we were called upon to give little speeches, off the cuff, on our favourites or rejects. I am no orator; everything I say needs rewrites. The fee was a lure, but a friend calculated that at the rate I was reading I was being paid about 20p an hour. So it mystifies me that I ever agreed to do it. Pure altruism on my part. Except I met a witty taxi-driver and assorted genial judges and organisers, collected a great many sewing kits from the hotel, and read perhaps two really good books.

I am in the dubious position of earning a living by reading and writing. This, despite the fact I'm not even sure I *like* books. Ever since my father panicked about my reading skills at six and commenced emergency Aesop's fable lessons at home, I have suffered from negative feelings towards books. Writing fiction myself has made me even more reluctant to read that of other people: only an exceptional novel relieves me of the habit of rivalry, or the impulse to edit the thing.

When reviewing, there is nothing as convenient as a nice (short) bad book, preferably full of quotable inanities. Since the reviewer's responsibility is to the potential reader rather than to the author (reviewers who are polite to authors either know them already or want to), it has often been my sad duty to warn people off a dreadful book. It is a joy! After all, writing a seriously bad book is a *crime* (against paper if not humanity, and especially against people who read slowly). The reviewer need feel no more compunction towards the author than a prosecutor worries about offending the defendant. And even if you say (as was said of Harold Brodkey), that *death* would have been a smarter career move than writing a novel, the author still benefits from the mention.

Praising, on the other hand, makes me feel foolish. I stiffen, become overly conscious of the praiseworthy author waiting in the wings for the necessary tribute. It is much easier here to say the Wrong Thing. Best love and be silent. The classic cop-out of the tentative flatterer is something like: 'This is probably the best black woman poet writing in America today.' The 'probably' is the final straw. And has the critic read all the poetry written today by black women? It might even be worthwhile taking a look at what they wrote yesterday.

Such categories, from the ghettoising to the grand ('nothing like it in the whole of 20th-century literature'), diminish books, as do comparisons to Jane Austen, Tom Sharpe and Rabelais, if what we're after is originality. In order to construct these categories, women get reviewed by women (if at all), blacks by blacks, and people named Chaim by other people named Chaim. It's the result of laziness (and prejudice) on the part of the literary editors, those suspicious guys (always men – women only make deputy editor) you see at parties.

I have added reason to doubt their abilities now, since the 46 books on our list were all selected by anonymous literary editors. If a Martian had been forced to consider the British entries, he/she/it would have assumed that there were no women writing in Britain. We're talking about Literature here, not Gender, I was told sternly when I brought the matter up. One judge claimed there was no sexism in the British literary scene. Silly me!

The British literary scene didn't come into it much in the end, since all four writers on the short-list were American: Norman Rush, Toni Morrison, Jane Smiley and Allen Kurzweil. The three losers get a free trip to Dublin for the ceremony, and the gratuitous rejection that failing to receive a prize entails. It's no joke getting one's hopes raised: you might never have *thought* of winning the Penrith Pedestrian Palindrome Competition, but once nominated you start to plan what you'd do with the eight quid. I was short-listed a few years ago for a £5,000 prize, and had visions of getting to Hong Kong. In the end they gave me a coffee machine.

As compensation for our trouble, Norman Rush fully deserves this prize. *Mating* is a generous account of an American woman's quest for love in Botswana. The flotsam and jetsam of her cultural influences are set against the complexities of African politics and, more tenderly, the intricacy of intimacy. Oh, I hate praising. Let's just say that as novelists go, male or female, white or black, American or otherwise, he's an original.

Grammar: comparisons

It's better ...

1 Work in pairs. Choose one of these pairs of topics to compare and discuss.

private/state schools
trains/buses
North American music/music in your country
English/Chinese as a world language
swimming in the sea/in a swimming pool

Choose one item to defend in each pair of topics, and try to convince your partner that the item you have chosen is the better of the two. Use a different comparative structure in each comparison. If necessary, look at the example sentences in the box below for an idea of some of the structures you could use.

Grammar reflection

> 1 I'd probably take with me a book I've read more often than any other book.
>
> 2 The reviewer need feel no more compunction towards the author than a prosecutor worries about offending the defendant.
>
> 3 Death would have been a smarter move than writing a novel.
>
> 4 A book that I found very moving and much more interesting than anything I'd read by any other South American writer.
>
> 5 They've made a film out of it but the film isn't as good as the book.
>
> 6 When reviewing there's nothing as convenient as a nice (short) bad book.

2 *more/less than*

What kind of word, phrase or sentence can follow comparisons with *than*?
Find examples of these in the sentences in the box.

as ... as ...

In comparisons, use *as* + adjective +
a a prepositional phrase beginning with *as*
b a clause introduced by the conjunction *as*.

Which of these two patterns do the examples in the box correspond to?

How do you make negative sentences with both *more/less than* and *as ... as ...* using *no, not* or *not nearly*?

Extension – submodifiers

Submodifiers with *than-* clauses

Look at the sentences in the box again. In sentence number 4 the speaker has used *much* before the comparative adjective *more interesting*. *Much* is used here as a submodifier. *Much* is one of a number of submodifiers which can be used both attributively and predicatively.

Example: *A novel that I found ...* **much more interesting** *than anything ...* (attributive use)

Compared to other South American novels, I found that book **much more interesting.** (predicative use)

Can you think of any other submodifiers that can be used instead of *much,* in the two sentences above?

Submodifiers with *as-* clauses

Submodifiers can also be used before *as.* Complete this list of submodifiers often used with *as ... as ...* in the following sentence:

The film is j – – t/n – – – – – y/a – – – – t/not – – – – –
as good as the book.

There is also a negative form of one of these, using *not.* Which one? Try out the two negative submodifiers in sentences 5 and 6 in the box.

Check your answers in the Grammar Reference on page 147.

Practice

The quality of life

3 Work in groups of four, and prepare to have a debate on this topic:

'The quality of life is far higher for most people today than it was 100 years ago.'

In pairs, prepare arguments either for or against the statement. Think about these things:

stress	illness	transport
quality of food	family life	human rights
war	education	environment

Now hold your debate. Try to use a submodifier in every comparison you make.

Speaking

Choosing a best-seller

Work in groups of four. You are a group of publishers working for a large company, which is not doing very well at the moment. You desperately need a best-seller to boost your company's image and sales.

By looking at the 'blurbs' (descriptions of books found on their back covers) below, decide which one of these books you would publish in the belief that it could become an international best-seller.

Now think of a suitable title for the book you have chosen. (The original covers of the published books can be seen on page 127.)

> She was a thin, lonely child with huge eyes and an extensive vocabulary of French foul language. Amongst the elegant middle-class British families holidaying in Dinard in 1926 – leading their privileged lives of secure routine pleasures – Flora was a ten-year-old misfit. Ignored by her self-absorbed parents, unloved, and pitied by the pleasant, stylish people in Brittany that summer, Flora was – peripherally – included in their gracious circles. And there, meeting kindly civilised people for the first time, she fell in love – with Cosmo – with Hubert – with Felix. It took forty years for the love affairs to be explored, consummated, and finally resolved.

> Macon does his best. He writes Armchair Tourist guidebooks that soothe the travel-hating businessman: keep wearing the non-crushable, stain-camouflaging grey suit and stick to Salade Niçoise in France – it's the one dish that's safe.
>
> Even when his son, Ethan, is murdered and his wife leaves him, Macon folds his anguish neatly back into place and adapts the household routine on to more efficient lines. So when he meets Muriel, dog trainer from the Meow-Bow dog clinic – thin, chaotic, outrageous, vulnerable Muriel – he considers that his defences against love and pain are in excellent working order.

> Desmond never did have much luck with women – except in getting them through their driving tests. Now a coach driver, he is at the most crucial crossroads of his life. His wife has thrown him out. The crisis serves only to deepen his despair over another failed liaison – until he elects to steer his coach on a spectacularly reckless quest for the son he has never seen …

Writing: blurbs

You are going to write the blurb for a book you know very well (preferably one you have read in English) and which you think other people in your class would enjoy reading.

Use the blurbs you have looked at here as a model. Most of them follow this pattern:

• Summary of the story
(The aim here is to give enough away about the story to interest readers and make them want to read the book, without giving away the whole story. Note the use of tenses in the blurbs.)

• Comments by the Press and critics
(Use the adjectives on page 86 and the back covers of the books on page 127. Comments should range from writing merely adjectives, to complete sentences about the writer's skill in style, characterisation, plot etc.)

When you have finished writing, read as many of the other blurbs as you can and pick out a book that you think you would like to read. Ask the person who wrote the blurb questions to find out more about the book.

Say the right thing!

Emphasising

1 Elsewhere in this book you have studied ways of giving more emphasis to what you want to say. (See sentence 1 below.) Now you are going to find out about other ways of changing emphasis.

Look at these pairs of sentences and tick the one which is more emphatic in each case. Explain which part of the sentence is now emphasised more strongly.

1 a I'm fairly flexible but I like people to turn up on time.
   b I am fairly flexible but I do like people to turn up on time.
2 a It was Jan who told me about the accident.
   b Jan told me about the accident.
3 a It's music for TV ads that she writes.
   b She writes music for TV ads.
4 a I remembered leaving my jacket on the plane when I got to customs.
   b It was when I got to customs that I remembered leaving my jacket on the plane.
5 a She fixed the car herself.
   b What she did was (to) fix the car herself.
6 a I think she's a very sensible person indeed.
   b I think she's a very sensible person.
7 a I don't like men who wear white socks at all.
   b I don't like men who wear white socks.
8 a The waiter came in carrying a huge bottle of champagne.
   b In came the waiter carrying a huge bottle of champagne.

Now match the sentences to these techniques for changing emphasis.

A Using full forms of modal verbs and auxiliary verbs in affirmative statements (*I did see you!*)
B Cleft sentences (*It is/was ... that ...*) (*What ... is/was, ...*)
C 'Emphasis' adverbs (*indeed, at all*)
D Fronting (*In came the waiter ...*)

Make a list of other emphasis words you know. Check your answers on page 127.

Conversion

2 Use the techniques from Exercise 1 at least once each in order to make these statements more emphatic. (More than one answer is possible, depending on the part of the sentence you decide to emphasise.)

1 They enjoyed their holiday in Denmark very much and they're going back there next year.
2 They took the decision to close down the reactor when the alarm bell rang.
3 Help yourself to a drink and make yourself comfortable.
4 A man wearing a ginger wig came into the room.
5 He didn't approve of the government's plans to privatise the railways.
6 They caught a later train and got to Salamanca at eight o'clock the next morning.

Discussion

3 Think about the things that you like and dislike about language learning and write a list of emphatic statements about them.

Work in groups. Without looking at your statements, discuss language learning. Try to use all the statements you prepared in the discussion.

"Well, you did say they should go outside and get some fresh air."

'Education is an admirable thing, but it is well to remember from time to time that nothing that is worth knowing can be taught.'

OSCAR WILDE

Vocabulary: education

1 List the following words under one or more of these headings:

1 school 2 university 3 assessment 4 qualifications

(*Note:* Match verbs with suitable nouns as you list the words.)

> Dip. BA exam grade MBA
> PGCE pupil take hall of residence
> detention MA degree fail sit lecturer
> curriculum PhD professor pass campus
> student GCSE teacher minimum leaving age
> discipline A-level uniform
> corporal punishment BSc seminar
> head teacher suspension read BEd module
> deputy head Students' Union drop out MSc

Work in groups. Choose a pair of words from the lists you have made and establish a connection between them. For every valid connection, you get one point. The next student chooses two words – not used before – that can be connected. The winner is the student with most points when all the word-pairs in the chart have been found.

Explain the difference

2 Can you explain the difference between these words?

a school/college
b nursery/crèche/kindergarten
c public school/state school/private school
d high school/comprehensive school
e boarding school/day school
f grammar school/comprehensive school

Discussion

A good education

Discuss in groups:

Which subjects do you think all children should study at school? Choose five subjects which you all agree are essential.

Apart from studying an adequate range of subjects, what constitutes a 'good education' in your opinion?

Make a list of the good and bad points of the education system in your country. Think about:

> exam system   school leaving age   university
> class size   subjects taught   quality of teaching
> hours of study   facilities

What could be done, where necessary, to improve the education system? Compare your answers with other groups.

The happiest days?

Many people have unhappy memories of their schooldays. Did you experience problems in any of these areas when you were at school?

• excessively severe discipline
• pressure to conform
• pressure to succeed
• choosing academic direction
• living up to parents'/teachers' expectations
• exams and assessment
• boredom

Discuss your answers in pairs, and add other problems you experienced – if any – to the list.

Reading

Before you read

1 Look at the photographs of children at different schools around the world. Do any of them show the sort of clothes many children wear to school in *your* country?

Some people defend school uniforms by saying that differences in wealth are less likely to be obvious. Do you think this is a satisfactory argument? What do *you* think about school uniforms? Discuss in groups.

While you read

2 You are going to read a text from the book *The Secret Diary of Adrian Mole Aged 13¾* by Sue Townsend. Read the text quickly and match the names and descriptions of the people. (Some of the descriptions can be matched to more than one name.)

Miss Sproxton
Pandora   a teacher at the school
Scruton   the headmaster of the school
Mrs Claricoates   Pandora's parents
Tania   friends of Pandora
Ivan   a girl Adrian likes very much
Nigel   the headmaster's secretary
Clair Neilson
Craig and Brett

Vocabulary comprehension

3 Find these words in the text. Then write which part of speech (noun, verb etc.) they are, and work out their meaning from the context. Finally, write a synonym or a definition for each one.

spotted	poached
tray	trooped
guts	flaunted
rallied	hot foot
folded	raged

Phrasal verbs

4 Find phrasal verbs in the text which have the same meaning as:

(*Saturday June 6th*)
call at someone's house
talk to all the people in a place
make arrangements or prepare for something
(*Sunday June 7th*)
like each other and have a friendly relationship
continue talking about something, often in an annoying way
change and become
(*Monday June 8th*)
give someone prior knowledge of something that was supposed to be a secret
(*Monday June 15th*)
give in and do something you don't really want to do

Reading

Friday June 5th

Miss Sproxton spotted my red socks in assembly! The old bag reported me to pop-eyed Scruton. He had me in his office and gave me a lecture on the dangers of being a nonconformist. Then he sent me home to change into regulation black socks.

Saturday June 6th

Oh Joy! Rapture! Pandora is organising a sock protest! She came round to my house today! Yes! She actually stood on our front porch and told me that she admired the stand I was taking! I would have asked her in, but the house is in a squalid state so I didn't. She is going round the school with a petition on Monday morning. She said I was a freedom fighter for the rights of the individual. She wants me to go round to her house tomorrow morning. A committee is being set up, and I am the principal speaker! She wanted to see the red socks but I told her they were in the wash.

Sunday June 7th

Pandora and the committee were waiting for me in the big lounge of her house. Pandora is Chairperson, Nigel is Secretary and Pandora's friend Clair Neilson is Treasurer. Craig Thomas and his brother Brett are just ordinary supporters. I am not allowed to hold high office because I am the victim.

Pandora's parents were in the wooden kitchen doing *The Sunday Times* Crossword. They seem to get on quite well together.

They brought a tray of coffee and health biscuits into the lounge for us. Pandora introduced me to her parents. They said they admired the stand that I was taking. They were both members of the Labour Party and they went on about the *Tolpuddle Martyrs. They asked me if the fact that I had chosen to protest in *red* socks had any significance. I lied and said I had chosen red because it was a symbol of revolution, then I blushed revolutionary red. I am turning into quite a liar recently.

Pandora's mother said I could call her Tania. Surely that is a Russian name? Her father said I could call him Ivan. He is very nice, he gave me a book to read; it is called *The Ragged Trousered Philanthropists*. I haven't looked through it yet but I'm quite interested in stamp collecting so I will read it tonight.

Washed red socks, put them on radiator to dry ready for the morning.

Monday June 8th

Woke up, dressed, put red socks on before underpants or vest. Father stood at the door and wished me luck. Felt like a hero. Met Pandora and rest of committee at corner of our road; all of us were wearing red socks. Pandora's were lurex. She has certainly got guts! We sang 'We shall not be moved' all the way to school. I felt a bit scared when we went through the gates but Pandora rallied us with shouts of encouragement.

Pop-eyed Scruton had been tipped off because he was waiting in the fourth-year cloakroom. He was standing very still with his arms folded, staring with poached egg eyes. He didn't speak, he just nodded upstairs. All the red socks trooped upstairs. My heart was beating dead loud. He went silently into his office and sat at his desk and started tapping his teeth with a school pen. We just stood there.

He smiled in a horrible way then rang the bell on his desk. His secretary came in, he said, 'Sit down and take a letter, Mrs Claricoates.' The letter was to our parents, it said:

Dear Mr and Mrs ....,
It is my sad duty to inform you that your son/daughter has deliberately flaunted one of the rules of this school. I take an extremely serious view of this contravention. I am therefore suspending your son/daughter for a period of one week. Young people today often lack sufficient moral guidance in the home, therefore I feel that it is my duty to take a firm stand in my school. If you wish to discuss the matter further with me do not hesitate to ring my secretary for an appointment.
Yours faithfully,
R G Scruton
Headmaster

Pandora started to say something about her O levels suffering but Scruton roared at her to shut up! Even Mrs Claricoates jumped. Scruton said that we could wait until the letters had been typed, duplicated and signed and then we had better 'hot foot it out of school'. We waited outside Scruton's office. Pandora was crying (because she was angry and frustrated, she said). I put my arm round her a bit. Mrs Claricoates gave us our letters. She smiled very kindly, it can't be very easy working for a despot.

We went round to Pandora's house but it was locked, so I said everyone could come round to my house. It was quite tidy for once, apart from the dog hairs. My father raged about the letter. He is supposed to be a Conservative but he is not being very conservative at the moment.

I can't help wishing that I had worn black socks on Friday.

Tuesday June 9th

My father saw Scruton today and told him that if he didn't allow me back to school in whatever colour socks I like he would protest to his MP. Mr Scruton asked my father who his MP was. My father didn't know.

Monday June 15th

The Red Sock Committee has voted to give way to Scruton for the time being. We wear red socks underneath our black socks. This makes our shoes tight but we don't mind because a principle is involved.

* Six members of a 'workers' union', exiled to Australia for seven years in 1834, for swearing an illegal oath.

Listing

Before you listen

1 Most languages have a 'standard' accent. For example, 'standard' English is spoken in many parts of Britain, but mainly in the south-east. Is there an equivalent in your language?

Which of these statements about accent and language do you agree with?
Discuss your conclusions in groups.

You are more likely to do better at school if you speak with a 'standard' accent.
'Standard' accents are boring because everyone sounds the same.
Professional people tend to speak with a 'standard' accent.
One of the reasons that educated people often speak with a 'standard' accent is that it is better for expressing complex ideas.
People should be proud to speak with the accent of the area where they were born.
People with a 'standard' accent are more likely to be respected.

First listening

 2 You are going to listen to an excerpt from the play *Educating Rita* by the Liverpool playwright, Willy Russell. The two main characters are called Frank and Rita. The first time you listen, concentrate on answering these questions.

1 What does Frank do?
2 Why has Rita come to see Frank?

Second listening

3 Listen and answer these questions.

1 What did Rita imagine public schools would be like?
2 What does Rita think of Frank using the same sort of language as her?
3 What were Rita's reasons for not becoming a 'proper' student?
4 Why does Rita want to change her situation?
5 What are her plans for when she has passed her first exam?

Pronunciation: vowels before -n

 4 Listen to the pronunciation of *difference* in this sentence from the play:

'Then I'll get a proper dress, the sort of dress you'd only see on an educated woman, on the sort of woman who knows the difference between Jane Austen and Tracy Austin.'

The vowels /ə/, /ɪ/ are *elided* (not pronounced) when they are preceded and followed by consonants in unaccented syllables.
Listen to the examples:

> certain   importance   absence
> caution   conscience   allusion
> appearance   golden

There are, however, exceptions to this pattern. Listen to these words and underline the vowels which are *not* elided:

> potent   tartan   London   medicine   Latin
> occasion   Washington   Hampton   student
> Saturn   confidence

Now listen and repeat.

Speech features: *ever*

Rita: You can't say that.
Frank: Why ever not?

Look up **ever** in the dictionary. What does it mean?

In addition to its use with the present perfect tense (e.g. *Have you ever been to France?*), **ever** is used to add emphasis to questions and statements in a number of other ways. Here are some of the more common uses of **ever** for this function.

• after *never*
• after comparatives with *than* and after superlatives
• with negative question forms and in negative statements (here it often expresses anger or surprise)
• to emphasise exclamations

Add **ever** to these sentences to make them more emphatic.

a 'Do you like chocolate cake?' 'Do I!'
b It was the most boring play.
c He never eats meat.
d How did you manage to get here during a transport strike?
e He is fatter now than …
f Don't you do that again!

Now listen and check your answers.

96

Grammar: reported speech

Late again!

1 Look at the situation in the illustrations, and report the conversation (in indirect speech) you think the two women had. Use these reporting verbs:

T58 Now listen to the original conversation and see if your version is accurate.

ask	complain
suggest	convince
apologise	explain
prefer	decide

A

B

C

D

E

F

Grammar reflection

2 Look at this range of types of reported speech from the reading and listening texts in this unit.

> A Reporting a statement
> B Reporting an order, a request or a piece of advice
> C Reporting thoughts and feelings
> D Reporting a question

Decide which of these four categories the sentences belong to.

1 Rita explained to Frank that her teachers had been unable to get her to study.
2 At one point Rita told Frank not to be stupid.
3 Rita intended to get a new dress when she had passed her first exam.
4 She wants me to go round to her house tomorrow morning.
5 I always thought they sounded great, schools like that.
6 Frank wondered why Rita had never become a 'proper' student.
7 They asked me if the fact that I had chosen to protest in red socks had any significance.
8 When she was at school, Rita preferred not to take it seriously.
9 Pandora's mother said I could call her Tania.
10 I told her they were in the wash.
11 Mr Scruton asked my father who his MP was.
12 Frank joked that proper students didn't read or study.

A Look at these patterns used for reporting a statement.

    a verb + *that*- clause
    b verb + object + *that*- clause
    c verb + *to* + object + *that*- clause

Which of the patterns listed do these verbs follow?

> answer   suggest   remind

(*Note:* *Suggest* can be used with two of the patterns listed. Which ones?)
After which verbs is it possible to leave out *that*?

B Reporting an order, a request or a piece of advice.

    verb + object + *to* + infinitive

C Reporting thoughts and feelings.

    verb + *that*- clause
    verb + *to* + infinitive
Which of the following verbs can be used ...?

1 only with *that*- clause
2 only with *to* + infinitive
3 with either of the above

Is it possible to leave out *that* in pattern 1?

> feel   agree   want   plan   believe   decide
> imagine   forget

A Reporting a question.

    verb + *wh*-word/*if* (often with *enquire*)
    verb + object + *wh*-word/*if*

What is the order of subject and verb in reported questions?

Check your answers in the Grammar Reference on page 148.

Practice

Conversion

3 Convert these sentences from the novel *Some Tame Gazelle* by the British novelist, Barbara Pym, into reported speech. Use the reporting verbs listed here once each:

> decide   plan   agree   feel   tell   ask
> believe   suggest   wonder   answer

1 'Don't you think you would be more comfortable in low-heeled shoes, dear?' suggested Belinda tentatively.
2 'I always think low-heeled shoes are so dowdy,' she said. 'Besides, high heels are definitely the fashion now.'
3 'Don't you like cauliflower cheese?'
4 'My sister and I are going to tea with Count Bianca.'
5 'It seems to me that you and Nathaniel have a great many tastes in common.'
6 'Oh, Harriet, you mustn't be so unkind!' protested Belinda.
7 'Why, yes, it must be nearly supper-time,' said Belinda, starting to put on her gloves. 'I must go.'
8 'What are you reading?' she asked, trying to change the subject.
9 'She was always interested in missions, if I remember rightly.'
'Oh, yes, she was,' said Belinda, thinking she might as well agree for a change.
10 'I think that English Literature and Theology can be happily combined,' said Olivia gracefully.

Candid Caller

4 Read the introduction to an opinion survey conducted by Tim Wapshott of *The Independent* newspaper.

USING the pseudonym Nosmo King, the Candid Caller got Britain fuming this week on the subject of smoking. His questions were: should Britain follow France's lead and introduce legislation banning smoking in public places? And, if you were in the non-smoking area of a restaurant and a fellow diner lit up, what would you do?

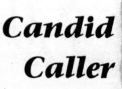

If you are in favour of people smoking in public places, look at page 117. If you are against it, look at page 118.

Read the views of the people interviewed.

Now discuss the issue of smoking in public, supporting your argument by referring to the views you read. (Use as many reporting verbs as you can when referring to the texts.)

Reading and Speaking

Here is the beginning and the end of a short story by the New Zealand writer, Joy Cowley.

The Woman Next Door

Six, perhaps seven, the child of the photograph, solid against the blur of a city, unsmiling in black and white.

She was old enough then to have learned that black and white were the non-colours, the everything and nothing that had no place in rainbows. She also knew that God was white and the Devil was black, while the in-between tones, the greys of the street in the photograph, belonged to the War.

And the child knew about War. It lay all the way between everything and nothing and covered the city so that no matter where one went there was no way of escaping it. It was a grey smoke that filled the air they had to breathe

Some time after that, Mrs Gessner moved away from the street. The child didn't see her leave. She came home from school and was met by Grandfather who gave her a brown paper parcel. Inside was the music box. The woman left it for the little girl, he said. She meant you, he said.

The child didn't know what to say. She felt as though she had been caught doing something wrong.

You know what your father would want you to do, Grandfather said.

Of course she knew. And as she put the music box on the fire, the aunts and uncles put their arms round her and told her she was a real little heroine, and that pleased her; but most of all she was pleased that she had made her father, who was living with the angels, very proud of his daughter.

Work in groups. You are each going to read one of five sections of the story. **Student A**, look at page 117; **Student B** page 118; **Student C**, page 119; **Student D**, page 120; **Student E**, page 121.

When you have finished reading, identify the picture which corresponds to your section of the story.

Now tell the rest of your group about your section, and without looking at each other's texts, decide the correct order for the extracts and the pictures. Finally, turn to the relevant pages (see above) and read the complete story in the correct order.

Writing: a review

Read this review of a novel.

IN BRIEF

GRACED LAND by Laura Kalpakian, Constable £13.99.
Miss Emily Shaw, young, pretty and educated, with wealthy parents and a big engagement ring, is doing a little light social work in St Elmo, California – 'the armpit of the nation' as her dinner party friends describe it. Though a member of a sorority, she knows nothing about sisterhood or love or life until she meets Joyce Jackson, her friend, Sandee, and her sassy teenage daughter, Cilla.

Joyce (born Rejoice) has exchanged the poor white's traditional consolation of religion for a life made rich by the music of Elvis Presley. Elvis died to redeem humanity, in Joyce's view – and if he ended his days a bloated addict, well, that was his Calvary. Joyce has kept rock'n'rolling in the face of all the disasters that existence in St Elmo has to offer, and

she is therefore a thorn in the ample flesh of Large Marge Mason, Emily's supervisor at the Welfare Department.

Emily's job is to run regular checks on Joyce's home to make sure that she is as manless and as moneyless as she claims. But after a single night down at the Cask and Cleaver, swilling beer bought on undeclared income and sweating to the beat, Emily Shaw discovers *Burning Love*.

If the message of *Graced Land* is fairly obvious, its fictional presentation is warm and funny, as full of vitality as a downtown dancehall when the King was at the height of his powers. What a shame that its cover is about as eye-catching as a dishcloth.

Julia Thorogood

© The Independent

What are the first three paragraphs about? What is the last paragraph about? What else could you include in a review? Overall, is the review positive or negative?

You are going to write a review of *The Woman Next Door*. You may find it useful to focus on these questions about the text:

- Which period is the story set in?
- Who are the main characters?
- What information do you gradually find out about Mrs Gessner?
- What tragic event changes the course of the story?
- How does the relationship developing between the little girl and Mrs Gessner change?
- What did the family do when they found out about her friendship with Mrs Gessner?
- What happened when Mrs Gessner left?
- What was Joy Cowley trying to say in writing the story?
- What did you like and dislike about the story?

Now write your review. Exchange completed reviews with other students and discuss any differences in opinion.

Improve your language learning:

Making mistakes

Choose the most appropriate answers in this questionnaire about mistakes and how to deal with them.

1 When I speak English I make mistakes
  a very frequently.
  b sometimes, according to the situation.
  c very rarely.
2 When I speak English, my main concern is
  a fluency.
  b accuracy.
  c a compromise between fluency and accuracy.
3 When I make mistakes when speaking English
  a I don't really care.
  b I worry about it but don't know what to do.
  c I have a clear idea about how to correct myself.
4 The most serious mistakes I make are
  a grammar mistakes.
  b vocabulary mistakes.
  c pronunciation mistakes.
5 In my opinion, mistakes in written work
  a are inevitable and there's not much you can do about it.
  b are a useful indicator of problems with my English.
  c are inexcusable at my level.

6 When my teacher gives back my written work
  a I check all mistakes and correct them in writing.
  b I have a quick look at the work and go over the mistakes in my head.
  c I don't usually pay much attention to the mistakes.
7 In class I think that my teacher should
  a correct all the mistakes I make.
  b occasionally correct me.
  c avoid correcting me so as not to discourage me.
8 When I hear another student make a mistake
  a I pay no attention.
  b I always correct him or her.
  c I draw his or her attention to the mistake if it is a consistent one, when the activity has finished.

Key and score

	a	b	c
1	2	3	0
2	2	1	3
3	0	2	3
4	2	2	1
5	1	3	0
6	3	2	0
7	1	3	2
8	1	2	3

Comment

Frequency of mistakes

1 If you chose a, you are probably over-critical and tend to worry too much about making mistakes. Although this could result in accurate language, it could also lead to a lesser degree of fluency.

If you chose c, you may not be self-critical enough, and probably make mistakes without realising it.

(*Note:* It is quite likely that the number of mistakes you make will vary according to the circumstances. For example, you may make more mistakes when you are very involved in a discussion; when you are discussing a subject which is unfamiliar to you, and you are unsure of the vocabulary needed; when you are angry, excited or tired.)

Fluency versus accuracy

2–3 The best answer is c. At an advanced level of English both fluency and accuracy are equally important. In recent years, teachers have encouraged students at lower levels of competence, not to become inhibited by the number of mistakes they make, and to concentrate more on communicating effectively.

But as a student becomes more proficient in a foreign language, the aim of learning should be to achieve near-native speaker competence. While not becoming obsessed with a high level of accuracy, you should concentrate more and more on speaking and writing accurately. Wherever possible, stop and correct yourself when you are aware that you are making a mistake.

Type of mistake

4 Many students take grammar mistakes more seriously than errors in vocabulary or pronunciation. At an advanced level, aim to try to eliminate all kinds of mistakes, but remember to be patient, and set yourself only realistic goals. (It is unlikely that most students will ever be able to pass themselves off as native speakers, unless they spend an extended period of time in an English-speaking country. Even then, they may not be able to correct a non-standard accent which they may have acquired much earlier in their learning of the foreign language.)

Written work

5–6 Mistakes in written work are sometimes easier to deal with than those made in spoken English, as the former are 'fixed' i.e. available for analysis later on. The best answer is 5b.

Correction

7–8 Teachers all have their own strategies for correcting mistakes – this depends on the type of activity the class is involved in, the size of the class etc.. Correction during a student's conversation can be discouraging and annoying, but you will do well to pay close attention to the useful corrective feedback *after* an activity.

Provided that students do not overdo it, or choose inappropriate situations for it, correction of others can be a worthwhile exercise. Even native speakers of a language occasionally help each other out when it is clear that they are having difficulty finding the right word or way to express themselves.

Vocabulary

Books

Look at these titles of books. What types of books are they?

1 *Egypt – The Rough Guide*
2 *T S Eliot* by Peter Ackroyd
3 *Passing On* by Penelope Lively
4 *A Murder of Quality* by John Le Carré
5 *The Penguin Book of Italian Verse*
6 *Moto Guzzi V-Twins* by Mansur Darlington
7 *Workout Advanced* by Paul Radley and Kathy Burke
8 *The Spy in Question* by Tim Sebastian
9 *Just Williams* by Kenneth Williams
10 *2001 A Space Odyssey* by Arthur C Clarke

Education

The italicised word in these sentences is wrong for the context. Write the correct word.

11 The head *professor* of the school was very angry.
12 People who study science at university get a *BA* when they graduate.
13 Students often live in a hall of *detention*, especially in their first year at university.
14 Parents who send their children to *private* schools don't have to pay for their education.
15 In America students go to *primary* school before they go on to university.
16 I *passed* a history exam yesterday morning but I don't know the result yet.
17 Students who go to a *boarding* school go home to their parents every evening.
18 Ann *fell* out of her university career when she met Mark.
19 The main university *set of buildings* is situated just outside the city.
20 The people who teach in British universities are called *professors*.

Grammar

Comparisons

Complete these sentences with an appropriate submodifier. (*Note:* More than one answer is possible.)

21 Clint Eastwood's new film is _____ more interesting than anything he has done before.
22 Compared to Indian food, English food is _____ less spicy.
23 It was not _____ as hot this summer as it was last year.
24 There are _____ as many students in this class as there are in the whole of the first year.
25 Since I started this job I have worked _____ harder.
26 This crossword puzzle is _____ more difficult than yesterday's.
27 The quality of life is _____ higher for most people today than it was 100 years ago.
28 _____ fewer people in Europe are having more than two children in the nineties than in previous decades.
29 _____ as many English people buy video recorders as Americans.
30 There are _____ more motorcyclists in Britain who use their machines all year round than there are in the rest of Europe.

Reported speech

Complete the sentences with one of these reporting verbs:

want	order	suggest	ask	intend
wonder	decide	persuade	tell	

31 I often _____ why people drive so aggressively in the city.
32 We _____ him that there were no vacancies at the moment.
33 Alan _____ that we buy our tickets a couple of hours before the beginning of the film.
34 I _____ to go for a walk after work but it started raining so I decided not to.
35 The policeman _____ me if I had been drinking.
36 Even though I had seen the play before, my friends _____ me to go to the theatre with them last night.
37 I thought Jeremy had _____ to leave the Civil Service.
38 The careers officer _____ me not to go to university, but I did and now I teach there.
39 Our friends _____ to visit us at Easter but we had to say no as we were going away.
40 The sergeant _____ the men to jump in the river and swim to the other side.

Check your answers by looking at the Answer Key on page 125.

'An actor entering through a door, you've got nothing. But if he enters through the window, you've got a situation.'

BILLY WILDER

Vocabulary: cinema and television

1 Look at these photographs. Which of them are the kinds of things only shown on television? Which can be seen both on television and at the cinema?

heavy	atmospheric	moving	subtle	corny

> heavy   atmospheric   moving   subtle   corny
> sensitive   harrowing   stylish   predictable
> stunning   thought-provoking   contrived
> plodding   tedious   far-fetched   pretentious
> fast-moving   schmaltzy

Now look at the film and TV reviews on page 117 and find six positive and six negative adjectives or phrases that the reviewers have used in their descriptions.

Explain the difference

3 Explain the difference between:

1 a sitcom and a comedy programme
2 a serial and a soap
3 a quiz and a game show
4 a feature film and a TV film
5 an animated film and a cartoon

Film

4 Write the words for these definitions.

1 the person who writes the script (story of a film)
2 the person who finances a film
3 the person who chooses the actors
4 the person who decides how a film is made
5 the person who operates the camera
6 the collective name for the actors in a film
7 the most important acting role
8 a subsidiary, but nevertheless important, acting role
9 a special 'film' word for the script
10 the audio element of a film
11 the names of people involved, which appear on the screen at the end of a film

Adjectives of criticism

2 Put these adjectives into two lists, those which have positive connotations (P) and those which have negative connotations (N). When you have listed all the words you know, check the meaning of any unknown words in a dictionary and add them to the list. Compare your list with a partner.

Discussion

Viewing habits

Discuss in groups:

How much TV do you watch every day?
Which programmes do you *always* watch, or *never* watch? (Use the adjectives from Exercise 2 to explain why.)
What types of films do you like?

Do you prefer watching films on TV or at the cinema?
What's the best/worst film you have seen recently, either at the cinema or on TV?
Use the vocabulary you have studied above to tell the rest of your group about these films.

Listening

Before you listen

1 What are the advantages and disadvantages of seeing feature films at the cinema, or on television? Discuss in pairs.

First listening

T59 2 You are going to hear Colin Goudie, a film editor at the BBC, talking about the relationship between video and cinema.
The first time you listen, make a note of the effects that video and television have had on film-making.

Second listening

3 Listen again and answer these questions.

1 Why do film directors have to take video into consideration when they make films these days?
2 What practical examples does Colin give of how this affects the way a director works?
3 Colin says that directors today 'don't have that eye'. What is he referring to?
4 How are films usually shown on TV? What exceptions does Colin mention?
5 What technological development will improve the way films will be viewed at home?
6 Why does he say that people will always go to the cinema?
7 Why are comedy films funnier at the cinema?
8 Why does Colin think that horror films are less scary at home?

25 ▶

Pronunciation: word boundary

T61 4 Listen to these extracts from the conversation with Colin Goudie. What happens to the sounds of consonants *-t, -d, -s, -z* and *-n* when they precede certain other consonants in conversational English?

1 … films are finance<u>d b</u>y television companies …
2 Therefore he composes hi<u>s s</u>hots with a view to television ratio.
3 … which is coming out thi<u>s y</u>ear in this country …
4 … no matter wha<u>t y</u>ou do with video at home …
5 … the horror film coul<u>d b</u>e more effective at home …
6 … it also ca<u>n b</u>ecome weaker because people will turn the sound down…

Now listen and repeat, concentrating on linking the words in the same way the speakers do.

> ### Speech features: *actually*
>
> The word *actually* is very commonly used when people speak English and it can have a number of uses:
>
> a to correct someone when they've misunderstood, or have wrong information
> b to introduce information – which may be unpleasant or unwelcome – gently. (This is often found in apologies and to express opinions politely.)
> c to confirm that someone else's assumption or information is correct
> d to contradict someone else's assumptions
> e to add further information
> f to introduce unexpected information
> g to express the difference between a 'real-life' situation, and one which exists in theory.
>
> T62 Listen to these extracts from the interview with Colin Goudie and decide which meaning *actually* has in each case.
>
> (On page 127 you will also find examples illustrating the other meanings.)
>
> Now try using *actually* as much as you can in a group discussion about new technology. Consider these points:
>
> • Colin Goudie mentions the new wide-screen and high-definition television. Would you buy one of these? Give reasons for your answer.
> • Recently the number of systems for playing music has increased and now includes vinyl records, compact cassettes, compact discs, digital audio tape, digital compact cassettes and mini-discs. What do you think of these developments and do/would you buy any of them?
> • In general, are you for or against this kind of technology?

Reading

Before you read

1 Discuss in pairs or groups:

What was the first film you ever saw at the cinema?

Which characters were your favourites on TV and at the cinema, when you were a child?

Do you like Westerns?

Why do you think Westerns are so popular with children and adults?

Do you know who these actors are? Have you seen them in any films?

While you read

2 The paragraphs and titles on page 105 come from two texts on the theme of Westerns. Work in pairs. Read each paragraph quickly and decide which text it comes from. Then work out the correct order of the paragraphs in each text.

Vocabulary comprehension

3 Look at these idiomatic expressions from the texts in their context. Discuss in pairs and work out what they mean.

Para. C (staged) a shoot out
Para. D laid siege to
Para. F (did) the bins
Para. G by the droves
Para. H (corporation) booty
firing on all cylinders
Para. I had a lie in
Para. K fled stage left

4 Find each of these words in the texts and work out their meanings and part of speech.

strode (*A*)	intermission (*I*)
upper stalls (*C*)	interval (*I*)
incredulity (*E*)	impersonator (*J*)
coveted (*F*)	outlaws (*K*)
attire (*G*)	

26 ▶

Reading

A The first main feature we had ever seen. Fantastic! Like visiting the Sistine Chapel after having only read the Thames and Hudson *Michelangelo* in braille. Then the actual Lone Ranger appeared. He strode out onto the stage in his pale blue suit amid shouts of 'Where's Tonto?' and 'Take off your mask!'

B In 1958 there was only one television in our street, and when the Lone Ranger made his weekly appearance it was like a mini-cinema in John Logue's front parlour with about twenty of us clustered round the little walnut cabinet.

C Hundreds of them assembled outside the cinema, and a group of Asian cowboys from Handsworth staged a shoot out in Grays Inn Road. Self-conscious in my normal clothes I seated myself at the rear of the upper stalls.

NOT THE LONE RANGER*

D Then came a very special occasion. Not only was the Ritz showing *The Lone Ranger and the Lost City of Gold* on the screen, but the Lone Ranger himself was going to make an appearance 'In Person'. My older brother and I immediately laid siege to our mother to let us go.

E As the film ended she faced the darkened cinema. When the lights came up the girl looked at the audience, her mouth slowly opened and on her face was an expression of incredulity.

F Our only hope for a TV of our own was our uncle John Hep who did the bins and could always be relied on for an old radio or gramophone. One day he excelled himself, turning up with a piece of furniture the size of a large sideboard which housed the coveted television set along with a radiogram and a place to keep your records.

MIVVIS† AT HIGH NOON

G A day of B-westerns brought in fans by the droves. Members of Western clubs from all over the country converged on a private cinema in Kings Cross. Each group was dedicated to a particular cowboy, be it Red Rider, Tom Mix or Randolph Scott. Their attire was that of their hero, complete with guns and leathers.

H It was corporation booty however, and it was only reasonable to expect that this early entertainment centre might not be firing on all cylinders. In fact the only parts that worked were the radio and the sound on the television. It was ours though, and Mrs Logue's parlour had been getting a bit rough lately. So we used to sit and listen and try to work out what was going on, which gave the Lone Ranger even more mystery.

I After the first two films there was an intermission. Ice cream and soft drinks were to be served. The ice cream girl must have had a lie in this Sunday morning, and she arrived towards the end of the film showing prior to the interval.

J My brother and I had already discussed the possibility of this not being the real Lone Ranger but an impersonator dressed up, and when our man appeared we knew. His trousers were too baggy.

K The armed and thirsty outlaws were rising from their seats and moving towards her with jangling spurs and cap guns. They had one thing on their minds and she was it. The punk ice cream girl with the Mohican hair cut fled stage left.

* The main character of a well-known American Western TV series of the same name.
† A type of ice-cream often sold in the cinema.

Grammar: participles

Sentence generation

1 Work in pairs. In five minutes, write as many logical variations as possible of the sentences below, by substituting words for those in italics. Make sure there is still an -ing participle in the new sentences.

1 We sat next to the TV, *listening to the Lone Ranger*.
2 *Seeing the crowd of cowboys*, the ice cream girl ran away.
3 *Having finished university*, I went to live abroad.
4 *Being a child with a rich imagination*, I often imagined that perfectly innocent people were spies or criminals.
5 I spent many hours during my childhood *watching bad Westerns*.
6 We looked at the *burning TV set* in the shop window with amazement.
7 The cinema was full of people *wearing cowboy clothes*.

Now compare with other pairs and see who has most sentences.

Grammar reflection

2 Look at these examples of participles.

1 It was like a mini-cinema in John Logue's front parlour with about twenty of us *clustered* around the walnut cabinet.
2 The armed and thirsty outlaws were rising from their seats and moving towards her with *jangling* spurs and cap guns.
3 She arrived towards the end of the film *showing* prior to the interval.
4 One day he excelled himself, *turning up* with a piece of furniture the size of a large sideboard.
5 *Feeling* self-conscious in my normal clothes, I seated myself at the rear of the upper stalls.
6 I spent many hours during my childhood *watching bad Westerns*.
7 My brother and I had discussed the possibility of this not being the real Lone Ranger but an impersonator *dressed up*.

Match the sentences in the box with these descriptions of the use of participles:

A Before nouns as adjectives, to describe general characteristics.
B Present participles as adjectives after nouns, to describe actions or circumstances at that particular time.
C In adjectival clauses to replace relative clauses. When the present participle is used, the clauses describe actions happening around the same time as the main verb.
D In adverbial clauses to give more information about the verb or the sentence as a whole. They often give the reason, cause or result.

Now explain the difference between these pairs of sentences.

1 Having made a cup of tea she noticed the letter on the kitchen table.
2 Making a cup of tea she noticed the letter on the kitchen table.

3 Developing countries are going through a period of great economic difficulty.
4 Developed countries are going through a period of great economic difficulty.

Rewrite these sentences using the word in brackets.

5 I met a woman riding a motorcycle. (who)
6 Having no money when I arrived, I had to wait for my agent at the station. (because)

Can you think of any other verbs like *spend, go* and *keep on*, which are followed by a verb + *-ing*?

Check your answers in the Grammar Reference on page 149.

Practice

First films

3 Complete this text about the writer's first visits to the cinema, using the verbs in the box in their participle form. (Be careful to use the correct form – either past or present.)

> miss take watch fire drown pass
> open play die ride move

White Square

I remember _____ flecks in the concrete _____ under the tips of my black button shoes and the flaked brown paint of the step of my pushchair. Then some grass, and a dark green van, and doors _____ at the back of it, and grey flat people _____ in a white square. Must have been the early 1940s, my mother _____ me for a walk near Bostall Woods during a gap in the bombing. Some Ministry of Something travelling information film. Towards the end of the war another memory. A trip to London to visit my 'Aunt' Josie. A bigger white square. A man _____ a ukulele and _____ a bicycle across the sky. Then a live magician on the stage; some singing; the flat white again and men _____ rifles across _____ buffalo at the rest of the herd. Afterwards I sat on the mat that smelled of dog, while my mother and Josie talked. About Josie's son _____ at sea and her daughter Irma's fiancé '_____'. He was in the Fleet Air Arm. I liked those words and repeated them often to myself.

Speaking

Work in groups. Imagine that you are film producers with an unlimited budget to make a film, either for TV or the cinema. Discuss the following:

1 Are you going to make the film just for the cinema or to be shown on TV, or both?
2 What genre is the film going to be?
3 Where are you going to get the story from? Are you going to adapt an existing novel or play? If so, which one?
4 Who are your leading actors going to be? Make up the ideal cast list.
5 Who do you want to direct the film?
6 Who would you choose to compose the theme music?

Choose a group spokesperson to report back to the rest of the class when you have finished.

Now form new groups of three. One of you is the head of a big studio, while the other two are writers who are trying to convince the studio boss to make 'their' film. The studio boss has to decide which film to make.

Writing: letter of protest

Read about plans for one of London's classic cinemas, the Parkway in Camden Town.

Cinema demolition vetoed

But developer says plans for Parkway will proceed

PLANS to demolish the art deco Parkway Cinema in Camden Town have been overwhelmingly rejected by Camden Council – but developer Bernard Sunley and Sons plc says redevelopment will go ahead.

Massive public opposition to the demolition of the cinema and all other buildings on the site bounded by Parkway: Arlington Road, Inverness Street and Camden High Street, ensured rejection was a formality at last week's Development Control Sub-committee meeting.

A public inquiry is due to open on September 8 into the proposed seven-storey office and cinema and leisure complex designed to replace the Parkway and Plaza cinemas, bingo hall, Post Office and branches of the Co-op and Barclays Bank.

Film director Terry Gilliam and fellow ex-Python Michael Palin are among those who have put their name to a 3,000-signature petition appealing for the cinema to be saved.

Plan a letter of protest about the closure of the cinema to the local newspaper, *The Hampstead and Highgate Express*.

Here are some ideas for the sort of language you could use.

State your reason for writing
I am writing to complain/protest/express my concern about …

Give your opinion of the plan
I really do think that …
I feel most strongly that …

Use rhetorical questions
Haven't we got enough shops in the town already? Doesn't the planning department realise how important the cinema is for the cultural life of the community?

Use irony
Maybe your aim is to safeguard citizens' lives by encouraging them to stay at home and watch TV rather than going out at night and risk getting mugged.

Ask for action
I would respectfully ask you to reconsider …
I would most strongly urge you to …

Closing sentences
Finally, I would like to repeat my plea for …
I would be interested to hear from others who share my concern …

Now write the letter (about 250 words) paying attention to correct layout. Organise your ideas logically into paragraphs, with a suitable introductory and closing paragraph.

Say the right thing!

Interrupting

When you are having a discussion in English, it is sometimes difficult to find exactly the right words to interrupt another person, especially if the discussion is heated! It is also important to use the right words according to how well you know the person you are talking to.

Number these expressions in order of formality.
(1 = informal, 10 = formal)

Sorry to interrupt you, but …
Excuse me, but …
Er, just a moment …
Hang on a moment …
Could I make a point there, …?
Now, listen to me, …
If I might make a point there, …
OK, but …
I'd just like to add something, if I may …
I'm sorry, but I …

Now listen to Part 1 and repeat, using the correct intonation.

Dealing with interruptions

2 Here are some ways of dealing with interruptions while *you* are speaking. Listen to Part 2.

Formal

I'm sorry, but { could you (just) let me finish?
if I could (just) finish?
If you will/would (just) let me continue …

Neutral

Sorry, I was (just) saying …
Just a moment, please …

Informal

Hold on
Hang on } a minute/second
Just

(Note the use of *just* in these expressions to add emphasis.)

Listen again and repeat.
You can modify the degree of formality of the language in both Exercises 1 and 2, by changing your intonation. Listen to Part 3. Note the difference between these ways of saying this sentence:

I'd just like to add something if I may …

Which of the two ways of saying the sentence is more abrupt and informal?

Situations

3 Work in pairs. Take turns to state your views on the topics listed. Interrupt each other and deal with each other's interruptions, using the language from Exercises 1 and 2.

- Cars with engines bigger than 2 litres should be subjected to a super-tax.
- Personal stereos should be banned on public transport.
- Public transport should be free in city centres to encourage people not to use their cars.
- Nuclear energy is the best and cleanest form of power for the future.
- Marriage is an obsolete institution.

Debate

4 Work in groups. Spend two minutes preparing your view on this topic:

'Families are the cause of most people's problems in life.'

Now discuss the statement. Interrupt each other when you have something to say, using the language you have practised. (Try to interrupt as often as possible!)

Read the bit again where I disinherit the whole family.

Ken Pyne

It's clever, but is it Art?

RUDYARD KIPLING

Vocabulary: art

1 Do you know the meanings of these words?
Choose five words that you know and explain them to another student.

> original   masterpiece   reproduction
> landscape   drawing   seascape   sketch
> subject   ink   title   print   gallery   poster
> museum   illustration   exhibition
> collection   watercolour

What's the difference?

2 Explain the difference between the following pairs of words.

1 abstract/representational
2 landscape/countryside
3 shape/pattern
4 portrait/still life
5 striking/moving
6 masterpiece/old master

Discussion

Painters and paintings

Discuss in groups:

Which do you prefer – paintings or photographs? Why?
What kind of paintings do you like? Is there anything you really *don't* like?

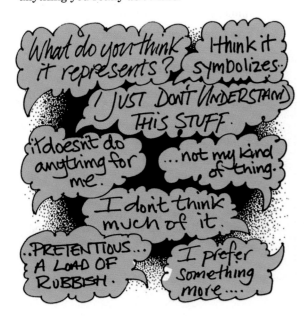

Colour

3 Re-order these words in terms of strength of colour. Compare your answers in pairs. (You will probably find there are some differences in your order, as response to colour is often subjective.)

> strong   subtle   brilliant   muted   vivid   deep
> soft   faint   bright   bold   intense   vibrant

How good are you at spotting great art? Look at these paintings and put them in order of preference.

In groups, discuss your order of preference and say what it is that you like or don't like about the paintings, using the language you have studied.

Do you recognise any of the artists? Look at page 126 to find out more about these works.

Listening

Before you listen

1 Look at these two paintings. One of them is a fake. Which one?

Discuss in groups:

Why do you think people fake paintings?
What's the difference between making a copy of an actual painting and painting something new in the style of a famous painter?
Which of these two types of painting is most likely to fool a potential buyer?
If fakes are technically as good as the original, do you think they should be sold for similar amounts of money?

2 You are going to hear an interview with Helen Valentine, Curator of Paintings at the Royal Academy in London. She talks about some of the works in the collection, and about the problem of fakes. Before you listen, read these statements and decide if you think they are true or false.

1 The Michelangelo sculpture was sold to the Royal Academy in 1836.
2 In the 19th century members of the academy bought drawings for art students to copy.
3 They sometimes bought fakes thinking they were original Michelangelos.
4 In the 18th century people would often sign a drawing which looked like the work of a famous artist, with that artist's name.
5 In the 18th century it was common practice to 'finish' incomplete statues.
6 It is more difficult to see if a statue is a fake than a drawing.
7 Studio assistants would often fake copies of their Master's work.
8 Modern fakers use materials from the same period as the work they are faking to make them look more authentic.
9 Auctioneers often spot fakes because of the materials used.
10 Most museums have one or two fakes in their collection.

First listening

T64 3 Listen and check your answers to Exercise 2.

Second listening

4 Listen again and answer the questions.

1 What do you find out about the Michelangelo sculpture at the Royal Academy?
2 Why did fakes find their way into the Royal Academy collection in the 19th century?
3 Why is it difficult to identify original Renaissance drawings?
4 What techniques do modern-day fakers use?
5 How do people at Sotheby's and Christie's spot fakes?

27

Pronunciation: compression

T66 5 Although some native speakers of English pronounce the central syllables of words like *actually* or *usually* as they are written /ʊə/, most people would use the 'compressed' pronunciation /ə/. Listen to the way Helen pronounces *actually*. Which of the two ways does she use?

In words like *brilliant* and *annual*, the pronunciation most commonly found is /brɪljənt/ and /ænjəl/.

In *automobile* the pronunciation /ə/ rather than /əʊ/ is more casual, but frequently found.

Listen and tick the pronunciation that you hear in each case.

	A (uncompressed)	B (compressed)
annual	/ʊə/	/jə/
valuable	/ʊə/	/jə/
extrovert	/əʊ/	/ə/
November	/əʊ/	/ə/
brilliant	/ɪə/	/jə/
actually	/ʊə/	/ə/
introvert	/əʊ/	/ə/
romantic	/əʊ/	/ə/

Now listen again and repeat.

T67 **Speech features: *say***

Listen to some extracts from the conversation with Helen and try to identify the meaning of *say*.

Now look at these other idiomatic uses of *say* and try to identify what they mean.

1 'Say, that's a good idea!'
2 'We have had very little say in plans for the new school.'
3 'Say the car breaks down on the way to the airport. What will you do?'
4 'I'm really fed up today.' 'You don't say!'
5 'So, as I say, I think paintings are often overpriced.'

Reading and Speaking

1 Read this section of a newspaper article about an art forger. Some of the
paragraphs relating to the trial of the man are missing.

Forger is a genuine success

TRADITIONALLY, artists paid their restaurant bills by dashing off a quick masterpiece on the tablecloth. That custom has now been refined and updated by the authorities in Stuttgart.

A master faker, who

Paragraph A

Wolfgang Lämmle caused anger and confusion when it was realised he had palmed off a number of drawings and paintings to well-known galleries and auction houses.

He produced home-grown versions of Egon Schiele, the Viennese painter of decadent nudes, and he manufactured works by many of Germany's best-known 20th-century artists. These were authenticated by experts, and sold for around £30,000.

From Steve Crawshaw in Bonn

He continued with this game for three years, from 1985 to 1988, and produced about 200 fakes during that time. He sold a number to leading galleries and auction houses.

When Lämmle was convicted in November, the judge said that he was giving him

Paragraph B

The court described Lämmle

Paragraph C

He was said to have been embittered by his failure to sell his own paintings, and because

experts were more interested in big names than in the paintings' intrinsic quality. The Stuttgart court appeared to sympathise with Lämmle's 'personal disappointment at the pricing methods of the art market'.

The fakes, initially confiscated by the court, will go on sale in Stuttgart next week. In case of confusion, Lämmle has been asked to add his own signature, so that each drawing and painting is now signed twice.

Prices for his work have risen sharply, as people fight to get a genuine Lämmle. But the artist insists that this is not important to him. He said he wants people to buy pictures 'because of interest in art'.

This meditative approach is not entirely new. Some years ago, under a self-portrait, Lämmle wrote: 'Every man is a criminal. But some are too lazy to commit crime.'

© *The Independent*

Write a sentence of not more than twenty words summing up the main circumstances of the case.

Role-play

2 Work in groups of three and choose one of the roles below.

Student A: You are the judge of Wolfgang Lämmle's trial. Listen to what the defendant and the prosecution have to say about the case and decide what punishment is appropriate.

Student B: You are Wolfgang Lämmle. Present a coherent argument explaining why you did the fake paintings, in order to be given a lighter sentence.

Student C: You are a lawyer for the prosecution, representing the people who bought Lämmle's paintings. They are very angry and not only seek compensation, but want the artist to go to prison for a long time.

Work with other people who have the same role as you and discuss what you are going to say when you meet your partners at a meeting.

Now get back in your original groups of three. Discuss the case, after which the judge will decide the sentence.

Writing: newspaper article

On the basis of the decision that the judge reached at the end of your discussion in Exercise 2, write the missing paragraphs of the newspaper article in Exercise 1. Begin the paragraphs with the words provided and include this information:

Paragraph A: details of any fine and/or prison sentence which Lämmle received.

Paragraph B: a summary of what the judge said about the sentence he passed and his reasons for passing it.

Paragraph C: a description of Lämmle and a summary of his reasons for making and selling the forgeries.

Now read the complete paragraphs on page 126.

Reading

Before you read

1 There are people who claim that they have received instructions from famous writers, composers and artists – who have since died – to create masterpieces, which are transmitted to them through a kind of 'spiritual communication' with the dead artists. In one case, a person who has written piano works by Mozart is unable to read music or play an instrument, yet experts who have seen her work believe it to be genuine.

What do you think of these claims?

While you read

2 Tom Keating was a British artist who became famous when his paintings, done in the style of the artist Samuel Palmer, were sold for large sums of money, as genuine works. In the extract from his autobiography *The Fake's Progress*, you will read about some details of his technique. Which of the following does he talk about? Read the text and tick those he mentions.

1 Ageing the varnish of a painting by heating it.
2 Using old frames and mounts for new drawings.
3 Signing paintings with a famous artist's name.
4 Making a drawing look old by adding artificial age marks.
5 Basing an oil painting on sketches from an old master's sketch-book.
6 Using exactly the same materials used by the artist.
7 Sprinkling dust on the back of a painting.
8 Using paper from the period when the original artist was alive.

Vocabulary comprehension

3 Find words in the text to match these definitions.

1 to mark the surface of something by rubbing or scraping
2 a work of art done quickly to make money rather than for artistic merit
3 meaningless marks made with a pen or pencil
4 a very small thin branch that grows out from a main branch of a tree or bush
5 deprived of food
6 to imitate or copy
7 large stiff feathers on a bird's wing or tail
8 cutting off the skin or top layer of something
9 fruit, especially apples, that have fallen from the tree
10 poured through a filter

28 ▶

Cockney rhyming slang

Tom Keating refers to a *Sexton* in line 31. This is rhyming slang; the original word is replaced by a phrase which rhymes with it. Rhyming slang was used by working class Londoners, but is less common nowadays.

In this case *Sexton* is short for *Sexton Blake*. Can you guess which word (rhyming with *Blake*) it has substituted?

Here are some other examples of rhyming slang and their 'translations':

whistle (and flute)	–	suit
apples (and pears)	–	stairs
plates (of meat)	–	feet
Barnet (Fair)	–	hair
Rosie Lee	–	tea
trouble and strife	–	wife

Turner – The Fighting Téméraire

Girtin – Durham Castle and Cathedral

Keating

All painters take from other painters and I chose Girtin because he is one of the greatest water-colourists this country has ever produced and I knew that I could learn a great deal from him. [1]

What little success I have had in fooling the art world is largely due to my use of the right materials. In the case of Girtin I would first find a rubbishy old 19th-century water colour of absolutely no value that had not been taken out of its frame since the day it was painted. With infinite care I would then steam the rotting brown paper off the back and lay it flat on a sheet of glass on my studio table. Then with equal care I tucked small squares of cardboard under each of [2] the rusty nails, so that I would not scuff the mount, as I eased them out with a pair of pincers. When eventually I'd taken the whole thing to pieces, I steamed the old potboiler off the mount and substituted my drawing – then put the whole thing back together again and sprinkled it with dust from the Hoover bag. Taking a frame to bits and putting it back together again was always far more difficult than painting the picture. As I have already mentioned I usually made some sort of scribble with the brush that the artist would never have made in a million years – a badly painted twig here or the wrong colour there, any small detail that would give it away.

Girtin died of tuberculosis in 1802 at the age of twenty-seven. 'If Tom Girtin had lived,' said Turner at his funeral, 'I should have starved.' [3]

I very much doubt whether Turner would have lacked admirers even if Girtin had lived on. But Turner recognised [4] his friend's genius and I agree that Girtin was the greater artist, at least at the time. Although I have done a few Sextons of Turner, I have always been more interested by Girtin.

In those early days all I wanted to do was emulate the masters. I felt that I could achieve this far more successfully [5] by using the same materials as they did. I have never wanted to make money out of their work with which to buy grand pianos or even a mouth-organ; I just wanted to learn to paint like them.

I remember once walking along the Thames foreshore at Greenwich, looking for a nice spot to set up my easel, when [6] suddenly I saw a dead seagull lying on the bank. Its grey wings were an inviting stock of quills and I wasted no time in detaching them from the skeletal remains and getting them back to my studio. That evening I washed and dried them, trimmed the feathers off the spine of the quill, cut the ends off obliquely, paring them carefully with a penknife.

In the garden of a friend's house there was a great walnut tree and the next time that I called on them I gathered up a big bag of windfalls, which I took home and simmered for ten hours in an old saucepan. By the end of this time the [7] water had turned into deep-brown bistre ink. When the mixture had cooled I strained it through a piece of silk and bottled it. It was with these simple tools that I made Rembrandt drawings on 18th-century paper; there was a bookseller in Blackheath who used to let me have the fly-leaves out of old leather-bound books that had fallen to pieces. When the ink was dry I would wet the paper with water and flick a spoonful of Nescafé into the air; as the [8] powder descended 'fox-marks' appeared as if by magic.

When you've done an old master it is a bit irresistible not to give it the appearance of age.

113

Grammar: *as* and *like*

Heads and tails

1 Match the two halves of these sentences.

1 I respect people who work with their hands, ...
2 He rides a motorcycle, as ...
3 As he was getting off the bus at the next stop, ...
4 My friend's garden is ...
5 My brother and I started work at seventeen ...
6 He drives a car like ...
7 As he was getting off the bus, ...
8 My friend's garden is as big ...

a ... as a farmyard.
b ... he saw an old man getting on.
c ... his father.
d ... like carpenters.
e ... he gave up his seat to the old man.
f ... like a farmyard.
g ... as carpenters.
h ... his father did when he was young.

Compare your answers in pairs.

Grammar reflection

2 Look at these examples of some of the uses of *as* and *like*:

---

1 I tucked small squares of cardboard under each of the rusty nails *as* I eased them out with a pair of pincers. *As* the powder descended, 'fox-marks' appeared *as if* by magic.
2 I just wanted to learn to paint *like* them. I felt that I could achieve this far more successfully by using the same materials *as* they did.
3 It was *like* a mini-cinema in John Logue's front parlour.

---

4 *As* I was no longer able to bend over ... I wasn't able to take on any restoring work.
5 I've worked here for ten years and I came here *as* a trainee assistant.
6 Keating learned a lot from artists *like* Turner.
7 I like photography almost *as* much as painting.

The uses of *as* and *like* are often confused. *As* can have many meanings. In which of the sentences in the box is it used

a to mean *because*?
b to mean *while*?
c to mean *in the same way as*?
d to state a person's role/job or the function of something?

As and *like* are both used to make comparisons. Which of them do you use

e with a clause?
f with a noun or pronoun?
g to express equality (before and after adjectives and adverbs)?

Check your answers in the Grammar Reference on page 149.

Practice

As or *like*?

3 Complete these sentences with *as* or *like*.

1 That car is superb. It's _____ a piece of sculpture.
2 He didn't come to the party _____ we expected.
3 Painters _____ Rembrandt are often copied by art forgers.
4 When I was a student I worked _____ a van driver during the holidays.
5 You should have left things _____ they were.
6 He made himself look silly behaving _____ that.
7 When we were younger we used this _____ our play room.
8 They got to the meeting late _____ their plane had been delayed.
9 _____ the train was coming into the station the people on the platform began to run towards it.
10 He wants people to think of him _____ a refined country gentleman but he certainly doesn't behave _____ one.

Similes

4 The writer Raymond Chandler was an expert at inventing imaginative similes in his work. In pairs, look at the sentences and complete them with the most suitable words or phrases from the box.

---

fresh orange pith
a fresh fall of snow at Lake Arrowhead
wild flowers fighting for life on a bare rock
a lazy fish in the water   a piece of carved wood
porcelain

---

1 She had little sharp predatory teeth, as white as _____ and as shiny as _____.
2 His brown face was as hard as _____.
3 A few locks of dry white hair clung to his scalp, like _____.
4 The white carpet that went from wall to wall looked like _____.
5 I hung there motionless, like _____.

Now work out some descriptions of your own using *as ... as ...* and *like ....*

a very blue sky
a gloomy squalid flat
a clean sandy beach
a greasy hamburger
a depressing grey day
an expensive red car

Writing: dialogue

1 Read this extract from the script of the film *Paris by Night*, and answer the questions.

> INT. FLAT: BEDROOM. NIGHT
> GERALD *is sitting in bed, reading a novel. He has half-moon glasses on and has a cardigan over his pyjamas.* CLARA *comes in, trying to seem casual, then sits down on the piano stool at the end of the bed. He does not look up.*
> GERALD: Well?
> CLARA: I think we should divorce.
> GERALD: Oh yes? (*He does not look up from his book.*) Why?
> CLARA: It's obvious, isn't it? None of us can live in this atmosphere.
> GERALD: Really? We always have.
> (*He is apparently mild. But as soon as* CLARA *speaks, he interrupts.*)
> CLARA: Look …
> GERALD: Oh, yes, I can see it would suit you. I'm an embarrassment. I'm getting old. I've seen you do it to everyone, since you were a girl. If they don't shape up, kick 'em out.
> CLARA: That's not fair.
> GERALD: (*Suddenly quiet*) I'll fight you for Simon. Oh, yes. In public. In the courts. In the papers. I've got nothing to lose. But you have. I'll get him.
> CLARA: You wouldn't.
> GERALD: I'll say what sort of mother you were. You didn't come home when he was in hospital. (*He looks at her.*) Well, did you? It doesn't look good.
> CLARA: (*Suddenly violent*) What do you want?
> GERALD: Very little. (*He goes back to his book, with a little smile.*) If you've got a man, I would like to know.

1 What is the relationship between Clara and Gerald?
2 Who is Simon?
3 What does Gerald threaten to do if Clara insists on a divorce?
4 Why do you think Gerald has 'nothing to lose' if the case becomes public, while Clara does have something to lose?
5 What evidence would Gerald use against Clara in an attempt to get custody of their son?

2 What are the characteristics of the way dialogue is written for a script, compared to speech in a novel? List three differences.

3 Look at this painting by the American artist, Edward Hopper.

Consider these questions, first on your own, then in groups.

What is the relationship between the man and the woman?
Where are they?
Why has the artist chosen to have the man reading the paper and the woman sitting at the piano?
Why aren't the two looking at each other?
What time of day or night is it?
What has happened?
What is going to happen?
What is the mood of the picture? Give three adjectives.
What do you think of the use of colour in the picture?

4 Imagine the conversation between the man and the woman, either just before or just after the scene in the painting.

Write the conversation as if you were preparing it as a film script of roughly the same length as the extract in Exercise 1. Before you begin, discuss these points in pairs or groups:

- The names of the two characters.
- What to write as directions before the scene, including a brief description of the characters and what they are wearing, and how they are sitting.
- Notes about the content of their conversation – Are they arguing? Does one of them want something from the other? If so, how do they go about getting it? How will the scene end?

(Don't forget that you can make your characters move, change expression, tone of voice etc. by including instructions in brackets before they speak.)

115

Vocabulary

Cinema and television

Underline the correct word in each case.

1 The film I saw last night was really *plodding / moving* and I fell asleep after the first half hour.
2 The most *thought-provoking / harrowing* film at the festival was a story of three old people living their last years peacefully on an island on the East Coast of the United States.
3 Annie really likes watching downhill skiing on TV as it's so *predictable / fast-moving*.
4 British people tend to like to watch *sitcoms / comedy programmes* on TV which are about people like themselves in funny situations.
5 The *cast / script* of the film contained some very well-known names, including Emma Thompson and Vanessa Redgrave.
6 The annoying thing about *soaps / serials* on TV is that they never end; they just keep on going, episode after episode.
7 Alfred Hitchcock was without doubt one of the greatest *scriptwriters / directors* of all time.
8 Directors who make *TV / feature* films don't usually have a very large budget and consequently can't attract famous actors.
9 The famous Russian director Eisenstein made some of the most *stylish / corny* films of his time, including *The Battleship Potemkin* and *Alexander Nevsky*.
10 *Mastermind* is probably the most respectable *quiz / game show* on British TV where people answer questions on general knowledge and a special subject which they choose themselves.

Art

Write the word corresponding to these definitions.

11 The name given to an authentic painting as opposed to a copy.
12 A place where you can go and see paintings.
13 A painting by a famous painter of a previous period.
14 The name given to paintings of static objects, for example, fruit or flowers.
15 The name used to describe a painting of the countryside.
16 A word used to describe a very good painting.
17 An adjective used to describe very strong colours.
18 An adjective used to describe very weak colours.
19 A painting which consists of shapes or patterns rather than a realistic representation of people and things.
20 The name given to the sort of picture found in books often to accompany text.

Grammar

Participles

Tick these sentences if the correct participle has been used. If the wrong participle has been used, rewrite the sentence using the correct one.

21 Finished the book, I decided to go for a walk along the seafront.
22 Alison came to the party, worn jeans and dirty T-shirt.
23 My brother got an electric shock when he was using a CD player connecting to the mains.
24 She kept on asking me to turn down the TV because she was doing her homework.
25 There was a man standing in the garden, half hidden by the bushes.
26 I felt very nervous, arrived at school on the first day of term.
27 She put the developing film in an envelope and sent it to the newspaper.
28 When I came home there were about twenty people sitting in my living room drinking tea.
29 Seeing the new play at the National Theatre, Humphrey wrote an article about it.
30 They managed to get out of the burnt car in time and put out the fire.

As and *like*

Rewrite these sentences using *as (... as)* or *like* instead of the words in italics. (In some cases you will have to make other changes to the sentence.)

31 *While* I was walking down the stairs I had the strange sensation someone was watching me.
32 I have a great respect for people, *for example* Mother Teresa, who devote their lives to helping others.
33 I had to pack up and go home *because* it started to rain very heavily.
34 William Turner, the painter, lived in London *when he was* a boy.
35 He behaved *in the manner of* a child and upset many people at the party.
36 I don't want to pay *the same price that* you did for my new stereo.
37 I want you to accept me *in the way that* I am, not *in the way that* you'd like me to be.
38 *Similarly to* most people I think Bridget Riley is one of the major influences in British painting of the 60s.
39 They built their own house *in the same way that* their friends did.
40 This fridge is *identical in its dimensions to* the one we have at home.

Check your answers by looking at the Answer Key on page 125.

Unit 2 page 18

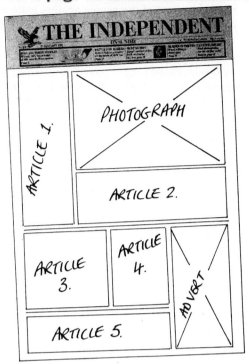

Unit 3 page 28

Group A: Prepare arguments in favour of package tours. These words may help:

carefree	limited time	cost	language
transport	new friends	accommodation	
sightseeing	reservations		

Unit 12 page 98

Read the views of the people in favour of smoking in public.

Mrs Gillian Ash of Durham: 'I'm not worried enough by smokers to have any views on a ban. If someone lit up next to me, I probably wouldn't say anything, either.'

Mrs. Mary Fagg of Nottingham: 'There's already a self-imposed ban in most pubs and restaurants now, and people do have the choice. As long as no one blows smoke in my face, I'm fine about it. If someone lit up at a table next to me, I don't think I'd have to say anything, my look would be enough.'

Mr John Benson of Kilburn, north London: 'I don't think Britain should introduce a ban since restaurants are public places and I think people should be able to do what they want in a public place. If someone lit up at a table next to me, I'd leave them alone, because I'm also a smoker.'

Unit 12 page 99

Student A

Perhaps she talked to her family about the music box. Later, she was unable to remember that either. But it seemed that the family, slow with grief, had dragged their thinking to the gap in the wooden fence. As an uncle nailed up the boards, they took the child before her grandfather who wanted to know how long she had been going next door. How long was long? Weeks? Years? She didn't know. Then Grandfather talked about King and country and the child's father. He talked to her seriously as though she were already grown up, the way he spoke to her uncles, only kinder. He had steel-rimmed glasses, and grey hairs growing out of his nose. She knew that she would give her dead father a pain that was much worse than drowning, if she ever went next door again.

Unit 13 page 102

Stories from an African Hospital
8.00 – 8.30 C4
Seven-year-old Gertrude Addo who suffers from tetanus is this week's case study from the Komfo Anokye hospital in Ghana. This painful documentary follows her progress after her poverty-stricken family – their income is 70p a day – has managed to scrape together the £7 it costs for the operation that will correct her deformed jaws. As a powerful indictment of the under-resourcing of health-care for the poor in African countries, this is perfect. Unfortunately, the grisly details of the surgery and the post-operative suffering of the little girl render it almost unwatchable, despite its happy ending. (RC)

Rugby World Cup Highlights
11.30 – 12.25 a.m.
Exciting extracts from the Fiji v Canada match introduced by David Bobin.

'Night on Earth' (15) (Jim Jarmusch, 1992, US) Winona Ryder, Beatrice Dalle, Armin Mueller-Stahl, Gena Rowlands, Giancarlo Esposito, Roberto Benigni, Isaach de Bankolé, Paolo Bonacelli, Matti Pellonpaa. 120 mins. Episodes 3–5 subtitled.
L.A. 7.07 p.m. Chain-smoking Ryder gets movie agent Rowlands in the back of her cab, and inadvertently persuades her she'd be right for a role Rowlands is casting. At the very same time, taxi drivers across the world are also having seemingly inconsequential encounters with their various passengers: in New York, East German exile Mueller-Stahl hands over the wheel of his car to Esposito; in Paris, Ivory Coaster de Bankolé discusses sight and sex with blind, beligerent Dalle; in Rome, raving Benigni confesses a carnal past to priest Bonacelli; and in Helsinki, melancholy Pellonpaa calms three drunks with a tale of infinite sadness. As the five sequential stories proceed towards their unexpectedly poignant conclusion, Jarmusch's gentle, offbeat comedy courses through a variety of moods inspired by national and cultural characteristics. As ever, there's a touch of the experimental at play, but it's also a film of great warmth. (GA)

High Noon
12.00 – 1.20 BBC2
(Fred Zinnemann, 1952, US) Gary Cooper, Grace Kelly, Lloyd Bridges, Katy Jurado, Thomas Mitchell, Otto Kruger, Lon Chaney jr., Henry Morgan, Lee Van Cleef.
What to make of a film that was scripted by a blacklisted writer (Carl Foreman), directed by an emigré from Nazi Germany (Zinnemann), and yet might easily be updated along the lines of 'Dirty Harry'? The film was clearly a seminal influence on Sergio Leone, and was hated by Howard Hawks, whose specific reposte, 'Rio Bravo', is undoubtedly one of the greatest Westerns ever made. Seeing it again, it is surprising how many familiar faces populate this remote railroad town; and what a spineless bunch they are! For all the conflicting allegorical/political readings it has inspired, it's a strikingly reductionist, disillusioned movie. It's a Western for people who don't like Westerns, a suspense film played out – quite brilliantly – in real time. Its real distinction lies in the editing, photography and score, and in the casting of Gary Cooper, who makes it seem much more weighty than it is (ironically, he was a friendly witness at

'City of Joy' (12) (Roland Joffé, 1992, GB/Fr) Patrick Swayze, Om Puri, Pauline Collins, Shabana Azmi, Art Malik. 135 mins.
East and West learn from each other in Joffé's film, and it's an interminable seminar. The fortunes of rickshaw man Hasari Pal (Puri) and American-doctor drop-out Max (Swayze) intertwine, but the acting styles are so divergent that they may as well be in different films. Max is selfish and suicidally sick of life, while Hasari has to fight for the daily bread to support his family. Together, they stand up to the razor-wielding bad guy (Malik). Presiding over the City of Joy school and clinic is Irish Joan (Collins), pushy, practical and derived from other movies. It's very old-fashioned stuff, with the impoverished Indian slum-dwellers working like cheerful chipmunks to build a better clinic, and a climactic monsoon on hand to bring out the best in everybody. Rotten.

'Basic Instinct' (18) (Paul Verhoeven, 1991, US) Michael Douglas, Sharon Stone, George Dzundza, Jeanne Tripplehorn. 128 mins.
Viewed from one angle, Verhoeven's troubled film is a gutsy, tough West Coast cop thriller with lashings of sex and obsession. Douglas's Nick Curran is yet another cop on the edge, who becomes slowly embroiled with the case and then the suspect when a former rock star is found murdered. Aided and abetted by Verhoeven's raunchy direction, Stone smoulders and snarls. If you like things unrestrained, hard, adult and off-the rails then Douglas and Stone are superb, and Dzundza delivers yet another classic, hard-boiled cameo. (Steve Grant)

Time Out

Unit 8 page 63

Situation 1 Roger had invited his boss and her husband to dinner a month before and had forgotten. He had had a hard day, so when they arrived he was in his pyjamas lying on the settee, having a drink and watching a video.

Situation 2 Mary had to give a teacher training talk in Sicily, which was very important as the Minister of Education would be present. She arrived at Palermo airport an hour and a half before the talk was due to start, wearing old jeans and a dirty sweater. Unfortunately her luggage containing her formal clothes and all her notes for the talk had gone to Reykjavik.

Situation 3 Rossana had been asked to take photographs at a colleague's wedding. She was the only photographer there. Unfortunately she lost the negatives after she had developed them.

Unit 7 page 58

Student A: You are Jeannine Stein, the Los Angeles journalist. You have observed the phenomenon with interest, but you are not sure if this is not 'just another fashion'. Try to find out just how sincere the stars are about ECG (Extreme Celebrity Guilt). Prepare some really searching questions.

Student B: You are Mark Fox, the owner of a shop which sells worn-out jeans at £1000 and boots at £600. Prepare arguments to defend your ideological position.

Student C/D: You are one of the Hollywood stars. Prepare to defend your position regarding your immense wealth and your problems of guilt. Be careful not to alienate the journalist, because you don't want any negative publicity.

Unit 12 page 99

Student B

Their neighbour had not appeared to be disturbed by the breaking of the windows. While the workmen cleared the fragments of glass and put in the new panes, Mrs Gessner carried on working in her garden. The face under the straw hat was flat and expressionless. The unlaced boots never hurried. Up and down the rows, day after day, those broad, freckled hands pulled weeds from the flowerbeds.

The child didn't speak but she often watched. She would lie in the grass on her own side of the fence and press her face against the palings, thrilled by her own daring. Dirty Hun, they'd said at school. Watch out or she'll get you. Spy, spy, string her up high. She would watch every movement and when it seemed likely that the brim of the straw hat was going to tilt in her direction, she would put her head down and crawl backwards until she was behind her Grandfather's bean frame, and she would stay there until the squat figure had moved away.

Unit 12 page 98

Read the views of the people against smoking in public.

Mrs Sharon Smoker of Bordon, Hampshire: 'Yes, I think a ban should be introduced over here. I gave up smoking more than seven years ago and passive smoking worries me. If someone lit up, I would tell them to put it out.'

Mr. John Cloud of Littlehampton: 'I always choose non-smoking areas when I dine in restaurants and would politely ask a smoker to stop if they were in the same section.
'I've had a leg amputated because I used to smoke and if I hadn't stopped smoking at once after the operation, I'd have lost the other one as well. I'm nearly 89 now and smoked for 40 years. Although I knew of the cancer risks, I didn't realise that the smoke also corrodes veins and blocks arteries.'

Mrs. Iris Hedges of Wimbledon, south London: 'I definitely think Britain should bring in a ban; I object to bieng a passive smoker and to my children being subjected to other prople's smoke. I would say something to a smoker in a restaurant, especially if my children were with me; they're aged seven and twelve and are very anti-smoking.'

Mr. Simon Butt of Taunton: 'I'm afraid I am a smoker, but I believe Britain should introduce a similar ban to the French in principle - although it's not the sort of thing one can really legislate for. I would say something to anyone smoking in a non-smoking area of a restaurant, and have done so already several times. It's perfectly O.K for me to pollute the atmosphere, I just don't like other people doing it.'

Unit 5 page 41

Student A

You are Peter. When you were at school and university you were very close to Jeremy, and you had a lot of good times together. You have always got on well with his girlfriends, but you don't like Lucy. There are a number of reasons for this:

– You think she has changed him and made him more materialistic.
– You think she took advantage of a moment of weakness on his part and grabbed the opportunity to marry him.
– You think she is bossy and manipulative.
– You can't see what they have in common, as she has very little education and shows no interest in music, art and literature which Jeremy always found important.

You stopped seeing Jeremy after the christening of his first son, where you were disgusted by the ostentatious show of wealth and the fact that Jeremy, an atheist, appears to have wanted to have a christening because it was the 'done thing to do'. It upsets you that you have lost your friendship and you'd like to do something about it.

Student B

You are Jeremy. You were very close to Peter at school and university. Since then you have grown apart, and you think it might be because of your marriage to Lucy. You married her just after your return from Argentina when you were feeling a bit lonely. But since then you have grown to love her and are grateful to her for having helped to give your life a sense of direction. You don't share many interests, but you don't think this is important in comparison to what the relationship gives you. You realise that Peter disapproved of your decision to have a christening for your child, but you think he is probably jealous of the money you have made and the success you are now enjoying. You're upset that he no longer comes to see you and would like to do something about it.

Student C

You are Lucy. You met Jeremy five years ago and immediately fell in love with him, even though you didn't have much in common, and felt slightly inferior to him. One advantage that you have is that you are more emotionally stable than him, and have given him a sense of security which has made a difference to his life. You are both very close now and have worked hard to make a success of the business which you started together. When you first met Jeremy he used to see a lot of his friend Peter, and you used to go out with them quite often. Jeremy used to drink quite a lot then, and especially when he was with Peter, which is one reason why you are relieved that they don't see so much of each other now. You suspect Peter is jealous of your relationship with Jeremy. You realise that it upsets Jeremy to have lost his friend, but you don't know what to do.

Student D

You are Sally. You went to university with Peter and Jeremy and have known them for a long time. By coincidence you went to school with Lucy, so you know her quite well too and started seeing her again when she started going out with Jeremy. You realise that there is friction between Peter and the couple but you don't really understand what is going on. You are keen to arrange a reconciliation between the two men, as you know that both of them are upset that they no longer see each other. Discuss the problem with each of the three people involved and try to find a way to get them to see each other's point of view.

Unit 1 page 11

Student A

And the barman says, 'Oh, all right then. Here you are.'
So, the barman pours loads of pints of beer and serves the whole bar.
Then the barman turns to the Martian and says, 'Right, that'll be £327.36 please, Sir.'
And the Martian says, 'Fine. Have you got change for a zonk?'

Unit 12 page 99

Student C

At school she watched the boys draw aeroplanes that resembled ducks laying eggs in flight, and she would feel the metal disc, named, numbered, on the string about her neck, and look up at the sky above the playground.

In the home the blinds were secured when sirens sounded, cups rattled on their hooks when trucks rolled past. Every morning the newspaper was unfolded over the kitchen table, plates covered with grey pictures, and above the toaster there was a voice that said, 'This is the BBC London calling. Here is the news.'

The child learned much by remaining silent through mealtime conversations but she never discovered who had thrown stones through Mrs Gessner's front windows. No one seemed to know. No one seemed particularly interested. Nor could she find out where Mr Gessner had gone. Certainly he wasn't fighting with the soldiers, for one day someone, an aunt, uncle perhaps, someone had said, 'Well, what would you do if they told you to go over and shoot your relatives?' And a grey sort of silence had settled in the room.

Unit 8 page 64

1 die   2 threw   3 spent   4 about to
5 cutting off a dog's tail
6 desperate final attempt
7 fall from a great height
8 soft, newly-grown hair
9 try to please by flattering
10 small wooden cage for animals
11 reducing an animal's ears in size
12 develop the same characteristics as
13 living in or owning a more expensive house
14 living in conditions of poorer quality than you are used to

Unit 10 page 82

What function do the verbs in these sentences correspond to in the list on page 82?

1 We could go on Friday.
2 Could you make out the bill, please?
3 Can you make me a copy of that?
4 I thought perhaps you might like to come too.
5 He might as well take the car.
6 Will you post this for me on the way to work?
7 You can borrow that pen if you want to.
8 Shall we talk about something different now?
9 I'd like steak and chips, please.
10 You may leave as soon as you have finished.

Student D

The child took to playing in the garden next door. Years later she would not be able to remember her first visit but soon she was crossing the fence so regularly that Mrs Gessner cut down some of the palings to make it easier for her. And because the child was older now, and in a new class at school, she no longer felt the need to confide in other children, or relatives, for that matter.

On warm afternoons she would sit under the apple tree by a mound of green fruit, or wander along the borders popping fuchsia buds, or kneel on the path urging snails to compete on a brick raceway. Mrs Gessner used to bring out the canvas chairs and they would sit, the two of them, drinking milk and eating biscuits with currants and lemon in them.

Then there were the days when they went into the house and the cool dark kitchen with its smells of apples and firewood and caraway seeds, and the child would climb up into the rocking chair, wriggling into a nest of cushions, while Mrs Gessner brought out the music box. It was of dark wood, carved, with a lid which framed trees and dancing deer; and when the lid was opened it was easy to tell why the deer danced like that, for from the emptiness of the box came a song of little bells, the same tune over and over until the lid was closed and Mrs Gessner was wiping the box on her apron and smiling, ya, is beautiful? Is beautiful? and the child was holding out her hands, begging for the music again.

Unit 6 page 50

Pair A: Read the texts quickly and write a comprehension question for each one. Each question must contain a passive verb.

Caribou and the timber wolf to resume battle

By Quentin Letts in New York

BATTLE is to be resumed between the Minnesota timber wolf and the caribou, which scientists are to reintroduce to the American Midwest 65 years after they were last seen there.

One particular herd from Canada's Slate Islands, in Lake Superior, goes through regular cycles of overpopulation, and it is from there that the 'exports' will be taken.

The success of the plan to re-establish caribou in Minnesota will depend on the ferocity and prevalence of the timber wolf, which prowls Minnesota to a density of one per 15 to 20 square miles.

Some Canadian biologists, quoted in the Smithsonian magazine, fear that this density is too great – it should not, they say, exceed one wolf per 39 square miles – for the caribou to succeed. A previous attempt to reintroduce caribou to Maine failed when the animals ate infected snails and contracted a fatal brain disease. Scientists hope to overcome this by releasing wild caribou into Minnesota – during the Maine experiment, the caribou used had been bred under controlled conditions.

With its majestic antlers and prized fur, the caribou was a symbol of the wildness of the pioneer days, but a natural target for hunters.

Eat my plates!

A TAIWANESE firm has good news for people too busy or lazy to wash dishes – it has invented what it claims is the world's first range of edible tableware. 'Our bowls and plates are made of oatmeal and can be eaten or thrown away after use,' said a spokesman for Taiwan Sugu. Production starts this week.

Girl mauled by pit bull terrier

A 23-month-old girl became the second victim in four days of an American pit bull terrier when she was savaged by her grandparents' pet while playing in their garden in Clayton Street, Bolton, Greater Manchester, police said yesterday.

Paula Holmes needed extensive surgery to her face after the attack on Sunday. The dog has since been destroyed. Last week a man was badly savaged by two pit bull terriers in Lincoln.

PARIS: Maigret, the fictional French detective, is to be revived for the seventh time in a new television series being made by the Paris company Dune. The company plans to make 104 episodes of the drama.

■PISA: Construction experts will sling 10 steel rings around the Leaning Tower of Pisa to prevent the monument from collapsing altogether, Public Works Minister Giovanni Prandini said. Sixteen months ago the tower was closed to tourists while experts worked out a programme to save it but this has not yet been decided.

Pair B: Read the texts quickly and write a comprehension question for each one. Each question must contain a passive verb.

Youth faces prison over US graffiti

LOS ANGELES: A teenager accused of spray-painting the name 'Chaka' in more than 10,000 public places from Los Angeles to San Francisco could be sentenced to five years in jail and fined $10,000. Daniel Ramos, 18, faces ten counts of vandalism. The graffiti ranged from a signature of thick, looping letters on lamp posts to colourful murals spread on walls.

Kisses and cuddles banned in China

BEIJING: Kissing, cuddling and holding hands are to be banned at Beijing University. Students have until October 5 to renounce what the Chinese authorities deem 'behaviour that corrupts public morals', according to a notice posted on the campus. Expressions of public dissent such as booing, whistling and unofficial gathering will also be banned.

Faulty heart valves put 350 at risk

By Jonathan Confino and Christine McGourty

A SEARCH is under way for 20 to 25 people in Britain who are thought to be fitted with a faulty heart valve made by an American company. In rare instances the valve can fracture and kill the patient.

More than 5,000 people in Britain were given valves made by Shiley, a subsidiary of drug company Pfizer, before they were withdrawn in 1986.

Those now thought to be most at risk are the 350 implanted with one of a batch made by an unnamed former employee – dubbed the 'phantom welder' by US government officials – whose faulty work has been blamed for the defects.

The company admits that 21 of the valves welded by worker number 2832 have already failed inside patients' chests and lawyers say 17 deaths have resulted.

Shiley says the valves are safe but has agreed to try to track users down.

Mr Philip Hedger, vice president of Shiley's European division said the risk of the valve breaking, although higher than normal, was 'still very low'.

Coach shooting

FIVE men were being questioned by Staffordshire police yesterday after a man was injured in a shooting on a coach at Stoke-on-Trent.

Group B: Prepare arguments against package tours. These words may help you:

independence   freedom   sense of adventure
cost   food   contact with local people
avoid crowds   spontaneity
choice of travelling companions

Student E
But nothing happened to her. Nothing. After a while the children at school lost interest in the story about the sounds of breaking glass in the middle of the night, and the mystery woman next door took on an ordinariness that defied the child's imagination. It did not seem right that a spy should put out tins of dripping for the birds or scratch down the back of her dress with a knitting needle. The child grew bolder. It was no longer satisfying to hide in the grass and stare. She came out into the open, walked along the fence, sometimes stood still and leaned on it. She met the woman's eyes, smiled when she smiled, even said hello.

Promise not to tell a living soul, she said to anyone at school who would listen. I talked to the spy.

Once she accepted a bunch of dahlias from the garden and was thrilled to find two earwigs in the petals. She took them to school next morning in a bottle and everyone looked. Oh yes, they were German earwigs, all right.

Then the child's father was killed. The man in the photograph on the mantelpiece was drowned at sea and everything about the child's house changed. It became quiet. People walked in it as though they no longer knew the way, and they talked in tired voices. Sometimes they would not leave the child alone. Sometimes they forgot she was there. The grey of war sat at the dinner table with them and curled upon their plates, making everything taste like the dead earth under houses.

Student B
This Martian goes into a bar, right, goes up to the bar, and says, 'Can I have a pint of beer, please?' And the barman says, 'No, no, sorry, sir. We don't serve Martians in here.'
The Martian says, 'What? You don't serve Martians?'
The barman says, 'No, get lost!'

Unit 10 page 80

Student A

Yellow

Yellow has been said to have a favourable effect upon human metabolism. In many studies of the biological action of light, however, it is generally found to be neutral (together with yellow-green). Because of the high visibility of yellow, it serves many purposes in safety. The hue is sharply focused by the eye, cheerful and incandescent in appearance.

In color conditioning, yellow will tend to appear brighter than white. It thus is useful in meeting unfavourable conditions of dim illumination or large, vaulty spaces.

Student B

The Significance of Blue

Blue has qualities that are antithetical to red. It seems to retard the growth of plants, to decrease hormonal activity, and to inhibit the healing of wounds. In its action upon the human organism it lowers blood pressure and pulse rate, though this effect may later be reversed.

Under the influence of blue, time is under-estimated and weights are judged as being lighter. Because the color has a naturally low saturation it may be used in almost any form – light, dark, pure, grayish. Being visually primary, however, it tends to be bleak if applied in too large an area. While blues are suitable for homes, they have not proved very successful in offices, industries, schools, hospitals, except as incidental areas and then in medium or deep tones. (Pale blue seems to 'bother' human eyes and to give a blurred appearance to adjacent objects.)

Because blue is a difficult color to focus, it is objectionable as a light source and low in attention-value. Yet blue is associated with dim light, is restful and sedate, and is an outstanding favourite throughout the world.

Student C

Greens in General

Yellow-green is generally neutral from the biological standpoint. Greens and blue-greens, however, are pacific and tend to reduce nervous and muscular tension. Psychologically, green represents a withdrawal from stimulus. It provides an ideal environment for sedentary tasks, concentration, and medication.

Bluish greens lack a primitive quality and are both pleasing and 'liveable.' The same virtues have been expressed for peach, and indeed the two hues beautifully enhance each other. Because blue-green is complementary to the tint of average human complexion, it provides a very flattering background.

Student D

Purple, Gray, White, and Black

Purple, being a blend of red and blue, the two extremes of the spectrum, is more or less neutral biologically. It is not suitable for large areas because it disturbs the focus of the eye. Of all hues, it seems to be the one dominantly aesthetic in its appeal.

White is the perfectly balanced color, clear and natural in its influence. Black is negative; gray is passive. All three are found to be emotionally neutral and fail to have much psychotherapeutic application except where negation may be the particular expression desired.

Student E

The Significance of Red

Red is perhaps the most dominant and dynamic of colors. Its energy has a strong influence on the growth of plants. It has been found to accelerate the development of certain lower animals, to increase hormonal and sexual activity, and to heal wounds.

In its action upon the human organism, red tends to distract the equilibrium of the body. It has been prescribed to treat sunburn, inflammation, rheumatism. It will act to raise blood pressure and pulse rate but may be followed by a reversal of these effects after a period of time.

Psychologically, red is exciting and increases restlessness and nervous tension. It represents an attraction to stimulus and as such provides an excellent environment for the creation (but not execution) of ideas. Under the influence of red, time is over-estimated and weights seem heavier. The color is most pronounced when strong light intensities are also involved. (Red is the first of all colors to fade out in dim illumination.)

Under practical situations, however, pure red can seldom be used; the full hue is too imperious and has too strong an after-image. Brilliant red has its value in commanding human attention, although a high frequency of color blindness among men introduces limitations. Modified forms of red – rose, maroon, pink – are beautiful and expressive, universally appealing, and deeply emotional. Variations of red are preferred by extroverts; therefore the color has a place in psychotherapy to bolster human moods and counteract melancholia. It helps to distract attention from within and to direct it outward.

Unit 1 page 11

Student C

The Martian says, 'Look, if I buy you a drink, will you let me have a drink as well?'
The barman says, 'Sorry, we don't serve Martians in here.'
The Martian says, 'Look, if I buy you and your wife and the people at the bar a drink, will you let me buy a drink?'
The barman says, 'No, sorry.'
So the Martian says, 'Look, all right, if I buy the whole pub a drink, will you let me buy a drink?'

In any writing that you do, it is important to check your work carefully to see if any rewriting is necessary – in other words, you need to be your own editor. Look at the following composition written by a student, and comment on

1 Style: Is it appropriate, i.e. too formal/informal generally, or only in particular areas?
2 Structure: Is there a clear introduction and conclusion? Are the ideas organised in logically organised paragraphs?
3 Linking expressions: Are the expressions used for linking contrasting ideas, and for listing ideas, appropriate?
4 Errors: Are there any vocabulary, grammar, spelling and punctuation errors?

Now compare your comments with those given below.

Package tours

Nowadays people have more money and free time than they had and spend their holidays in various ways. Package tours are very popular, so there are a bunch of travel agents which provide us varied package tours. If you just go to a travel agent, and choose your kind of tour, then everything will be arranged, including hotels, transport and food. It is terribly handy, isn't it? Whats more, (the) package tour enables the people who find difficulty in a foreign language go abroad very easily. On the other hand if you really want to know the true charm of the country it will be very difficult to have it in the package tour for two reasons.

First of all, the package tour is so well organized that everything go just as we expect, in other words, it could be boring.

Secondly, if we choose the package tour, we don't have to make a deliverate effort to get to know the place, which means that there are a few opportunities to talk to local people. A tour in which we have enough time to talk to them, will be something pleasant to look back on, I belive.

However, as far as I am concerned, what is the most important thing is to be open-minded, when you visit somewhere. It doesn't matter whether you make a package tour, so long as you can do this. Most strangers will be as freindly as you are, because they are 'curious' about you too. This means package tours can have the same effect as travelling by yourselves.

Yoko II

Package tours

Nowadays people have more money and free time than they had and spend their holidays in various ways. Package tours are very popular, so there are a bunch of travel agents which provide us varied package tours. If you just go to a travel agent, and choose your kind of tour, then everything will be arranged, including hotels, transport and food. It is terribly handy, isn't it? Whats more, (the) package tour enables the people who find difficulty in a foreign language go abroad very easily. On the other hand if you really want to know the true charm of the country it will be very difficult to have it in the package tour for two reasons.

First of all, the package tour is so well organized that everything go just as we expect. In other words, it could be boring.

Secondly, if we choose the package tour, we don't have to make a deliverate effort to get to know the place, which means that there are a few opportunities to talk to the local people. A tour in which we have enough time to talk to them, could be something pleasant to look back on, I belive.

However, as far as I am concerned, what is the most important thing is to be open-minded, when you visit somewhere. It doesn't matter whether you make a package tour, so long as you can do this. Most strangers will be as freindly as you are, because they are 'curious' about you too. This means package tours can have the same effect as travelling by yourselves.

Learning check

Score: Less than 10 – You need to work harder at your English!
10–15 – You obviously have some large gaps in your knowledge of the language you have studied.
15–25 – Average. You should look carefully at the mistakes you have made and go over those points again.
25–35 – Good. You have absorbed most of the things you have studied in these two units.
35–40 – Excellent.

Units 1 – 2 page 21

Humour
1 practical   3 teased   5 sexist   7 slapstick
2 really   4 telling   6 racist

The Press (Some variation possible)
8–10 newspaper, magazine, periodical
11–13 editor, correspondent, picture editor
14–16 sport, foreign, leader

Present tenses
17 sends   21 sends   24 is sitting
18 comes   22 wait   25 says
19 decides   23 is getting   26 are you doing
20 puts

Past tenses(1)
27 said   31 was   34 got
28 decided   32 had hired   35 were doing
29 found   33 were having   36 had been
30 had

The noun phrase (Some variation possible)
37 A four thousand pound gleaming red car parked outside the house.
38 A long train journey to London.
39 The forty-three year old man with a beard from Twickenham.
40 A pretty girl whose name was Rita.

Units 3 – 4 page 37

Life choices
1 boredom   4 kick   7 thrill
2 responsibility   5 stability   8 freedom
3 career   6 rat race

Another country
9 grumble   12 curious   15 discrimination
10 fascinated   13 cope with   16 moan
11 bureaucracy   14 culture

Past tenses (2)
17 was   22 has been living
18 took   23 has previously written
19 worked   24 published
20 has also worked   25 was
21 has lived   26 also published

The future (No fixed answers, but the verb tense must be the same as in the example sentences supplied.)
27 I'll be working for my father next summer.
28 My bus leaves at six o'clock tomorrow morning.
29 I'm meeting Betty outside the cinema at eight o'clock on Thursday evening.
30 I'm going to make dinner then do some ironing.

31 I think I'll take the bus home.
32 I think the pound will get stronger in the coming year.
33 It's going to be sunny later this afternoon.
34 I want to go and live in a foreign country.
35 I will have passed the CAE exam by the end of the year.

Adjectives (One mark for the correct adjectives and one for the correct order.)
36 a luxurious leather armchair
37 an interesting little village
38 hot Indian food
39 a tall sun-tanned man
40 an important historical film

Units 5 – 6 page 53

Communication
1 supercilious – condescending
2 eloquent – articulate
3 tactful – diplomatic
4 opinionated – dogmatic
5 pompous – self-important
6 abrupt – brusque
7 tolerant – open-minded
8 reticent – reserved

The family
9 parents   12 fell in love   15 upbringing
10 relatives   13 got married   16 partner
11 extended   14 get engaged   17 adopted

Verbs with -ing and to + infinitive
18 –
19 –
20 I tried to see him last night but he was out.
21 I used to play football every Saturday morning when I was a child.
22 We need to buy a new plug for the television.
23 –
24 I'm trying to learn French at night school.
25 –

Wishes
26 wouldn't ask   29 were   32 didn't give
27 hadn't gone   30 had phoned   33 could
28 could   31 had gone

Passives
34 Hotel bills have to be paid the day before departure.
35 The National Gallery is being restored at the moment.
36 Fifty people have been invited to the reception.
37 I phoned the police when I found out the painting had been stolen.
38 Next year our salaries will be paid in sterling.
39 Many oil wells in Kuwait were damaged during the Gulf War.
40 Smoking is now allowed in this part of the building.

Units 7 – 8 page 69

Style
1 dishevelled   4 elegant   7 match   10 gaudy
2 suit   5 craze   8 dowdy
3 tacky   6 dress down   9 lovely

Money
11 thrifty   15 well off   18 tight-fisted
12 spend-thrift   16 splash out   19 destitution
13 hard up   17 in the black   20 short-changed
14 charitable

The article

21 the	23 the	25 a	27 the	29 a
22 the	24 the	26 the	28 the	

Conditional sentences

30 is	32 were	34 read
31 had	33 would not have happened	35 didn't like

Inversion

36 Not only	38 Such	40 Only
37 Hardly	39 Never	

Units 9 – 10 page 85

The home

1 shack	5 motel	8 penthouse
2 bungalow	6 houseboat	9 terraced house
3 mansion	7 apartment	10 bedsit
4 maisonette		

Moods

11 world	14 beans	17 moon	20 down
12 dumps	15 mood	18 mood	
13 fed	16 dollars	19 sulk	

Question tags

21 shall we?	24 shall I?	26 will they?
22 did they?	25 hadn't you?	
23 will you?		

Relative clauses

27 (that/which)	30 who/that	33 who
28 which	31 (that/which)	34 who
29 whose	32 which	35 which/that

Modal verbs

36 can	38 –	40 should
37 –	39 must	

Units 11 – 12 page 101

Books

1 guidebook	5 anthology	8 spy story
2 biography	6 manual	9 autobiography
3 novel	7 textbook	10 science fiction
4 thriller		

Education

11 teacher	15 high/secondary	18 dropped
12 BSc	16 took	19 campus
13 residence	17 day	20 lecturers
14 state		

Comparisons

21 far/much/a good deal/very much/infinitely/considerably/a lot/lots
22 far/much/a good deal/considerably/a lot
23 nearly/quite
24 nearly/almost/just
25 far/much/a good deal/very much/infinitely/considerably/a lot/lots
26 far/much/a good deal/very much/infinitely/considerably/a lot/lots
27 far/much/a good deal/very much/infinitely/considerably/a lot/lots
28 far/a good deal/considerably/a lot
29 Just/nearly/almost
30 far/a good deal/considerably/a lot/lots

Reported speech

31 wonder
32 told
33 suggested
34 intended
35 asked
36 persuaded
37 decided
38 advised
39 wanted
40 ordered

Units 13 – 14 page 116

Television and film

1 plodding	6 soaps	
2 thought-provoking	7 directors	
3 fast-moving	8 TV	
4 sitcoms	9 stylish	
5 cast	10 quiz	

Art

11 original
12 gallery/museum/exhibition
13 old master
14 still life
15 landscape
16 masterpiece
17 brilliant/vivid/bright/intense/vibrant
18 muted/soft/faint
19 abstract
20 illustration

Participles

21 Having finished …
22 … wearing jeans …
23 … a CD player connected to …
24 –
25 –
26 … arriving at school …
27 … the developed film …
28 –
29 Having seen …
30 … the burning car …

As and *like*

31 As I was walking down the stairs I had the strange sensation someone was watching me.
32 I have a great respect for people like Mother Teresa, who devote their lives to helping others.
33 I had to pack up and go home as it started to rain very heavily.
34 William Turner, the painter, lived in London as a boy.
35 He behaved like a child and upset many people at the party.
36 I don't want to pay as much as you did for my new stereo.
37 I want you to accept me as I am, not as you'd like me to be.
38 Like most people, I think Bridget Riley is one of the major influences in British painting of the 60s.
39 They built their own house as their friends did.
40 This fridge is as big as/the same size as the one we have at home.

Answers: Mainly *a*
You are quite an impulsive person with extravagant tastes. You've obviously never learned about budgeting and seem to think money grows on trees. You may run into problems if you are ever broke.

Mainly *b*
You seem to be quite well-balanced in your approach to money and finances. You save and budget but still let yourself go occasionally and enjoy life. You shouldn't run into any serious difficulties.

Mainly *c*
Oh dear! You're not a very pleasant person, are you? You're much too worried about and obsessed with money. Relax and live a little. You'll have to change your ways if you want to have any fun – or any friends – in five years' time.

Unit 2 page 18

Unit 14 page 109

Details of the paintings
A Doreen Wilcox: 'White Boat' – little-known artist from Richmond-Upon-Thames, England.
B Untitled painting by Giorgio Rava – part-time artist in Omegna, Northern Italy.
C David Hockney: 'Afternoon Swimming'
D A Tom Keating fake 'The Artist as Rembrandt with Titus' done in the style of Rembrandt.

Unit 4 page 36

Some 400 miles south west of Sri Lanka lie The Maldives, an independent republic of 4,000 tiny coral islands scattered across the translucent blue waters of the Indian Ocean.

In this unique environment, where visiting another hotel means taking a boat, only about 200 of the islands are inhabited – some by simple fishing communities, others with just one small tourist hotel.

Here the visitor will find a tranquil, unspoilt setting of gleaming white beaches ringed by vivid coral reefs teeming with rainbow coloured fish – a haven for the watersports enthusiast and for those seeking to do nothing more than totally unwind with the emphasis on sunshine, the beach, the ocean and simple living …

Unit 14 page 111

Paragraph A
A master faker, who two months ago received a suspended prison sentence and was ordered to pay £16,000 in compensation, has been given permission for some special fundraising. In order to pay up, he will auction off his own fakes.

Paragraph B
When Lämmle was convicted in November, the judge said that he was giving him the minimum punishment for his offence. Almost admiringly, the judge commented that Lämmle had shown 'a hefty dose of Swabian slit-earedness'. (to be schlitzohrig, or slit-eared, is to be sly and cunning.)

Paragraph C
The court described Lämmle as a 'passionate painter', and accepted that he was motivated, above all, by his desire to score points against the art establishment.

Unit 11 page 92

Emphasis words which can be added to statements to make them more emphatic, include the following:

surely   even   by all means
really   simply
truly   actually above all

Unit 13 page 103

Further examples of *actually*:

a   'So you're 43 tomorrow?'
     42, actually.'

b   'See you on Saturday!'
     'Well, actually. I'm not coming …'

c   'Did you have a relaxing holiday?'
     'Yes, I did, actually – lay in the sun all day.'

d   'Did your interview go well?'
     'No, it was awful, actually.'

e   'I heard the music was good last night.'
     'Yes – actually, it was the best jazz I've heard in a long time.'

f   'How's Mary doing in her new job?'
     'She's been fired, actually.'

g   'It sounds a good idea, but I don't think it'll actually work.'

Unit 11 page 91

Here are the original covers of the books.

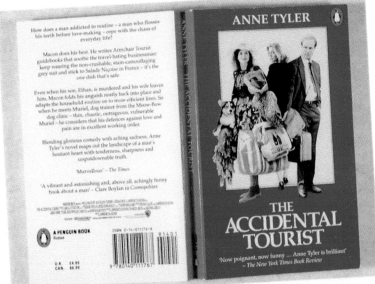

One day while I still lived in St. Paul, I got a bad toothache from biting on peanut brittle and endured it until two o'clock in the afternoon, afraid to look for a new dentist. My old one was a Lutheran who went to India to fix teeth in rural areas, and I was afraid I'd get a real St Paul Catholic dentist, impervious to pain, one who believed that St. Paul in his epistle to the Anesthesians says that agony can be offered up for God's glory, but instead I found a young woman dentist who gave me Novocian and gas and relaxed me so deeply I almost drowned from the spray on the drill, but it was painless. It put me right in a hopeful mood to get a haircut. Ordinarily I'd have gone to Walt's barbershop on Como and said, The usual, and gotten an earful of wisdom about fishing, but he got out of barbering in 1967. Since then I had wandered from shop to shop, looking, hoping. I drove up Grand Avenue and saw a shop called "Hair One Day and Gone the Next—Personal Hair Stylists," and walked in. It was all done in black and white: tile floor, chairs, white walls, black ceiling. The magazines were all about expressing the True Woman Inside You, even the men's magazines were about that. A young woman came around the corner. Yeah? she said. I said, "Uh, you're probably booked up, you wouldn't be able to get me in right away, would you," turning away. Her hair was pink; it looked like she wasn't getting all her vitamins, or was getting some she shouldn't.

"No, I can take you now. My name's Candy."

She was chewing gum. She looked about seventeen. We went to a black cubicle and she sat me in a little black chair. There were stuffed pandas and kangaroos. She put a red silky cloth around me and ruffled my hair and said, 'Uhh, howdja like it?" I almost said, The usual, but to look at Candy there didn't seem to be a usual. I said, "Oh, just a trim around the edges and not too short." I tried to sound like it wasn't important. I was brought up to believe beauty is not worth thinking about, what's important is your soul, your mind—you don't want to be a fifty-dollar haircut on a fifty-cent head. But I was feeling hopeful.

She started to cut. She wore a couple dozen plastic bracelets on her hands that clattered in my ear like an old John Deere combine. She didn't talk except once, to ask, "Do you live around here?" I said no. She seemed satisfied to know that and said no more until she unpinned the smock and handed me my glasses. I put them on and saw in the mirror an old old clown. She hadn't painted big blobby lips or a red nose on me but the hair was right. All I needed was a pair of exploding pants.

"How's that?' she said. "That's fine,' I said. I was ashamed to complain, which would imply that I had imagined she could make me look nice. "That's sixteen dollars," she said. I gave her a twenty. "Keep the change," I said. A twenty-five-percent tip. Just because a man looks ridiculous doesn't mean he can't pay extra for the privilege. I bought a Twins cap at the drugstore. "Care for some hair cream?' the woman said. Drove home, and walked in the door, steaming mad just like all of us Wobegonians get mad, about twenty minutes after the fact, angry retorts coming to mind too late to be retorted. My wife took one look at me as I took off the cap and she said, "You have the most beautiful green eyes, do you know that?"

1 ▶ Unit 1 page 7

You are going to hear Jean describing a very embarrassing thing that happened to her when she was younger. Look at these pictures and try to predict the correct order before you listen.

2 ▶ Unit 1 pages 8–9

A Work with a partner who has read a different text. Read your text again and write six comprehension questions which focus on the most important information. Exchange and answer the questions.

B Prepare a summary of the first text you read. (maximum 100 words)

3 ▶ Unit 2 page 14

T8 Read this summary of the second part of the interview with Tony McGrath of *The Observer*. Then listen to the interview and underline six mistakes in the summary.

After they had signed the contract, they were surprised to be told that Madonna would select the pictures herself and they would have no choice in this. The pictures were given to the editor of the paper in New York at another secret meeting. Unfortunately Tony only got them at the last moment before the publishing deadline, and they turned out to be black and white copies of the originals, and were of very poor quality. They argued with the publishers and finally got the originals six days before the publication deadline. Martin Amis went to New York and interviewed the photographer Steven Maysell about the pictures, and the interview was published with the photos in the magazine. On the day they were published the newspaper's circulation increased by 17,000 copies. In Tony's view, big purchases like the Madonna photos do a lot in the long term to increase sales of the newspaper.

Now write a sentence correcting each of the six mistakes.

4 ▶ Unit 2 page 16

A Part 1

Which paragraphs do the following sentences summarise?

a The qualities of a good paparazzo.
b Incidents which illustrate the dangers of the profession.
c The difference between photographers and paparazzi.
d How some people have tried to deal with paparazzi.
e The author's view of the best attitude to them.
f An example of why a good paparazzo earns more than the average photographer.

Now do Part 2 on page 130.

T2 Now listen and check your predictions.

Part 2

What is the connection between these people and paparazzi? (Where more than one answer is possible, the number of answers required is given after each name.)

Federico Fellini
Massimo Sestini (2)
Ayrton Senna
Princess Caroline
Mandy Smith
Jackie Onassis (2)
Dudley Moore
Princess Stephanie
Madonna (2)

A someone who has reacted to paparazzi
B no connection with paparazzi
C driving style required by Sestini
D inventor of the term *paparazzi*
E victim of paparazzi
F owner of a photo agency
G famous paparazzo

B Answer the questions and support your answers by referring to the text.

1 What evidence is there in the text to suggest that the writer is, or was, a paparazzo?
2 Do you think the writer admires paparazzi?
3 Which are the most important qualities of a paparazzo?
4 On which occasion do you get the impression that the writer disapproves of them?
5 What are the author's conclusions about paparazzi and the famous?
6 What is the public's attitude to paparazzi, according to the writer?

5 ▶ **Unit 3 page 23** ━━━━━━━━━

[T12] Listen to Jonathan (*J*) and Louise (*L*) talking about hitchhiking experiences. Write *L* or *J* next to these excerpts from the sentences according to the story that they belong to.

1 in Switzerland …
2 three people …
3 raining …
4 in Crete …
5 drove off with their bags …
6 'Get out the car …'
7 'Come and stay at my place …'
8 turned off across the fields …
9 put their bags in the back of the car …
10 after an hour they stopped …
11 pulled up at a big house …
12 'I'll take you along the road …'
13 the boot was locked …

Now choose one of the stories and listen again. Make more complete notes, then write an account of the anecdote.

6 ▶ **Unit 3 page 24** ━━━━━━━━━

A True or false?

1 Ted Simon says that you can't really get to know the world if you travel by boat or plane.
2 Most round-the-world travellers go to Asia first.
3 He was sure that he would get to Cape Town by 24 February 1974.
4 He had been to Africa before.
5 It was raining on the night of his departure.
6 The people at the *Sunday Times* had tried to discourage him from going on the journey.
7 Before he left he had a strong desire to give up the idea of the journey and go back to his job.
8 He put the bike on the train to get to the English Channel.

B Answer the questions.

1 How do you have to travel if you really want to get to know the world, according to Ted Simon?
2 What was Ted Simon's main reason for choosing the route that he did?
3 Why did he choose to go to Africa first?
4 Which countries were impossible for him to visit and why?
5 Why did he decide to visit India last of all?
6 Why did he think it was 'foolishness' to collect information about the countries on his journey?
7 Why did he feel 'utterly defeated' when he was standing outside the *Sunday Times* offices on the day of his departure?
8 How did he feel as soon as he set off for the coast?

7 ▶ **Unit 4 page 30** ━━━━━━━━━

[T17] Look at these incomplete sentences from an interview with another traveller. Then listen and complete the sentences with the words you hear.

1 Er … living in most … I suppose _____ really …
2 I haven't lived in a culture like that and it's very interesting _____ 'cos there's nothing I could relate to, …
3 Very interesting the way _____, live erm, it was nice.
4 Japanese people don't like foreigners very much, so _____ was extremely difficult …
5 How do you feel about _____ live there?
6 It was a very interesting experience to feel what it was like _____ actually.
7 'Is Japan the only country you've lived in so far?' 'No, I've lived _____.'
8 Erm, I think _____ actually, I really like Spain.
9 I'm thinking of going _____. Maybe I'll go for two, or something like that.
10 I don't know, I think _____ but I couldn't say for a hundred, you know a hundred percent.

8 ▶ Unit 4 page 32 ━━━━━━━━━━━━━━━

A Match the names and the descriptions.

> 1 Doctor Paulcke
> 2 Davos
> 3 Javed Ahmad
> 4 Morignone, Les Arcs
> 5 Werner Fritz
> 6 Dominique Rambaud
> 7 Branger family
> 8 Grindelwald, Vorarlberg

a Director of Alp Action
b places damaged by avalanches
c area where new developments are banned
d founders of modern skiing industry
e representative of International Centre for Alpine Environment
f resort with world's first funicular
g Director of Austrian National Tourist Office
h early German skier

B Choose the best answer by referring to the text.

1 Alpine farmers stopped working the land
   a to go skiing.
   b to sell it to the skiing industry.
   c because they were poor.
   d because it snowed more often.
2 The most important natural barriers to avalanches are
   a forests and rivers.
   b trees and leaves.
   c cut grass and trees.
   d uncut grass and leaves.
3 Construction of new resort facilities is not possible
   a in Italy and France.
   b in all parts of Austria and Switzerland.
   c in all the Alps.
   d in parts of Austria and Switzerland.
4 Dominique Rambaud claims that the attitude of the French and Italians to the problems caused by ski developments is one of
   a indifference.
   b interest.
   c hostility.
   d amusement.
5 The writer thinks that the French will have many environmental problems caused by skiing
   a in a few years' time.
   b very soon.
   c in the distant future.
   d next year.

9 ▶ Unit 5 page 39 ━━━━━━━━━━━━━━━

T21 You are going to hear someone talking about being conned by a very able salesman. Read the questions, then listen and answer them.

1 What did Vina and her family buy from the man?
2 What fundamental mistake did Vina make when she first decided to buy the goods?
3 Why was she unhappy with what she bought?
4 How does the man avoid prosecution?
5 What reasons does Vina give for having bought goods from the man?
6 Why won't other companies solve the problems Vina has run into?

10 ▶ Unit 5 page 42 ━━━━━━━━━━━━━━━

A Complete these sentences with information from the text.

1 _____ cites an example where two people from different cultures had a misunderstanding over ways people of their culture react to injury.
2 Another example in the text describes how an _____ woman was offended by a _____ couple when they ignored her in a restaurant.
3 In order to be able to cope with cramped living conditions _____, people tend to ignore the existence of their neighbours.
4 _____ feel offended if people don't talk to them when they pass near them.
5 _____ made a film called _____ about the problem of communication in relationships.
6 One of the conclusions of the film is that we keep trying to communicate despite our frequent failures, because we need _____ and _____.

B Answer the questions.

1 Why is there a greater danger of misunderstanding between people of different nationalities?
2 What do you learn from the text about British people's attitudes to talking to people they don't know?
3 What do you learn from the text about American expectations about communication between strangers?
4 How has the environment affected social attitudes in Japan?
5 What, according to the writer, are the similarities between attempts at international agreement and personal relationships?
6 Can you explain what Woody Allen was trying to say in the joke quoted in the text with which he ended *Annie Hall*?

11 **Unit 6 page 46**

T26 Read these statements, then listen to the conversation about Caroline's family and decide if the statements are true or false. Give reasons if you think they are false.

1 Caroline is one of three children.
2 Caroline was spoilt when she was a child.
3 Caroline felt pressure to do as well as her older brother.
4 She feels that her father was justifiably strict with her when she was younger.
5 She left home to go to university.
6 Caroline feels under an obligation to maintain close contact with her parents.
7 Caroline's grandmother lives with her parents.
8 Caroline accepts that she may have to look after her parents when they get old.

12 **Unit 6 page 48**

A Decide if these statements about the text are true or false. Give reasons for your answers.

1 Robin Skynner invented the Family Systems Exercise in 1972.
2 The exercise is now used at the Institute of Family Therapy as part of the treatment of couples with difficulties.
3 The aim of the exercise is to show how people are unconsciously attracted to each other.
4 The best time to do the exercise is when people don't know each other at all.
5 When people who have done the exercise report back, they find they chose people with similar families to their own.
6 Robin is convinced that the fact that there are always similarities between the families of the people who choose each other, is proof that people are attracted to each other unconsciously.
7 The first time he tried the exercise, Robin was worried about the people who wouldn't find a partner or group.
8 People who didn't find a group felt rejected as a result of participating in the exercise.
9 People in the group who came together last were all orphans.
10 The most convincing thing about the activity for Robin was the similar background of the members of the last group who got together.

B Write a short (100 words maximum) summary of the ideas outlined in the text.

13 **Unit 7 page 55**

T30 Rob went for a colour consultation with House of Colour some time ago. He now talks to Alice Prier about the reaction he got from his friends afterwards. Read the questions, then listen and answer.

1 What was the most positive result of the consultation for Rob?
2 Which 'major reaction' has he experienced from other people?
3 What does Alice Prier think about the idea of wearing clashing colours?
4 How did working for House of Colour change Alice's attitude to colours?
5 What does Rob say about the frequency with which he wears his clothes?
6 Why does Alice talk about colour co-ordinated 'dusters'?
7 Why is Rob doubtful about decorating his house in 'his' colours?
8 Who are better at choosing colours, according to Alice – men or women?

14 **Unit 7 page 56**

A Find the names which match these descriptions:

1 Three stars who ate humble food in public to demonstrate their solidarity with the world's hungry people.
2 The owner of a shop which sells expensive secondhand clothes to the stars.
3 The owner of a shop which sells cheap secondhand clothes to the stars.
4 The names of a famous film star and her friend who were nearly thrown out of an expensive restaurant for the way they were dressed.
5 Two men who have had success in predicting trends.

B Read the relevant sections of the text again and summarise what Jim Trenton, Mark Fox, Jeannine Stein and Lance and John say about the phenomenon of 'dressing down'.

"Well, we haven't made a very good start have we, Mrs Turnstone?"

T35 You are going to hear a man called Denis, who used to be one of London's homeless, talking about how he found out about *The Big Issue* and how it has changed his life.

Read the statements carefully, then listen and choose the best alternative:

1 When he found out about *The Big Issue* Denis was
   a sleeping on the streets.
   b staying in a hotel.
   c staying with friends.

2 Denis found out about *The Big Issue* from
   a a policeman.
   b a friend.
   c a vendor.

3 the number of people selling *The Big Issue* now is about
   a 26,000.
   b 260.
   c 2,600.

4 At the time of the recording the magazine had been going for about
   a a year and a half.
   b a year.
   c two years.

5 The main job of the *Outreach* team is to
   a settle disputes between vendors.
   b sell *The Big Issue*.
   c improve relations with the police.

6 Vendors of *The Big Issue* sometimes argue with beggars because they
   a steal the beggars' money.
   b discourage people from giving money to the beggars.
   c don't want to be considered as beggars themselves.

7 Denis says that the police
   a are tolerant towards vendors.
   b often have trouble with vendors.
   c have a good relationship with vendors.

8 Denis now
   a sometimes sells *The Big Issue* but works mainly in an office.
   b spends all his time in an office.
   c still sells *The Big Issue* and also works in an office.

A Read the text quickly and match the names of the owners, their pets and the things that the owners have bought for them.

An American couple	a sheepdog
Miss Robins	a hamster
Nina Campbell	a luxurious hutch
Lord Snowdon	a three-storey town house
Marion Elliot	an expensive grave
a ginger cat	a papier mâché basket
a King Charles Spaniel	a luxurious kennel
an angora rabbit	

B True or false?

1 The writer says that the rise in pet food sales shows that pets are having an easier time than humans during the recession.

2 During the election campaign the Liberal Democrat Party promised voters they would defend animal rights if they won.

3 Owners of pets in Japan have to use a special credit card or cheque book to pay for pets' luxuries like water beds and flushing toilets.

4 The New York couple sued the Long Island Pet Cemetery because their dog was not buried in the right place.

5 Although she has called her pet rabbit Rosemary, Miss Robins is not sure if it is a male or a female.

6 Ferrari the hamster prefers sleeping on the second floor of his house than on the third floor.

7 Lord Snowdon thinks it is more important to give dogs a luxurious kennel rather than pat and stroke them.

8 George the cat is going to live in a replica of the Taj Mahal.

9 Eric Lansdown's bird cages are not made for people who want to keep birds.

T41 You are going to hear a conversation between Jo and Jonathan about the advantages and disadvantages of living in the city and the country. Make a list of the things that you expect to hear.

Now listen and tick the things on your list that Jo and Jonathan mention. What other advantages and disadvantages do they mention?

18 ▶ Unit 9 page 74

A Write the number of the paragraph in which you find this information:

a A comparison between babies' and adults' ability to communicate.

b Comment on the real value of some typical products of society, when seen from outside.

c A description of an idyllic country scene.

d A comparison of different types of stress.

e A description of a small but interesting community in Britain.

f Details of a psychological illness which some children suffer from.

g The writer's claim that people in cities will never be happy.

h Criticism of the narrowness of people's social groups in cities.

B Read the text again and answer these questions.

1 What was the reason for the writer's visit to the Boro River?

2 What does he say about the stress in cities, and the stress of people living in the area he visited?

3 In what way does the writer claim that living in large, highly concentrated groups is damaging to us?

4 Which piece of modern technology does the writer frequently refer to as being a negative influence in the lives of city people? How does it affect them, in his opinion?

5 Does he give an idyllic picture of life in primitive society?

6 How would he answer the claim that 'country life limits people's social lives'?

7 According to the writer, how do your priorities change when you live further away from the comforts of modern cities?

8 What advice does he offer to people who have become caught up in the system and values of city life?

19 ▶ Unit 10 page 79

T47 Listen to Jonathan and Joanne talking about moods and answer these questions.

1 What makes Jonathan moody?

2 What makes his mood worse?

3 How does he get out of it?

4 What can happen to make Jonathan's mood change?

5 What does he say about people's attitude at work to his moods?

6 What happens if he goes home and he's in a bad mood?

20 ▶ Unit 10 page 80

A In which order do you find the following information in the text? Number the points 1 – 9.

a Appropriate lighting and colour for manual tasks.

b The influence of colour on the mentally disturbed.

c The author's policy regarding colour research.

d The future of colour research.

e The centrifugal action of colour and light.

f Colours for schools.

g The centripetal action of colour and light.

h Appropriate lighting and colour for sedentary occupations.

i The effect of illumination on localised work tasks.

B Read the text again more carefully and make notes about the items listed in Exercise A.

Now expand your notes into a series of statements.

21 ▶ Unit 11 page 87

T51 Val asks Bhasi about the three books he would take to the desert island. Listen and answer the questions.

1 Which books does Bhasi imagine everyone will want to take?

2 How does he classify these books?

3 Which books would he like to take?

4 Why does he choose the first book he mentions?

5 What information do you find out about the second author Bhasi mentions?

6 What do you find out about the content of this book?

7 Why does he like the poet that he mentions?

8 What do you find out about this poet's attitude to traditional poetry?

22 ▶ Unit 11 page 88

A Complete the sentences with the best alternative.

1 As first prize for winning the *Irish Times* – Aer Lingus competition Norman Rush won
   a a trip to Dublin.
   b a large sum of money.
   c 46 new books.
   d a contract for a new book.

2 The reason why Lucy Ellmann decided to judge the competition was
   a to make money.
   b to get a free trip to Dublin.
   c because she likes reading new books.
   d as a favour to the organiser.

3 When she was very young, Lucy Ellmann
  a used to read a lot.
  b was forced to read by her father.
  c hated reading.
  d wasn't very good at reading.
4 Lucy Ellmann reviews books
  a to help new authors.
  b to help publishers.
  c to help readers.
  d to make a lot of money.
5 Lucy Ellmann finds it difficult to review good books
  because
  a she doesn't know what to say.
  b she rarely reviews good books.
  c praising is more difficult than criticising.
  d she is jealous of writers better than herself.
6 There were
  a no British entries in the competition.
  b only American entries.
  c no British prize-winners.
  d no British male entries.
7 Lucy Ellmann entered a competition herself a few years
  ago and
  a won first prize.
  b didn't win a prize.
  c went to Hong Kong to collect her prize.
  d won a prize which disappointed her.
8 Lucy Ellmann thought that Norman Rush's prize-
  winning novel *Mating* was
  a good, but not the best entry.
  b interesting but difficult to praise.
  c a poor novel but the best entry.
  d the best novel in the competition.

B Answer the questions.

1 What were the positive and negative aspects of judging
  the competition, for Lucy Ellmann?
2 What evidence can you find in the text that Lucy
  Ellmann is a novelist herself?
3 How does the writer feel about books in general?
4 Which books are easier to review in her opinion, and
  why?
5 What is Lucy Ellmann's explanation for people
  reviewing books which are written by people like
  themselves?
6 What does the writer say about sexism in the British
  literary world?
7 What happens when a writer enters a competition and
  how is this reflected in her own experience?
8 What is the writer's opinion of the novel which won first
  prize in the competition she judged?

23 ▶ Unit 12 page 94

A Decide if these statements are true or false. Give
reasons if you think a statement is false.

1 Adrian would not have protested about not being able to
  wear red socks if it had not been for Pandora's interest
  in the matter.
2 Adrian is strongly attracted to Pandora.
3 Adrian's parents get on well together.
4 Pandora's parents are of Russian origin.
5 *The Ragged Trousered Philanthropists* is about stamp-
  collecting.
6 Adrian is scared of the headmaster, Mr Scruton.
7 Pandora cried because she was confused and
  embarrassed after the events in the headmaster's office.
8 Adrian regretted getting involved in the protest.
9 Adrian and his friends lost their struggle to be
  nonconformists.

B One of the most difficult things to understand in another
language is humour. The text you have read would make
most native speakers of English smile. Can you explain
what is funny about these things?

1 The names Adrian uses for some of the characters.
2 Adrian's use of language.
3 His description of Pandora's parents, their home and
  lifestyle.
4 The book Pandora's father lent Adrian.
5 The shift in Adrian's attitude to the protest.
6 The conversation his father had with the headmaster.
7 The outcome of the incident.

24 ▶ Unit 12 page 96

T55 Listen to another excerpt of the play *Educating Rita*. The
first time you listen, choose the best description of the
topic Frank and Rita are discussing.

a The connection between Peer Gynt and British TV.
b Rita's home life.
c The myth of working class culture.

Now listen again and complete these sentences. Stop the
cassette where necessary.

1 I was doin' her hair and I …
2 I wish I could go off …
3 Well, we've …
4 They'll tell you they've got culture as …
5 There's like this sort of disease …
6 An' like the worst thing is that y'know …
7 They just tell them …

Listen again and write a short paragraph (100 words)
summarising what Rita says.

25 ▶ Unit 13 page 103 ━━━━━━

⌑60 Listen to Colin Goudie again and make notes about what he says about:

- his career at the BBC
- working with poor materials
- the advantages of working with video
- how he edits film and video
- his best documentary
- how to judge the quality of editing in a film
- the disadvantages of working with video
- technological developments in editing

26 ▶ Unit 13 page 104 ━━━━━━

A Match the descriptions on the left with a name or names on the right.

1 Famous cowboys	a Uncle John Hep
2 The location of a private cinema	b Tonto
	c The Ritz
3 A hairstyle like that of an American Indian	d Randolph Scott
	e Tom Mix
4 The owner of a TV	f John Logue
5 A person who worked for the local authority	g Red Rider
	h Kings Cross
6 The cinema which showed a Lone Ranger film	i Mohican
7 The Lone Ranger's partner	

B Answer these questions.

Mivvis at High Noon

1 Why did the writer of the article sit 'at the rear of the upper stalls'?

2 Why didn't the ice cream vendor realise that the cinema was full of cowboys?

3 Why did she run away when she saw who was in the audience?

Not the Lone Ranger

4 How did the writer get his first TV?

5 Why did the writer find it 'reasonable' that his first TV didn't work very well?

6 Why were the writer and his brother prepared to put up with their malfunctioning TV rather than watch the Lone Ranger at John Logue's?

7 What was the advantage of listening to the Lone Ranger without the picture?

8 Why does the writer compare his visit to the cinema with a visit to the Sistine Chapel?

9 How did the writer and his brother know that the person who appeared on stage at the cinema was not the real Lone Ranger?

27 ▶ Unit 14 page 110 ━━━━━━

⌑65 Every summer in London the Royal Academy organises its Summer Exhibition. Listen to Helen Valentine talking about the exhibition and answer the questions.

1 What are the names of the two committees which select works for the Summer Exhibition?

2 Who are the Royal Academicians and how are they chosen?

3 How many works are submitted to the committees for consideration?

4 How are the works assessed?

5 Who decides what to hang and where?

6 Who has the last word about what is to be included?

7 What happens when they have finished the selection of works?

28 ▶ Unit 14 page 112 ━━━━━━

A True or false?

1 Tom Keating copied other painters in order to learn more about painting.

2 He was very successful at passing off his paintings as originals, partly because he used the right materials.

3 He used to stick his own drawing over the top of old 19th-century watercolours.

4 Keating found that painting a picture was easier than framing it.

5 He deliberately put a 'mistake' in the painting to show that it was not an original by the artist whose style he was imitating.

6 In Keating's opinion, Girtin was a great artist, but Turner was even greater.

7 Keating made his own bistre ink because he didn't have enough money to buy commercially produced ink.

8 He found it difficult not to give his paintings the appearance of being old masters.

B Re-read the text and make notes about the following:

1 Tom Keating's materials

2 Keating's copies of Girtin

3 Thomas Girtin

4 Tom Keating's Rembrandt drawings

Unit 1

Present tenses

Here are the main uses of the present simple and present continuous tenses. (See The future, page 139, for further uses of the present tenses.)

A General time

The present simple is used to describe habitual on-going activities and permanent situations (states).

> *Most Londoners commute to work every day.*
> *My sister works for a small company in Walton. She lives near the town centre.*

It is often used with time expressions *always, never, usually, sometimes, often, occasionally, rarely, normally, generally, every so often, (every) once in a while / month / week, once or twice a week* etc..

B General truths

The present simple is also used to describe things that are considered to be always 'true'.

> *The earth rotates in a clockwise direction.*
> *Exercise, rest and a balanced diet all contribute to good health.*

C Temporary situations

The present continuous is used to describe situations or activities which are not permanent, but in progress only for a limited period, 'around this particular time.'

> *I normally drive to work, but I'm taking the bus at the moment (because my car's being repaired).*
> *He's not going out a lot these days (because he's quite busy).*
> *I'm studying at a language school in Dublin now (although I'm an engineer and I usually work in Frankfurt).*

It is often used with time expressions *at the moment, these days, now* – and more formally – *currently, at this time.*

(Note: The situations are not necessarily in progress at the moment of speaking, but refer to a period of time around it):

> *You'll have to use the other computer – Rob's using this one to do his reports.*
> *I'm reading a new book by Toni Morrison.*

D Talking about something happening at the moment of speaking

The present continuous is also used to describe something in progress now.

> *He's having a bath at the moment – can I take a message?*

Time expressions often used are *(right) now, at the moment.*

E Progressive change

The present continuous is used to describe situations which are in the process of changing and developing.

> *People are becoming more and more dependent on technology.*
> *She's getting better, but she's still in hospital.*

It is often used with time expressions *nowadays, these days, currently, presently* etc..

F To express irritation or annoyance

The present continuous is used for this purpose.

> *He's always / forever / continually phoning me and complaining about something.*

G Dramatic narrative

The present tenses are often used instead of the past tenses in stories, jokes, anecdotes etc. to create atmosphere and make the narrative livelier. (See The past continuous, page 138, for further information about dramatic narrative in description.)

> *So this guy goes into the pub, and he's sitting at the bar when this parrot suddenly appears, and says …*

H Synopses of books, films, plays etc.

Present tenses are frequently used for this purpose. (See Past tenses, page 138, for further information about this.)

> *A woman in her thirties goes to spend her holidays at a lakeside hotel in Switzerland. She is lonely and is hoping to find adventure …*

I Commentaries

Note the different uses of the two present tenses in commentaries – especially sports events or public ceremonies – usually broadcast on radio or TV. The present simple is usually used for short, quick actions, for example in rugby commentaries:

> *Jones passes the ball to Andrews, he passes it to Baines …*

The present continuous is used for longer-lasting actions, for example in horse-racing commentaries:

> *Blue Judge is coming up to second place now … and there's Thunderbird pounding up behind him, and the gap between them is closing …*

J Demonstrations, instructions, describing sequences

The present simple is used for each individual action, while the present continuous is used for actions of longer duration, and for the background activity.

> *First you peel and finely chop a clove of garlic, and you fry lightly in olive oil. Then you add one thinly sliced onion. While the onion is frying slowly, you mix the remaining ingredients …*

There are many verbs that are not usually used in continuous tenses, or that change their meanings if they are used in these tenses.

> *What are you thinking about?* (= mental activity)
> *What do you think of this?* (= opinion)

Here is a list of some of these verbs:
being *be exist*
perception *see hear taste smell*
appearance *look like seem appear*
likes and dislikes *like dislike hate love prefer*
thinking *forget know realise imagine believe think*
possession *have own belong to contain*

Unit 2

Past tenses (1)

Here are the main uses of the past simple and continuous tenses.

The past simple

Events and situations in the past

The past simple is used to describe short, completed events as well as longer-lasting situations.

> *Cheryl went to the window and called out to Paul.*
> *When I was a student, I spent a year in Viareggio, which is near Pisa.*

The past continuous

A Background information

The past continuous and the past simple are often used together for this purpose. While the former describes a longer, background activity, the latter is used for the shorter events that happened during this time.

> *He was working in Spain when he met his wife.*
> *I was doing some gardening when all of a sudden I came across a human skull …*
> *What were you doing (when you heard the news)?*

B Description

The past continuous is used to set the scene against which shorter actions are described (by the past simple).

> *It was a stormy night. The wind was howling and the rain was beating against the windows. Sarah heard a noise downstairs, and grabbed her gun …*

C Temporary situations

(See The present continuous, page 137, for further information.)

> *I was living with friends at the time.*

D Expressing ideas more politely or tentatively

The past continuous tends to give a more formal, therefore more polite or hesitant tone to a sentence.

> *I was wondering if you could lend me your umbrella.*

The past perfect simple and continuous

The past perfect simple is used to describe an event which occurred before another event or situation even earlier in the past.

> *Before he left New York, he had telephoned the car-hire company in Montreal, so that there would be a car there for him when he got to the airport.*

If the order of events needs to be emphasised, the past perfect tense should be used.

> *As soon as he had saved enough money, he bought a new computer.*

But if there is unlikely to be any ambiguity about the order of events, it is not necessary to use the past perfect.

> *After we got home, we sat in the garden and read the newspapers.*

After and *before* are often used in this type of sentence.

(Note: It is preferable to use the past simple for a sequence of verbs after the first verb in the past perfect.)

> *Their house was very well built. They had used the very best materials in the construction. The wood came from Canada and the ceramic tiles, from Italy. They bought the …*

The past perfect continuous is used instead of the past perfect simple to emphasise the idea of 'duration', or an activity in progress.

> *They had been working for Siemens in Germany before they returned to England.*
> *I had been rewriting the essay for several days before I finally handed it in.*

The noun phrase

Noun groups can be the subject or complement of a verb, or the object of a preposition.

> *The inn at the edge of the lake was very popular with the tourists.*
> *I sat down on the chair beside the roaring fire.*

More information about a noun can be given by using modifiers in front of it or qualifiers after it.

Modifiers can be

• another noun (thereby making a compound noun): *hotel – tourist hotel*
(Notes: The pronunciation of compound nouns varies, although the stress usually occurs on the first noun. Some common compounds are written as one word – *seaside*, others with a hyphen – *swimming-pool* – and others as two words – *tourist hotel*. Unfortunately there are no rules governing this.)

• an adjective: *hotel – cheap hotel*

• a determiner (*a, the, my* etc.): *hotel – my hotel*
(See The article, page 142, for more information.)

Qualifiers can be

• a prepositional phrase: *a hotel – a hotel with a swimming pool.*

• a relative clause: *a hotel where I once stayed*
(See Relative clauses, page 145, for more information.)

Unit 3

Past tenses (2)

The present perfect simple

Here are the main uses of the present perfect simple.

A Situations or repeated actions which began in the past and are still continuing

I've lived here all my life (= I still live here)
He's taken the same train to work for years.
(= he still does this)

B Completed past actions and events where there is no mention of a specific time

The present perfect simple is used to emphasise the experience, rather than <u>when</u> it happened. Note the connection of the past and the present in these sentences:

I've been to Italy.
(= So now I have some knowledge of the country)
She's climbed Everest.
(= so now she is a very experienced climber)

It is often used with adverbials *ever, never, often* etc..

(The past simple tense is used for past experiences where the time is mentioned, or at least 'understood'.)

Did you see that new comedy show last night on TV?

The present perfect simple is also used to express 'more recent' past.

A *Have you seen the new MD yet?*
B *Yes, I've just seen him in the corridor.*
C *I've already met him.*

It is often used with adverbials *just, yet, already*.

(Note: In American English, the following sentences would be acceptable):

Did you see the new MD yet?
Yes, I just saw him in the corridor.

The present perfect simple or continuous can be used to comment on past situations, results of which are evident now. (See B below.)

You've been on a diet! (= you seem thinner now)
I haven't been sleeping well. (= that's why I look tired)

The present perfect simple or continuous?

A Temporary activities and situations which are still continuing

The present perfect continuous is usually used for this purpose, although the present perfect simple is also acceptable in certain cases.

I've been working / I've worked in advertising ever since I left school.
He's been seeing a lot of her lately.

B Completed activities and situations

Note the different tenses used to express activities and situations which are completed or on-going.

What have you been doing? (= activities engaged in up to now)
What have you done today? (= completed)
I've been writing a book. (= I'm still writing it now)
I've written an article for a magazine.
(= completed)

(Note: Certain 'momentary action' verbs, when used in continuous tenses, express the idea of something happening repeatedly.)

I've cut my finger. (single action)
I've been cutting flowers. (repeated action)

(See Present tenses, page 137, for verbs which are not usually used in the continuous tense except as participles, or with a different meaning.)

Unit 4

The future

In English there is no 'one future tense'. There are several different forms to choose from, depending on what is being expressed. Below are the most frequently used forms, together with their most common uses.

A going to

1 **Plans/intentions**
going to + infinitive is used to talk about both short and long-term future plans and intentions, which are quite definite.

I'm just going to stay in and watch a video tonight.
Silvia and Jaime are tired of living in Madrid. They're going to move near the sea. (= they've discussed the issue and have made a definite decision)

Note: The verbs *plan* (to ...) and *intend* (to ...) are often used as more formal ways of expressing the above.

2 **Prediction**
Going to is normally used for predicting the near future when there is some present evidence of what is likely to happen.

She's going to faint (because she looks pale and dizzy).

(Note: For reasons of style, we generally use the present continuous instead of *going to* with the verbs *go* and *come*.)

He's going to Spain.
She's coming to the party!

B Present continuous

The present continuous is used to talk about short-term and longer-term arrangements and appointments made in the future.

> *I'm seeing Luis on Friday after work.* (= we've spoken to each other and arranged to meet, and we've probably decided on a time and a place.)

Compare this tense with the use of *going to* for plans/intentions (see A1, page 139):

> *Silvia and Jaime are moving to Alicante.*
> (= they've made a decision to move from Madrid, and now they've made the necessary arrangements, i.e. sold their flat, bought a flat in Alicante, etc..)

> *Marcello and Laura are going to get married.*
> = they've discussed it and have decided to do this)
> *Marcello and Laura are getting married.*
> (= they've decided where and when; they've invited people etc..)

This tense is often used with a time or date.

> *They're getting married / moving in June.*

C will

1 Prediction

Both *going to* and *will* are used for future prediction. Predictions using *going to* are based on something concrete that we can see or hear now; predictions using *will* are based on our interpretation of facts, or knowledge of a situation in general.

> a *She's going to faint* (because she looks pale and dizzy).
> *She'll faint* (because she always faints when she hasn't eaten for a long time).

> b *He's going to win!* (= he's in the lead)
> *He'll win.* (= He's the best so far)

> c *There's going to be a war.* (= all the evidence points to this)
> *There'll be a war.* (= from my knowledge of history and current affairs, I can tell this)

(Note: Predictions with *will*, though quite definite, are based on the speaker's interpretation only.)

2 Future intention

Will is used for decisions about the future (usually near future) made at the moment of speaking.

> *The rain's stopped. I think I'll go for a walk.*
> *'Julia's back from her trip.'*
> *'Oh, good. I'll give her a ring.'*

> *We need some more blank cassettes.'*
> *'Okay, I'll get some today.* (= I'm deciding how)
> *I know. I'm going to get some today.* (= I already decided to do it earlier on)

3 Formal reporting of planned events

On TV and radio news reports *will* is often used to report planned events.

> *The Mayor will open a new hospital on Saturday.*

(See also Future continuous below.)

4 Future fact

Although it is generally impossible to be absolutely certain about the future, there are aspects of the future which are considered to be fact. *Will* is used to express this.

> *The sun will rise tomorrow / Babies will be born / People will die.*

Will used as a modal auxiliary verb also has several other uses not connected with future prediction or intention.

D Future continuous

1 Activity in progress at a particular point in time in the future.

> *Just think. This time next week, I'll be lying on a beach in Greece.*
> *Don't phone her in the morning. She'll be working.*

2 Events that take place in the normal course of everyday life.

> *Give me John's watch.*
> *– I'm seeing him tomorrow.* (= we've arranged to meet.)
> *– I'll be seeing him tomorrow.* (= I work with him and I see him every day, in the normal course of events.)

3 Formal reporting of planned events
(See C3 above.)

E Future Perfect

This form is used to say that something will have been completed by a certain time in the future.

> *'I need the dress by Friday.'*
> *'Don't worry. I'll have finished it by then.'* (= we don't know when it will be finished, but the important idea is that it will be finished before the time specified.)

F Present simple

This form is used for fixed schedules, timetables, itineraries.

> *Autumn term starts on 23 September.*
> *You fly to Amsterdam, and from there you go by coach to …*

(Note: This form is not used for personal arrangements. See The present continuous, page 137, for this use.)

Unit 5

Verbs with *to* + infinitive/-*ing* clause

1 Some verbs can be followed by either of these patterns, without a change in meaning, e.g. begin, start.

• *Like/hate/love/prefer* are usually used with *to* + infinitive, when there is an implication that this is the 'right' or 'wise' thing to do.

> *The boss likes staff to get in on time every day.*
> (= these are his standards)

These verbs are also used to talk about habitual activity.

> *I like to get up late on Sunday mornings, get the papers and have a big breakfast. I hate getting up early on weekends …*

2 Some verbs have different meanings according to whether we use *to* + infinitive or -*ing*.

• *forget/regret/remember*

with -*ing* clause when we are referring back to an event after it has happened:

> *I remember putting my keys down somewhere but I can't remember where.*
> *I regret not having spent more time with him.*

with *to* + infinitive when we are referring forward to an event:

> *Don't forget to cancel the milk.*
> *I forgot to cancel the milk before we went away.*
> *Please remember to call him.*

(Note: *Regret* is used with verbs like *say/tell/inform* in a formal written and spoken style, when the speaker wants to apologise for what is about to be said.)

> *I regret to inform you that your application has been refused.*

• *try*

> a *I tried to speak to a policeman.* (= made an effort to speak to a policeman but probably didn't succeed)
> b *I tried speaking to a policeman.* (= actually spoke to a policeman)

In a the meaning is 'to make an effort'. In b the emphasis is on 'experimentation'.

• *need*

> a *My hair needs cutting.*
> b *My hair needs to be cut.*

The examples mean the same but the -*ing* form is more common in spoken British English.

• *go on*

> a *Alison went on to become a journalist.* (= she became a journalist after doing something else)
> b *Alison went on working as a journalist.* (= she continued to work as a journalist)

• *used to/be used to*

> a *We're used to getting up early.* (= accustomed to it now)
> b *We used to get up early.* (= it was a habit in the past, but it isn't any longer)

Unit 6

Wishes

There are four main types of 'wish':

A A regret that a present or general situation is not as we would like it to be

To find out which tense to use after *wish* with this meaning, imagine a sentence describing the undesirable situation, then 'going back' a tense.

> *My hair's too curly.* ⟶ *I wish my hair wasn't so curly.*
> *I don't have a car.* ⟶ *I wish I had a car (but I can't afford one now).*

(Note: In formal English, *were* is often used in the third person singular.)

> *I wish he were more honest.*

B A regret that something happened or didn't happen in the past

Again, imagine a sentence describing what happened, and then 'go back' a tense.

> *I got angry (and hit the headmaster).* ⟶ *I wish I hadn't got angry (and hit the headmaster).*

C A desire for someone to change or to do or stop doing something, or for a situation to change

This form can refer to the present and/or future. *Would* or *wouldn't* are used after the verb *wish*.

> *I wish you wouldn't smoke as much.* (= I'm asking you to stop or cut down, although I realise that it won't be easy)
> *I wish he wouldn't smoke as much.* (= it is not easy but I keep asking him to stop and I hope he will)
> *I wish he didn't smoke so much.* (= I don't like him smoking but I've tried and failed to make him stop.)

With *wish* + *would/wouldn't* there is a feeling that there is some possibility for change, however small – and a desire for that change to happen. With *wish* + past simple it is felt that there is little possibility for things to be different now.

D A wish that someone was able to do something which they can't do

When a wish is unlikely to be fulfilled, for reasons beyond someone's control, *could* is used.

> *I wish you could spend the weekend with us, but I suppose if you've got to work there's nothing we can do about it.*

The Passive

The passive voice is more commonly used in English than many other languages. It is often used in more formal reporting. Here are examples of the tenses formed with the passive voice:

A Present simple passive

She is picked up after work every day.

B Present continuous passive

He's being interviewed for the job this morning.

C Past simple passive

Henry was thrown out of the hotel for not paying his bill.

D Past continuous

When I arrived, Richard was being questioned by a policeman.

E Past perfect passive

The newspaper had been delivered before I got up this morning.

F Present perfect passive

My car has been stolen!

G Future passive

They will be married on Saturday.

H Future perfect passive

By this time next week we will have been told who is buying the company.

Here is a summary of the points raised by the questions in Unit 6 about the use of the passive.

The passive is used when you want to focus on or emphasise the person or thing affected by an action, rather than the person doing the action.

Thirty-five people were killed by a bomb planted by terrorists in the city centre.

You may decide not to mention the agent because:
• you don't know who or what it is

The car was stolen from outside his house last night.

• it's not important to know

We were told there would be a private bathroom for every room.

• you don't want the listener to know who did the action

The video in room 3 has been broken.

• the agent has been mentioned before

He was a very fast worker and the windows were all painted before we got back from holiday.

• It's understood who the agent is

He was sentenced to five years' imprisonment. (by the judge)

• The agent is 'people in general'

Milk can be bought at the shop on the corner.

If the agent is mentioned, when using the passive, the emphasis is then placed on the agent. This may be because you want to refer back to it in the next clause.

I was arrested by a security guard, who later admitted that he had made a mistake.

With is used after a passive verb when the instrument used to perform an action is emphasised.

It had been cut with a knife. (= not with a pair of scissors)

The verb *get* can be used instead of *be* as the auxiliary in informal English.

We get paid on the 25th of every month.

(Note: The passive can only be used with transitive verbs – verbs which can have an object – but there are some transitive verbs which are not usually used with the passive: *have, let, get, like*.)

Unit 7

The article

Here are the most important rules to remember when using the article:

the
• when a noun being referred to has already been mentioned in the conversation

I saw a man coming up the path to the house. It was the man I had seen at the station the day before.

• when both the speaker and listener know what is being referred to (because it has been mentioned earlier, or is generally understood)

I was talking to Geoff about the time we went to Brighton.

• when specifying which thing is being talked about

The bus that is supposed to leave at six is always late.

• when talking about something which is unique in the world or of which there is only one in a particular place

The sun was shining brightly when I got up.

• when making a generalised statement about things in a scientific or technological context

The bicycle is going to become more and more important as a means of transport in future.

• when talking about classes or kinds of entertainment

I love the theatre / cinema.

• when talking about musical instruments

She plays the piano very well.

• with proper nouns used as people's names

We spent a fascinating evening with the Bowens.

• with some proper nouns referring to some geographical places, countries, mountain ranges, regions, rivers, seas, oceans

the Panama Canal, the Shetland Isles, the Alps, the Far East, the Adriatic Sea, the Pacific Ocean, The Thames

(Note: *Lake Geneva, Regent Street, Northern England*, but when referring to general classes or groups of people, *the* is not omitted: *the French, the handicapped, the poor*.)

a/an
- when a countable singular noun is mentioned for the first time

> *They rented a car.*
> *She's an artist.*
> *What an incredible film!*

Note: *A/an* can replace plural countable nouns when referring to something in general:

> *Children/A child respond(s) to guidance.*

and when referring to 'one of ':

> *I met a cousin of yours yesterday.* (= we don't say exactly which cousin)

no article
- when referring to things in general (plural countable nouns or uncountable nouns)

> *Cats and dogs make good pets.*

(Note: With plural countable nouns or uncountable nouns, *some/any* can be used without changing the meaning significantly):

> *Would you like (some) tea?*
> *Have you got (any) children?*

- between a preposition and noun in certain everyday phrases

> *at school/in hospital/at night/by plane* etc..

- with certain categories of nouns – subjects, leisure activities, names of meals, abstract nouns

> *She studies literature, enjoys tennis, chess and pottery.*
> *Would you like to have dinner?*

Unit 8

Conditional sentences

A Situations which are generally true or which happen often. (zero conditional)

Form: main clause = present simple or present perfect
     if-clause   = present simple

> *If you go through a red light, a camera takes your photo and you get a fine a few days later.*
> *If she's had a bad day at work, she tends to take it out on me.*

The present continuous is not usually used in both clauses:

> ~~*If he is going fishing and he isn't catching much, he is getting angry.*~~

When there is a present simple or present continuous tense in the main clause, an imperative is often used in the *if*-clause:

> *Wake me up tomorrow morning, if you want a lift to work.*

B Talking about a situation which you know does not exist, or which is unlikely to exist.

Form: main clause = conditional
(*would/could/should/might*)
                    + infinitive
    if-clause   = past tense

> *If Britain was further north, there would be more snow in winter.*
> *I should be very surprised if he came to the party.*

It is also possible to use *were* instead of *was* with the first and third person singular in the *if*-clause (and this is the case in advice expressions):

> *If my nose were a little shorter, I'd look a bit like Michael Jackson.*
> *If I were you, I would speak to her about it.*

Would is not normally used in the *if*-clause except when it means 'would be willing to':

> *If you would give me an answer soon, I would be grateful.*

To make the situation even more unlikely, *were to* can be used instead of the past simple in the *if*-clause:

> *If you were to find a diamond in your garden, what would you do?*

C Talking about a situation when you do not know whether it exists or not, or when it is unlikely to exist.

Form: main clause = conditional or modal
     if-clause   = present simple or present perfect

> *If his theory is right, then it would be possible for humans to live on other planets.*

This kind of conditional form is also used to make offers; the *if*-clause comes second in the sentence and often ends with a modal:

> *I'll help you, if I can.*

D Talking about a situation which may exist in the future.

Form: main clause = future simple (*will*)
     if-clause   = present simple or present perfect

This type of conditional can express several functions, such as suggestions, warnings, predictions, promises or threats.

> *If you're going to see that film, you'll need to get there early.* (suggestion)

Will is sometimes found in the *if*-clause, when it implies 'insistence' or (lack of) willingness:

> *If he will go out without a coat, of course he'll get cold.* (prediction)
> *If Annie won't take you, I will.* (promise)

Form: main clause = conditional perfect (*would* + *have* + past participle) or *could have* / *should have* / *might have*

if-clause = past perfect

> *If they had known it was going to rain, they would have stayed at home.*

Notes:

When the first verb in an *if*-clause is *should*, *were* or *had*, it is possible to leave out the word *if*:

> *Should you come to Barcelona, give me a ring.*

Should or *happen to* can be used separately or together to emphasise that something is unlikely to happen, or will happen by chance:

> *If you should / happen to pass by a newspaper kiosk, will you buy me a newspaper?*

Unless can be used to mean 'if…not':

> *You needn't come to work on Saturday, unless you really want to.*

Inversion after adverbial expressions

Inversion is used to give or add emphasis in sentences.

hardly … than, no sooner … when
The past perfect tense is used here, and the subject and verb at the beginning of the sentences are inverted. (Note the words used to introduce the second clauses.)

> *Hardly had I got into bed, when there was a knock at the door.*
> *No sooner had she started her new job when the company moved to Basingstoke.*

little
The present simple or past simple can be used.

> *Little do / did I know, that she'd been lying all this time.*

so … that, such … that
When used to measure the quantity or quality of something, *so* or *such* at the beginning of a sentence can be followed by the adjective, adverb or noun group being 'qualified.'

> *So fast was the new train that I arrived two hours earlier than I expected to.*
> *Such is the brightness of the sun here that I have to wear my sunglasses all day.*

Negative adverbials
Negative adverbials are often placed at the beginning of a sentence where inversion is used.

> *Rarely / Seldom / Never / Nowhere have I seen such a lovely view.*
> *Not until the next day did we meet the owner of the hotel.*

> *Not since the 20s has someone made a recording of this symphony.*

Expressions with *only* and *no*
Inversion takes place after expressions such as *not only*, *only*, *at no time*, *on no account*, *under no circumstances* etc..

> *Not only have we missed the plane, but there are no other flights until tomorrow.*
> *Only after we'd finished the meal did I realise I'd forgotten my wallet.*
> *At no time did I say I would accept these conditions.*
> *On no account / Under no circumstances should you leave the building without signing out at reception.*

Unit 9

Question tags

Question tags are usually added to statements, not questions.

> *You're a student, aren't you?*

In most cases a negative statement has an affirmative tag, and vice versa. (See 1 below.)

> *He isn't very tall, is he?*
> *He's tall, isn't he?*

Here is a summary of the form for question tags.

1 Use the same tense in the statement and the tag.

If *to be* is in the statement, it is repeated in the tag.

> *You were here, weren't you?*
But: *I'm going, aren't I?* (Not: ~~amn't I~~?)

If there is an auxiliary or modal verb (except *have to*) in the statement, it is repeated in the tag.

> *You haven't got flu, have you?*
But: *He has to go, doesn't he?*

When there is no auxiliary, modal verb or *to be* in the statement, the tag uses *do* / *did*.

> *You live here, don't you?*

2 Imperative statements often have tags using modal verbs such as *will, can't, can, could, would*.

These question tags can make a statement more polite, or can express anger more strongly, depending on intonation used.

> *Open the door, will you?*
> *Just listen for once, won't you?*
> *Come on, stand up, can't you?*
> *Get me some stamps too, would you?*

(Note: When the meaning expressed in the imperative is negative, only *will* is used in the tag):

> *Stop shouting, will you?*
> *Don't tell anyone, will you?*

3 Note the agreement in the following sentences, between the subject and the tag.

> *There are three people coming for dinner, aren't there?*
> *Someone stole your bike, didn't they?*
> *Nobody saw me, did they?*
> *Nothing went wrong, did it?*

4 In informal English, the subject and verb are often omitted from the statement.

> *Lovely day, isn't it?*

5 To agree or disagree with a question expressed by a tag, pay attention to the verb in the statement, not in the tag.

> *You enjoyed the play, didn't you?*
> *Yes, I did.* (Not: *Yes, I didn't.*)

Use

The intonation used with question tags determines their meaning. A rising intonation means the speaker is unsure of the facts, and is asking for information.

A falling intonation shows that the speaker is sure of something but is checking details or seeking confirmation.

A more tentative and therefore polite tone can be given by using a negative statement with an affirmative tag:

> *You couldn't lend me a pound, could you?*

The pattern: affirmative statement + affirmative tag can express surprise, anger/sarcasm, concern or interest.

> *She's resigned, has she?* (surprise)
> *So you think you're an expert on this country's political situation, do you?* (sarcasm)
> *You're moving out, are you?* (concern)
> *He's going to the States, is he?* (interest)

If this pattern is used when checking information, it usually indicates that the speaker is fairly sure about the information already.

> *You're about 35 are you?* (fairly sure)
> *You're about 35, aren't you?* (less sure)

Relative clauses

Defining relative clauses

These are clauses which are used to explain which person or thing is being talked about, and are essential to the meaning of the sentence.

> *The aim that most city people have at the weekend is to get out to the countryside.*

After people, use *that* or *who*.

> *The man that/who I saw in the garden was about fifty.*

After things, use *that* or *which*.

> *The bag which/that* I wanted to buy as a present for her had been sold.*

* *That* is more commonly used in spoken English.

(Note: *Who/that/which* can be either the subject or object of the verb in the relative clause.)

> *The man who came into the room was tall and thin.*
> *The man who you saw here yesterday is a reporter.*

In formal English *whom* is used when a person is the object of the relative clause.

These pronouns can be left out when they are the object of the relative clause:

> *The man you saw here yesterday is a reporter.*
> (Not: *The man came into the room was tall.*)

After times, use *when*.

> *The accident happened at a time when there weren't many people about.*

After places, use *where*.

> *He comes from a place where it's very hilly, so bicycles aren't very popular there.*

The relative pronoun can also be the object of a preposition in a relative clause. In this case the preposition is at the end of the clause:

> *She's the only person (that) I ever write to.*

Non-defining relative clauses

These are clauses used to give extra information about the person or thing being talked about. The clause is not necessary in order to identify this person or thing.

After people, use *who* when the person being described is the subject of the relative clause.

> *Bill, who had already been late twice, was called to the manager's office that morning.*

When the person being described is the object of the relative clause, use *who*, or in formal English, *whom*.

> *Her favourite author is Alison Lurie, who/whom she first heard about from a friend.*

After things, use *which*.

> *I work at the BBC, which is in Wood Green.*

In non-defining relative clauses it is not possible to use *that* instead of *who/whom/which*, or to leave out the relative pronoun.

Extension

Other clauses introduced by *which*
A relative clauses can be introduced with *which* when referring to the 'whole situation' which is being described in the main clause.

> *They gave me a set of golf clubs for my birthday, which was very kind of them.*

many/most/some/one of ...
A relative clause introduced by these words, is followed by *which* or *whom*, when a group of people or things in the main clause has already been mentioned, and is being referred back to.

> *The bus stopped and a crowd of people got off, many of whom were carrying cameras.*

Unit 10

Modal verbs

(As this is a vast area of grammar, this section provides only a basic framework. It would be advisable to consult a thorough Grammar reference book for further information.) The following are the main functions of modal verbs:

A Obligation/necessity

1 *must* and *have to*

In spoken English, *have to* and *have got to* are the most commonly used forms. *Must* is used to give more emphasis and to make the sense of obligation stronger.

> *You must go and see a doctor.*
> *I have to visit my aunt in hospital tonight.*

Must expresses the idea that the obligation comes from the speaker, not from someone else.

> *I must lose some weight.*
> *You really must give up smoking.*

When the obligation has been imposed by someone other than the speaker, *have to* is used.

> *I have to be at work by 9 a.m.* (= these are rules imposed on employees)
> *I have to give up smoking.* (= the doctor says so)

To describe habitual obligations, *have to* is normally used.

> *Every morning I have to sort out the mail, check the answer machine and distribute the faxes, before I can have a cup of coffee.*

The past form of *must* is *had to*. The future form is either *will have to* if the focus is completely on the future:

> *You will have to dress more smartly when you start that job.*

or *must*, if the focus is more clearly on the present:

> *You must be home by ten tonight.* (= I'm telling you this now)

(*Mustn't* for prohibition – see B below.)

2 *need*

To express the fact that there is no obligation, the following forms are used:

> *I needn't go.* (more formal)
> *I don't have to/haven't got to go* (informal)

Questions about obligation generally use *have to* and *need to*.

> *Do I have to/need to get a visa?*

(Note: *Must I get a visa?* is also acceptable, but sounds unnecessarily formal.)

needn't have/didn't need to

Compare the difference between these examples in the past.

> *The guests needn't have cleared up after the party – the staff would have done it the next day.* (= it wasn't necessary for the guests to do it, but they did it all the same)
> *I didn't need to go to the dentist after all – my toothache disappeared.* (= it wasn't necessary to go to the dentist after all; I realised this and so I didn't go)

B Prohibition

Mustn't means there is an obligation <u>not</u> to do something.

> *You mustn't drive off before the traffic lights turn green.*

C Mild obligation

Present – *should/ought to*

> *You should try and finish that report before you go home.*
> *You ought to visit your parents a bit more often.*

(Note: *Ought to* has a moral connotation, and implies that something is 'the right thing to do'.)

Past – *should have/ought to have*

> *I should have written to Howard weeks ago.*
> *She ought to have had the car serviced last week but she didn't have time to take it in.*
> *He shouldn't have told everyone about their affair.*

(See also E below.)

D Possibility

General time: *can*

> *Students can get a lot of fun out of studying grammar.*

Present/Future: *could/might/may*

> *He could/might be in the library. Have you checked?*
> *They may have to sell their house soon.* (*May* is slightly more formal, and slightly more 'certain' than *might*.)
> *We might move to Paris next year.* (*Might* is slightly less 'certain' than *may*.)

Past: *could/may/might have*:

> *He could/might/may have caught a later train.*
> *She could/might/may be Norwegian. I think I recognise the accent.*

E Suggestions/Advice

could

> *We could go for a walk in the park.*

shall

> *Shall we wait and see if it stops raining?*

might

> *You might like to try the Chicken Kiev, madam.* (very polite)

should/ought

> *You should take them to court for breach of contract.*
> *You ought to see a doctor about those headaches.*

(Note: *Ought to* implies a stronger conviction in something than *should*.)

F Probability

should/ought to

> *We should get to the hotel by about eight o'clock.*
> *Fred ought to know what time classes begin.*

should have/ought to have

> *He should have got to Moscow by now if his plane was on time.* (I am fairly sure he has got there.)
> *Alice ought to have received the payment yesterday.* (She has probably received it.)

must

> It's late and she's still not here. She must have missed the bus.

can't

> It can't be Stephen. (He's on holiday in Venice.)
> = a single event
> It couldn't be Judy. (She doesn't finish work till much later.) = habitual activity

G Instructions and requests

could/would

> Could/Would you give me my bill, please? (more polite request)

H Ability

can/can't

> She can/can't play the guitar very well.
> I can help you, if you like. (When used with a future reference, can could imply 'willingness'.)

Be able to is used instead of *can*, with *going to*, *used to* etc..

> I will be able to swim 30 lengths by next month.
> I used to be able to speak German quite well.

could (general ability in the past)

> When he was a boy he could do all sorts of magic tricks.

be/was able to (specific ability in the past)

> I couldn't/wasn't able to get you a ticket, I'm afraid.
> He was able to escape by digging a tunnel under the wall.

(*Couldn't* is not possible here; *be able to* in this sense means 'managed to, despite difficulty'.)

I Permission

can (saying what is allowed)

> You can only swim here if you are wearing a bathing-hat. (allowed)
> You can't cross the road if the red light is showing. (not allowed)
> You can borrow my car this evening. (giving someone permission)
> Can I go out tonight? (asking for permission)

may (saying what is allowed)

> Customers may take glasses out into the garden, if they bring them back in again when they have finished. (allowed – formal)
> You may leave early today. (giving someone permission – formal)
> May I smoke? (asking for permission – polite/formal)

(Note: *Could* and expressions such as *Do you mind if …?* are more commonly used than *may*.)

could (asking for permission)

> Could I have a look at your newspaper? (polite)

Unit 11

Comparisons

more/less

Comparisons using *more/less … than …*, can be followed by

• a noun: *Henry is more/less intelligent than his brother.*

• an adjunct: *The drought this year has been more/less severe than in any other year.*

• a clause: *Michael Douglas is more/less famous than his father was.*

(Note: You can make negative sentences of the examples above by putting *no* or *not* before *more*: *Henry is no/not more intelligent than his brother.* There is a difference in meaning. The use of *no* implies that Henry and his brother are of the same intelligence, while *not* implies that Henry is less intelligent than his brother.)

as … as …

In comparisons with *as* + adjective, the second *as* can be followed by

• a pronoun: *This car's as big as yours.*

• a clause: *You're as young as you feel.*

(Note: Negative sentences can be made by using *not* before *as* and the meaning becomes the same as 'less … than …')

> This car's not as big as yours.

Submodifiers

With *more/less*
Submodifiers can be used to strengthen or weaken more and less. Here is a list of commonly used submodifiers:

considerably   very much   a good deal   great   vast
infinitely   (formal)
much   far   a lot   neutral   lots (informal)

> Arthur is a good deal more interesting than I had imagined.
> They are considerably less well-off than their neighbours.

With *as … as …*
Here is a list of submodifiers used before *as*:

just   quite   nearly   almost

> William is just as inquisitive as his father was at that age.
> I'm almost as fat as he is.

It is possible to use *not* in front of *nearly* to mean 'much less … than …'

> You're not nearly as suntanned as I am.

and *not* in front of *quite* to mean 'nearly as …'.

> Teresa's not quite as tall as her mother.

Unit 12

Reported speech

When reporting what people say in English it is common to paraphrase what they say or use 'reporting verbs' to summarise. Here is a list of some common reporting verbs and their different patterns.

A Reporting a statement

1 verb + *that*-clause

> *He suggested (that) we leave.*
> *She said I had to fill in another form and come back later.*

say/answer/reply/suggest/explain/argue/complain/insist etc.

That can be omitted after most verbs but not after *answer, argue, explain* or *reply.*

Suggest cannot be followed by an infinitive, but it can be followed by *-ing*-clause:

> *He suggested leaving.*

Insist can be followed by *on + -ing:*

> *Russell insisted on paying for me.*

2 verb + object + *that*-clause

> *They told me that there was no work for me.*

tell/remind*/inform/convince/persuade etc.

That is often omitted after *tell.*

(* See also D below.)

3 verb + *to* + object + *that*-clause

> *He explained to me that he would be late.*

admit/suggest/say/explain etc.

Here is a summary of the main differences between *say* and *tell*:

Say is not used with a hearer as the direct object of the verb.

Tell is not used without the hearer as the object of the verb.

Tell cannot be used with *to* before the hearer.

B Reporting an order, a request or a piece of advice

advise/ask/order/persuade/recommend/remind

Verb + object + *to* infinitive

> *They ordered me to get out of the car.*

C Reporting thoughts and feelings

feel/believe/imagine/understand etc.

1 verb + *that*-clause

> *I knew that she would turn up sooner or later.*

That can be omitted after these verbs. (Compare A1 above.)

intend/plan/want etc.

2 verb + *to* + infinitive

> *She doesn't want to go out this evening.*

3 verb + *that*-clause/*to* + infinitive

agree/decide/hope/expect etc.

> *I hoped that she would remember me.*
> *She hopes to go to university next year.*

D Reporting a question

1 (*Yes/No* questions) verb + *wh* -word/*if*

> *I asked if they would like something to drink.*
> *I enquired (as to) whether/where they wanted to go that day.*

Ask also follows this pattern:

ask/wonder/enquire etc.

verb + object + *wh*- word/*if*

> *I asked them if they knew the man in the photograph.*

2 General questions

> *They asked us where we were going.*

Unit 13

Participles

Participles are sometimes used after certain verbs, like *go* and *keep on*.

> *She keeps (on) ringing me up in the middle of the night.*

(For more information about verbs and the clauses that follow them, see Unit 5.)

Participle clauses can be used to describe simultaneous actions.

> *Singing and dancing, the crowd cheered as the team came on to the field.*
> *That man talking to the policeman is my husband.*

Participle clauses can be used to describe actions happening around the time of the main verb.

> *Sitting down, I opened the letter and read it.*

(Note: To emphasise that one action followed another, use *having* + past participle at the beginning of the sentence):

> *Having had a shower I got down to preparing dinner.*

Participles occurring at the beginning of clauses have the meaning 'because'.

> *Thinking that the lesson had already begun, I went to the canteen for a coffee.*

Participles are sometimes used as reduced relative clauses.

> *When he opened the door, Tom was surprised to see a man wearing a gorilla suit.*

Participles are used as adjectives to describe an action still happening or which has just happened.

> *A mother was dragging her screaming child out through the doors of the supermarket.*

The present participle is used for the action still happening, while the past participle is used for the finished action.

> *The damaged building was later demolished.*

Unit 14

as and *like*

As can be used to mean 'because'.

> *As he had never been to Berlin before, he bought himself a street map.*

As can also be used to mean 'while'.

> *As the sun was setting, the trout started to rise.*

As is used with a clause, and means 'in the same way as'.

> *Rob has learned to make furniture as they did before the invention of power tools.*
> *He is a good pilot, as his father was.*

As is also used when we are describing a person's job or the function of something.

> *I used a pile of books as a table and put my mug of tea on top.*
> *When I was a student I worked as a furniture porter in a big store in Kingston.*

Like is followed by a noun or pronoun and means 'similar to'.

> *He is quite like his sister in many ways.*

Like can be used to mean 'for example'.

> *Tennis players like Agassi earn a phenomenal amount of money.*

Note: In American English, and increasingly, in informal spoken English, *like* can be used with a clause.

> *Nobody can sing Jamaica Say You Will like Joe Cocker can.*

As is used before and after adjectives and adverbs when saying how similar people or things are.

> *She was as happy as a lark.*

(For detailed information about comparisons see Unit 11.)